THE WEEKEND WOODWORKER®

Projects for the HOME CRAFTSMAN

THE WEEKEND WOODWORKER®

Projects for the
HOME
CRAFTSMAN

**Cabinets and Chests • Tables and Chairs •
Kitchen Projects • Accents • Outdoor Projects • Toys**

Selected by the Editors of Rodale Books

Illustrations by Sally Onopa

Rodale Press, Emmaus, Pennsylvania

Copyright © 1993 by Rodale Press, Inc.

Printed in the United States of America on acid-free ∞, recycled ♻ paper

This book is being simultaneously published by Rodale Press as a book entitled *The Weekend Woodworker Annual 1993*.

If you have any questions or comments concerning this book, please write:
Rodale Press
Book Readers' Service
33 East Minor Street
Emmaus, PA 18098

Library of Congress Cataloging-in-Publication Data

The weekend woodworker : projects for the home craftsman : cabinets and chests, tables and chairs, kitchen projects, accents, outdoor projects, toys / selected by the editors of Rodale Books ; illustrations by Sally Onopa.
    p.   cm.
   ISBN 0-87596-593-8 hardcover
   ISBN 0-87596-575-X paperback
   1. Woodwork.   I. Rodale Books.
TT180.W3462 1993   92-32816
684'.08—dc20   CIP

Executive Editor: Margaret Lydic Balitas
Senior Editor: Jeff Day
Editor: Bob Moran
Writers: Kenneth S. Burton, Jr., Bob Moran, David Page, David Schiff, Rob Yoder
Copy Manager: Dolores Plikaitis
Copy Editor: Sarah Dunn
Office Manager: Karen Earl-Braymer
Editorial assistance: Susan Nickol

Art Director: Anita G. Patterson
Book Designer: Robert E. Ayers, PUBLICATION DESIGN
Book Layout: Peter A. Chiarelli
Cover Designer: Darlene Schneck
Cover Photographer: Mitch Mandel

Photo Credits: The photos on pages 2, 9, 15, 19, 24, 35, 46, 50, 80, 86, 93, 99, 181, 218, and 226 are reprinted by permission of ICA bokförlag, Västerås, Sweden. All other photos are by Mitch Mandel.

Cover Projects: The projects shown on the cover include (clockwise from bottom left): Spoon Holder (page 55), Shaker End Table (page 141), Painted Cupboard (page 200), Wall-Hung Corner Cupboard (page 211), and Doll Bed with Storage Chest (page 245).

Distributed in the book trade by St. Martin's Press

2 4 6 8 10 9 7 5 3 1 hardcover
2 4 6 8 10 9 7 5 3 1 paperback

CONTENTS

Contributing Craftsmen

ICA bokförlag, Västerås, Sweden (Kitchen Clock, Cookbook and Spice Shelf, Serving Tray Cart, Folding Tray Table, Towel Shelf, Stacked Shelf, Shelf and Pegs, Rice Paper Screen, Garden Trellis, Outdoor Recliner, Two-Wheel Wagon, Outdoor Bench, Step Stool, Lisa's Chest, Bathroom Cabinet, Rocking Horse)

Kenneth S. Burton, Jr. (Window Box, Seesaw, Coopered-Front Cabinet, Low Bookcase)

Steve Clerico (Hall Table)

Phil Gehret (Quilt or Drying Rack)

Brent and Linda Kahl (Open Wall Box, Candle Box, Dovetailed Blanket Chest)

Joe Kovecses (Contemporary Jewelry Box)

Fred Matlack (Fishing Rod Rack)

Jean Nick (Doll Bed with Storage Chest)

David Page (Three-Person Bench)

Bobbie Ralphs (Limberjack, Hand-Held Table Tennis, Marble Tilt Game)

David Schiff and Rob Yoder (Shaker End Table)

Rick Wright (Jelly Cupboard, Spoon Holder, Sofa Table, Painted Cupboard, Wall-Hung Corner Cupboard)

Darryl Yeager (Child's Tool Box, Helicopter)

INTRODUCTION

There are a lot of reasons for messin' around in a woodworking shop. When the woodworking editors at Rodale Press ask readers why they work wood, we hear reasons such as "It satisfies a creative urge," and "It gives me a sense of achievement." But most often we hear, "Beats me; I just get a kick out of it," or "It's just plain fun," or "Hey, I don't think about why, I just do it."

Maybe you're one of the woodworkers who knows why he heads for the shop, and maybe you're one who just does it. In either case, it's a good bet that you get more satisfaction out of a project that presents a bit of a challenge than you do from one that you could do in your sleep. It's also a good bet that your projects in the last six months are more complex and show better craftsmanship than the projects you did a few years ago. The two bets are not really very different. Projects that challenge us also make us better craftsmen. The reasons why we work wood are not really very different either. Satisfying a creative urge *is* just plain fun, and most of us get a kick out of a sense of achievement.

The projects that we've included in this book cover a broad range of complexity and are suited to a broad range of skills. Projects like the Open Wall Box and the Shelf and Pegs are both quick and easy. They're a good place for the novice woodworker to begin. They're also a good place for the more advanced woodworker to strive for totally flawless execution. Projects like the Candle Box are quick but offer a bit more of a challenge. The Fishing Rod Rack and Lisa's Chest are medium-size projects that are quite easy to make, while the Spoon Holder and the Wall-Hung Corner Cupboard require intermediate skills. A few of the projects, like the Coopered-Front Cabinet and the Hall Table, will introduce you to techniques that are less common. You'll find projects on which to practice recently acquired skills. Others will explore new territory for you. A few may be beyond your skills for the time being, but be patient. They won't run away, and you'll be ready for them before you know it.

To make the learning process fun instead of a source of frustration, we've included special step-by-step instructions for many of the techniques you'll use in this book. Each technique appears in a project that uses it. If another project requires the same technique, we'll refer to the technique and tell you what page to find it on. We've also listed these special techniques in the Contents so you can find them if you're working on a project of your own design.

We've produced a book that will help you have fun while leading you to new levels of skill. If you have suggestions for making our woodworking books even better, let us know. There are as many ways to put together a book as there are ways to put together a drawer. We'd like to do it the way *you* prefer.

PART ONE

KITCHEN PROJECTS

KITCHEN CLOCK

Every kitchen needs at least one clock, whether it's for timing eggs or for helping to get everyone going on time. This clock combines contemporary simplicity with country warmth for a look that fits almost anywhere.

The parts of the clock are all quite small, making this a great opportunity to use up cutoffs of nice wood from some other project. At most you may have to glue up 7 inches of width for the clock face. If you know your way around your shop, you should be able to make this clock in a few hours.

1 **Select the stock and cut the parts.** Select the wood for the clock face and body. If necessary, glue up pieces to make the face, but remember that the face is the most prominent part of any clock. Glue lines may detract from its appearance. Cut the parts to the sizes specified by the Cutting List. Lay out the face with a compass and mark the center clearly.. Cut the circle with a band saw or coping saw. You can also rout the circle with a jig like the one shown in "Routing Circles" on page 6. Sand the edges smooth.

EXPLODED VIEW

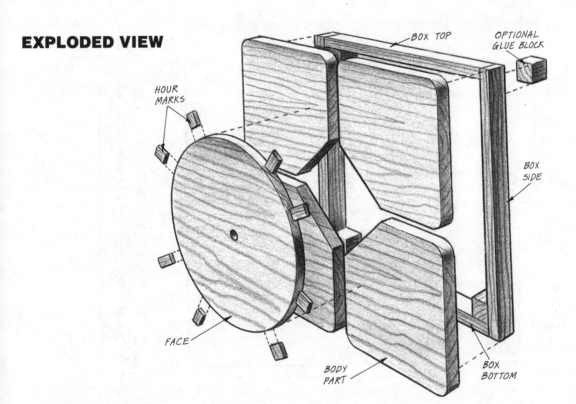

BOX TOP

OPTIONAL GLUE BLOCK

HOUR MARKS

BOX SIDE

FACE

BODY PART

BOX BOTTOM

CUTTING LIST

Part	Quantity	Dimensions	Comments
Face	1	¼″ × 7″ dia.	Your choice of wood
Body parts	4	½″ × 5¼″ × 5¼″	Same as face
Hour marks	8	⅛″ × ⅜″ × ½″	Same or contrasting wood
Box sides	2	½″ × ¾″ × 10¼″	Same as hour marks
Box top/bottom	2	½″ × ¾″ × 9¼″	Same as hour marks
Glue blocks	4	¾″ × ¾″ × ¾″	Optional

Hardware

1 clock movement, ⅝″ × 2⅛″ × 2⅛″. Available from Precision Movements, 2024 Chestnut St., Emmaus, PA 18049. Part #309, regular shaft.

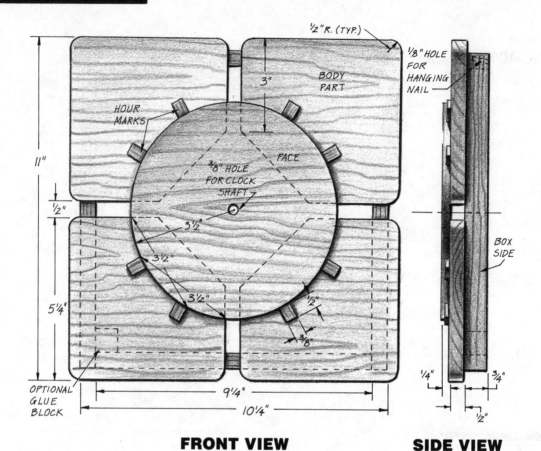

FRONT VIEW   **SIDE VIEW**

2 **Lay out the body parts.** Arrange the four body parts into a square on your workbench and put the face on top of them. Play with the arrangement of the five parts until the combination of grain patterns pleases you. Mark the 12 o'clock position on the back of the face. Mark the corners of the four body parts that come together at the center of the clock. Label these four parts clockwise 1, 2, 3, and 4 so that you can reassemble them correctly later. On one of the body parts, lay out the corner cutoff and three ½-inch-radius corners, as shown in the *Front View*.

3 **Cut out and shape the body parts.** Stack the four body parts on top of each other with the corners marked for the center of the clock on top of each other. Make sure the part with the laid-out corner cutoff is on the top of the stack. Stick the parts together with double-faced tape. Saw off the center corner and round-over the other three corners. A rasp and sandpaper will round-over the corners if you don't have a band saw to cut them.

Separate the four parts and finish sand their front surfaces. Relabel them if you sand off the labels.

4 **Make the box.** The shallow box on the back of the clock is mostly hidden from view. If you're using a wood like Eastern white pine that doesn't split easily, you can assemble the box with 1-inch finishing nails. Use two nails in each joint. Set the nails and fill the holes.

If you decide not to nail the box together, saw out four ¾ × ¾ × ¾-inch glue blocks. Glue the blocks flush with each end of the box top and box bottom. When the glue is dry, glue the box sides to the top and bottom, as shown in the *Front View*.

5 **Attach the face.** Rip four spacers ⅜ inch × ½ inch, each about 3 inches long. Use these spacers to position the four body parts ½ inch apart on your workbench. Make sure the labels 1, 2, 3, and 4 are arranged clockwise. Now center the face on the body and trace around it lightly with a very sharp pencil.

Finish sand the face and glue it to the body. Apply the glue sparingly to both surfaces, position the face inside the light pencil tracing on the body, and hold it in place for a minute or so until the glue grabs. Put a weight on the face to clamp it. (You can try to use conventional clamps if that will make you feel better, but remember this is a kitchen clock, not Boulder Dam.)

6 **Make the hour marks.** Saw some scrap to the thickness and width of the hour marks. Choose a piece long enough to make the eight markers, plus several extras. Sand the piece smooth, then saw the markers to length and sand the ends.

SHOP TIP: Lay out a ½-inch radius by tracing around a quarter. It's not a perfect ½-inch radius, but it's close enough. If you're laying out a ⁷⁄₁₆-inch radius, use a nickel.

7 **Lay out and attach the hour marks.** Lay out the hour marks, as shown in the *Front View*. Fasten them in place with hot-melt glue so you won't have to wait for regular glue to dry again.

8 **Attach the box.** Center the box on the back of the body and mark its position. Make sure the exposed end grain on the box is at the top and bottom, not on the sides where it would be visible. Apply glue to the joining surfaces and secure the box with spring clamps.

9 **Finish the clock.** Finish the clock with your favorite wood finish. Drill a ⅜-inch-diameter hole for the clock shaft through the center of the face. Install the clock movement and hands. The movement comes with a black rubber washer which you install between the movement and the face. The brass washer and nut go on the outside to secure the movement to the clock.

To hang the clock, drive a 1-inch finishing nail halfway into the wall at a slightly downward angle. Drill a ⅛-inch hole in the back edge of the top of the box at a corresponding upward angle. Make sure this hole is accurately centered from left to right. Slip the hole over the nail.

ROUTING CIRCLES

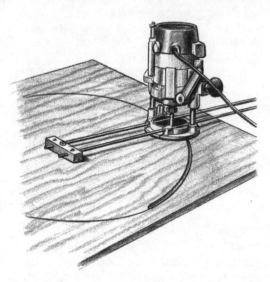

There are many ways to cut circles in wood. The best method depends on many things, including the size of the circle and the tools you own. The method described here is good for using a plunge router to cut circles from a few inches to a few feet in diameter. The technique uses an easily made, tiny jig to guide the router in cutting accurate, smooth-edged circles. The only materials required are a hardwood scrap and three #8 × 1-inch roundhead wood screws.

The jig provides a pivot point that can be adjusted along the router fence guide rods that come with most routers. Cutting the circle is much like drawing a circle with a compass or trammels, except that the router bit cuts a circle instead of a pencil drawing one.

1 **Measure your router.** Begin by taking three measurements from your router, as shown in *Guide Rod Dimensions:* the diameter

of the rods (D), the height of the rod holes above the bottom of the router base (H), and the center-to-center spacing of the holes (S).

2 **Lay out the rod holes and screw locations.** Saw a piece of hardwood scrap to ¾ × ¾ × 8 to 10 inches and sand the four surfaces smooth. Draw a line on each surface,

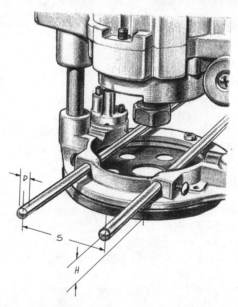

GUIDE ROD DIMENSIONS

dividing the stock in half. Mark one surface "Top" and the opposite surface "Bottom." Lay out the screw and rod holes, as shown in *Hole Locations.* One of the screws will act as the jig's pivot. The other two will tighten the jig on the guide rods.

3 **Drill the screw and rod holes.** Drill the rod holes the same diameter as the rods or very slightly larger. These two holes must be parallel to each other. Bore them on the drill press if you have one; otherwise, hold a square to the jig near the hole and drill parallel to the square. Try the rods in the holes. If they don't slide easily through the holes, run the bit back and forth in the holes a few times until they do.

At each of the three screw locations, drill shank holes the full diameter of the screw shanks halfway through the jig. If your screws are threaded full length, drill these shank holes the outside diameter of the threads. The screws must not grip the wood in the shank holes. Drill pilot holes $\frac{7}{64}$-inch in diameter (for #8 screws) the remainder of the way through the jig.

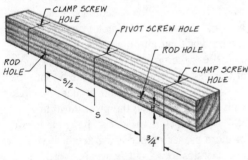

HOLE LOCATIONS

4 **Thread the screw holes.** Clamp the jig firmly from side to side in a vise to prevent any chance of it splitting. Thread all three screw holes by driving the screws all the way in until the screw head is seated on the top of the jig. The screws will project out the bottom of the jig. Remove the screws.

5 **Slot the ends of the jig.** A slot at each end of the jig allows the clamp screw to flex the wood enough to clamp firmly on the guide rods. First, cut the jig off ¾ inch beyond the clamp screw holes at both ends. If your guide rod holes fit the rods fairly closely, a $\frac{1}{16}$-inch wide slot will be sufficient and you can cut the slots quickly and easily on the band saw. If the rods are a bit loose in the holes, cut the slots the width of the kerf of a table saw blade. To cut them on the table saw, adjust the blade to cut 2¼ inches deep. Adjust the fence to center the kerf on the rod holes. Either hold the jig in a tenoning jig or screw it to an 8 × 8-inch block of scrap, as shown in the *Kerf Detail,* when making the cut.

6 **Trim the screws.** The clamp screws must be cut off so they don't scratch the workpiece, and the pivot screw must have the tip ground to a threadless point. Begin with the clamp screws. Put the rods in their holes and insert the clamp screws. Tighten the clamp screws until the jig grips the rods. There's no need for the rods to be vise-tight in the jig—in fact, overtightening the screws risks splitting the jig. Just snug the screws down. Now cut the screws off flush with the bottom of the jig. If you'd like, you can grind the screws off, but be careful not to overheat them and scorch the wood. In practice, it's just as easy to saw the screws off with a hacksaw and then file them flush with the jig.

Loosen the clamp screws and slide out the rods to make it easier to work on the pivot screw. Drive the pivot screw all the way in. Saw or file it off so only about ⅛ to $\frac{5}{32}$ inch projects beyond the bottom of the jig. File away the threads on the projecting part of the screw, then file what remains to a point. Make the point fairly sharp and slender without being too delicate. Don't worry if ⅛ to $\frac{5}{32}$ inch seems like more pivot point than you will need; loosening the screw will reduce the projection of the point.

(continued)

ROUTING CIRCLES—CONTINUED

To use the jig, assemble the rods in the router and the jig on the rods. Slide the jig along the rods until the distance from the pivot point to the nearest cutting edge of the router bit equals the radius of the circle to be cut. Tighten the clamp screws in both the jig and

KERF DETAIL

the router. Lay out the center of the circle on the back side of the workpiece so the pivot screw won't mar the front side.

There are several ways to hold the workpiece while cutting the circle. The easiest is to put it on one of the foam routing and sanding pads that are readily available from most woodworking tool mail-order stores. Larger pieces can be clamped on the corner of the workbench. Position the piece so that you can rout a little more than half of the circle, then rotate and reclamp the stock. If the workpiece is small, you can temporarily stick a block of wood to it with double-faced tape or hot-melt glue and clamp the block in a vise. Make sure the bit won't cut into the block or the vise.

Press the pivot screw into the workpiece at the center mark and plunge the bit into the workpiece. Guide the router around the circle with one hand holding the pivot down firmly.

If the stock is thick, cut the circle in two or more passes of increasing depth. If you have many circles to cut out, it will be worth your while to buy and use a spiral upcut router bit (available from Woodworker's Supply, 5604 Alameda Place NE, Albuquerque, NM 87113). It plunges easily, cuts a smooth edge, and tends to pull the router snugly against the stock.

COOKBOOK AND SPICE SHELF

Not only are these shelves simple to build, they also simplify life in the kitchen. They provide a surprising amount of storage in a minimal amount of space at a very convenient location. The wide middle shelf holds your cookbook open to the current recipe. The top shelf holds all the spices you'll need. Trays, small tools, and containers are close at hand on the bottom shelf.

The shelves come to us from a European contributor and reflect both modern European taste and European standard materials sizes. To simplify construction, we've changed the dimensions of the project parts to conform to standard lumber sizes in this country, so look to the drawings rather than the photo for guidance. You'll find that the project as we've drawn it comes very close to the project as photographed, but a few trivial details are slightly different.

The construction is very straightforward. Simply cut the stock to size and screw the parts together. If you can buy ½-inch-thick wood or plane 4/4 (four-quarter) stock to ½ inch thick yourself, you can make the entire project out of solid wood. The alternative to solid wood shelves is ½-inch plywood. If you use plywood, get 5-ply or 7-ply plywood with no voids. You might want to cover the ends of plywood shelves with edge banding to hide the laminations.

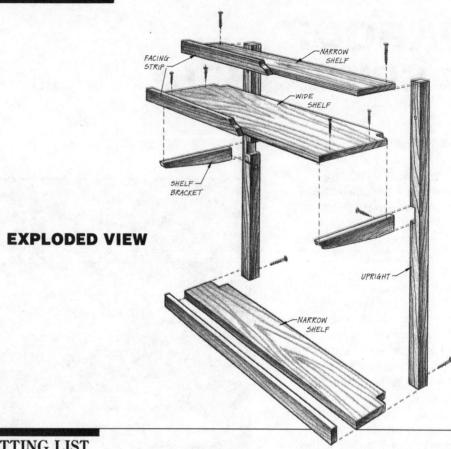

EXPLODED VIEW

Labels on illustration: FACING STRIP · NARROW SHELF · WIDE SHELF · SHELF BRACKET · UPRIGHT · NARROW SHELF

CUTTING LIST

Part	Quantity	Dimensions	Comments
Narrow shelves	2	$\frac{1}{2}'' \times 4\frac{1}{4}'' \times 24''$	Solid wood or plywood
Wide shelf	1	$\frac{1}{2}'' \times 8\frac{1}{8}'' \times 24''$	Solid wood or plywood
Facing strips	3	$\frac{1}{2}'' \times 1'' \times 24''$	Solid wood or plywood
Shelf brackets	2	$\frac{1}{2}'' \times 1\frac{1}{4}'' \times 8\frac{1}{8}''$	Solid wood or plywood
Uprights	2	$1'' \times 1'' \times 25\frac{1}{2}''$	Solid wood

Hardware

4 flathead wood screws, #8 × 2″
6 flathead wood screws, #8 × ¾″
Cup hooks, sized to fit your cups (optional)

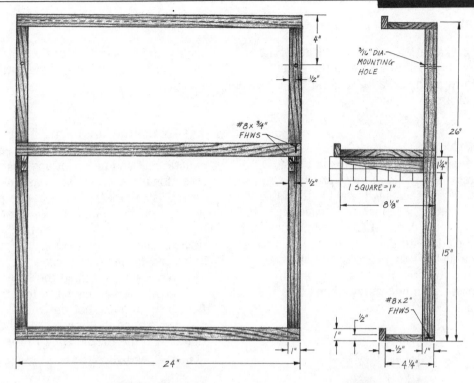

FRONT VIEW   **SIDE VIEW**

1 Select the wood and cut the parts. Since nothing in the joinery of this project will keep the parts from warping, look for clear, straight-grain stock. It stays flatter than stock with knots or other defects. Cut the parts to the sizes specified by the Cutting List. You can resaw thicker stock to ½ inch thick for the facing strips and shelf brackets. See "Resawing on the Table Saw" on page 13 for detailed instructions. If you can't get 5/4 (five-quarter) stock for the two uprights, cut three pieces of ¾-inch-thick stock so that they are 1¼ inches wide × 27 inches long. Glue them together to make a piece 1¼ inches thick × 2¼ inches wide. When the glue is dry, saw the two uprights from this larger piece.

2 Make the shelves. Saw out the notches in the back corners of the two lower shelves, as shown in the *Shelf Notch Detail.* You can cut the notches with a handsaw or in repeated passes with a dado blade. Glue the facing strips to all three shelves.

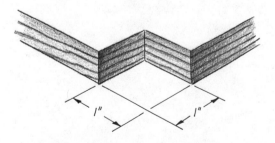

SHELF NOTCH DETAIL

11

3 **Make the shelf brackets.** Saw the shelf brackets to the shape shown in the *Side View*. Sand the edges to clean up the saw marks.

4 **Notch the uprights.** Lay out the shelf bracket notches in the uprights, as shown in the *Upright Notch Detail* and the *Side View*. On the table saw, set up a ¾-inch-wide dado blade to cut ½ inch deep. Guide the uprights past the blade with the miter gauge. It will take at least two passes to make each notch. Cut the notches very slightly smaller than necessary, then plane the brackets to fit. If you don't have a dado

blade, cut the shoulder of the notches with a backsaw, and chisel away the waste.

5 **Assemble the parts.** Test assemble the shelf. While it is assembled, countersink and drill pilot and shank holes for the screws. The easiest way to do this is to drill the holes in one pass with a combination bit, available at most hardware stores. If you drill the holes with regular bits, drill ⁵⁄₃₂-inch shank holes and ³⁄₃₂-inch pilot holes.

When you've drilled the holes, glue and screw the various parts together. Attach the top and bottom with 2-inch screws. Attach the brackets to the uprights, and the middle shelf to the brackets, with ¾-inch screws.

6 **Apply a finish.** Finish the shelves with your favorite wood finish. Drill a ³⁄₁₆-inch mounting hole in each upright, as shown in the *Front View*. If you like, you can screw cup hooks to the underside of the wide shelf.

7 **Hang the shelves.** Even though these shelves are designed to sit on the counter, you should screw them to the wall so they don't tip over. Your hardware store can recommend fasteners for just about any kind of wall.

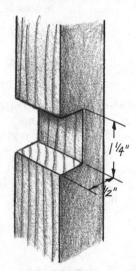

1¼"

½"

UPRIGHT NOTCH DETAIL

RESAWING ON THE TABLE SAW

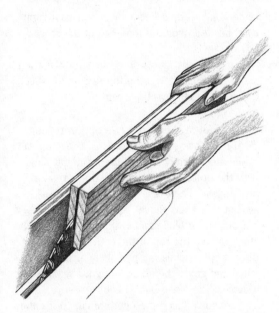

Very few woodworkers can go out and buy wood less than ¾ inch thick. Yet very often, for either practical or aesthetic reasons, a project needs thinner wood. In fact, the clunky appearance of some woodworking projects is a direct result of using thick boards where thinner ones would have been fine.

The woodworker who owns a thickness planer can plane his stock thinner. If that requires removing much more than ⅛ inch of stock, however, the process is time-consuming, wasteful, and produces a huge pile of chips to dispose of. A far better solution is to saw the stock thinner, a process called *resawing*.

The idea of resawing is intimidating to many amateur woodworkers. It needn't be. Resawing can be quite successful with the typical, home-shop, 10-inch table saw. Before you start, make sure of a few things:

• The stock must have one truly flat side and two straight edges, square to the flat side.

• The stock must be free of internal stresses caused by uneven moisture, improper kiln drying, or abnormal growth. You can make sure the moisture is uniform by wrapping the stock in plastic for several weeks before resawing. As a practical matter, other stresses can only be discovered by trying to resaw the board; if it tends to warp and twist, pinching the blade, try a different piece.

• The saw motor must have adequate power *for the depth of cut and width of kerf*. This doesn't mean that a moderately powered saw can't resaw a 6-inch-wide board. It does mean that you may have to cut it in successively deeper passes. The depth of cut should allow the stock to be fed a foot in no more than 2 or 3 seconds without slowing down significantly.

• The blade must be designed specifically for ripping and have no more than 24 teeth. Combination blades are seldom suitable for resawing. They lack the gullet depth needed to carry away the waste. As a result, they overheat and then warp. A ripping blade, on the other hand, is designed for this kind of work and will let you make surprisingly deep cuts. If you're buying a blade just for resawing, consider a thin-kerf ripping blade. The narrower kerf requires less power.

• The blade must be sharp and clean. If not, it will overheat, warp, and bind in the kerf.

• The table saw fence must be rigidly fixed parallel to the blade.

(continued)

RESAWING ON THE TABLE SAW—CONTINUED

Here's a step-by-step look at resawing.

1 **Attach a tall auxiliary fence to the table saw.** Make an auxiliary fence out of a ¾-inch-thick, flat, stable material like particleboard or good plywood. Make the fence 5 to 6 inches wide and as long as your table saw fence.

Fasten it to your table saw fence with flathead stove bolts and wing nuts. (Table saws usually have holes in their fences for this purpose.) Countersink the stove bolts slightly below the surface of the auxiliary fence. Make sure the auxiliary fence is perpendicular to the saw table by shimming as necessary with pieces of masking tape.

2 **Install the rip blade.** Select a clean, sharp rip blade with no more than 24 teeth and install it on the table saw. Adjust the depth of cut to ¹⁄₁₆ inch more than half the width of the board to be resawed.

3 **Adjust the fence.** Set the fence to cut the desired thickness plus ¹⁄₁₆ inch—this will give you a little extra stock for cleaning up the cut. Check to make sure the fence is parallel to the blade and perpendicular to the table. Make any necessary adjustments. Don't hesitate to use whatever shims or clamps are needed to lock it firmly in proper alignment.

4 **Make the first cut.** It will take at least two cuts, one from each edge, to resaw the board. To make the first pass, hold the flat side of the stock firmly against the fence with a push stick. Push the stock forward with your other hand. Even though the blade is buried in the wood, keep both hands away from the blade area. Keep a finger or two of your right hand hooked over the top edge of the stock and the fence.

If the blade slows down significantly when fed at a normal rate, stop the saw and reduce the depth of cut by 50 percent.

5 **Saw again from the opposite edge.** Turn the stock end for end. Hold the same face of the stock firmly against the fence but now with the other edge down. Feed it across the blade again. The pressure holding the stock against the fence should be applied to the stock in front of the blade and in the upper half of the stock, above the top of the cut. As the end of the cut approaches, stop pushing against the fence and guide the stock straight ahead. Keep it against the fence but without pressure.

If you reduced the depth of cut to maintain blade speed, raise the blade and finish the cut.

6 **Clean up the cut.** Even the best blade may not do a perfect job. Clean up the resawed surface on a jointer or planer, if you have one. If not, hand plane, scrape, or belt sand the surface smooth. If you're edge-gluing resawed boards, glue them together before you smooth them.

Boards more than six inches wide can be resawed on the typical 10-inch saw. Cut as deeply as you can from each edge, then finish with a handsaw. A well-sharpened hand rip saw, guided by the table saw kerfs, will cut quite rapidly. Carpenters and furnituremakers before the advent of power tools were not supermen, but they did have a higher regard than most of us for sharpness in their tools.

SERVING TRAY CART

A perfect complement to your screened porch or deck, this serving cart rolls around on four casters. It is just right for serving cold drinks on a hot day.

The cart features two removable trays, each with a bentwood rim. Don't be put off by the bending process—it couldn't be easier. The thin rims are bent right on the tray bottoms and are nailed in place. There are no forms to make or pieces to steam. The cart shown has a high-gloss painted finish for maximum protection from spills. The frame is made of poplar and the trays have poplar rims and birch plywood bottoms. The entire project is joined with screws, which makes it very easy to assemble.

1 **Select the stock and cut the parts.** Select the wood for the cart frame. Cut the legs and cross members to the sizes specified by the Cutting List. Cut two 16½-inch squares of cabinet-grade birch plywood for the tray bottoms. You'll cut them to circles later. Don't cut the tray rim pieces yet.

SHOP TIP: To make crosscutting easier, screw an extension fence to your miter gauge. The extra length makes the work easier to guide. When cutting several pieces to the same length, clamp a stop block to the fence the needed distance from the blade. Hold each piece against the extension fence and tightly against the stop block to make each cut.

2 **Cut the lap joints.** The cross members of the cart frame are joined with a lap joint, as shown in the *Lap Joint Detail*. Cut the joint with a dado blade on your table saw.

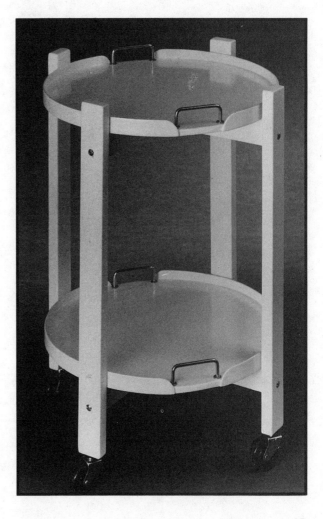

EXPLODED VIEW

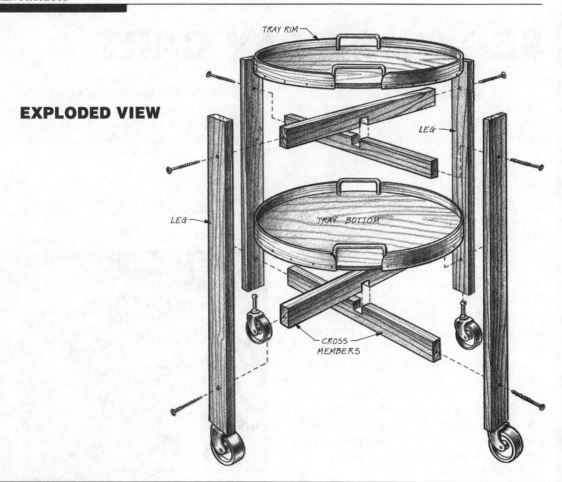

TRAY RIM

LEG

LEG

TRAY BOTTOM

CROSS MEMBERS

CUTTING LIST

Part	Quantity	Dimensions	Comments
Legs	4	$\frac{3}{4}'' \times 1\frac{3}{4}'' \times 23''$	Poplar
Cross members	4	$\frac{3}{4}'' \times 1\frac{1}{2}'' \times 17''$	Poplar
Tray bottoms	2	$\frac{3}{8}'' \times 16\frac{3}{8}''$ dia.	Plywood
Tray rims	4	$\frac{1}{8}'' \times 1'' \times 24''$	Poplar

Hardware

8 roundhead wood screws, #8 $\times$ 2½″
¾″ wire brads
4 swivel casters. Available from The Woodworkers' Store, 21801 Industrial Blvd., Rogers, MN
  55374-9514. Part #24026.
4 handles. Available from The Woodworkers' Store. Part #30460.

3 **Attach the legs.** Drill $\frac{3}{32}$-inch pilot holes in the ends of the cross members and $\frac{5}{32}$-inch clearance holes through the legs, as shown in the *Side View*. Sand all the parts. Glue the lap joints, then screw the legs to the cross members with #8 × $2\frac{1}{2}$-inch roundhead wood screws.

4 **Cut the tray bottoms to shape.** Lay out an $8\frac{3}{16}$-inch-radius circle on each plywood tray bottom. Cut out the tray bottoms and sand the edges smooth. You'll get perfect circles that require a minimum of sanding by using a jig like the one described in "Routing Cir-

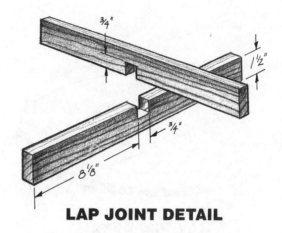

LAP JOINT DETAIL

cles" on page 6. As you sand, keep the edge square to the surfaces. A stationary disk sander works well for this.

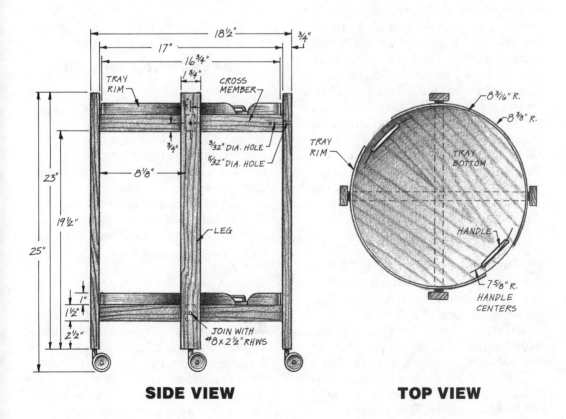

SIDE VIEW   **TOP VIEW**

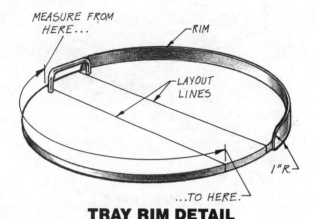

MEASURE FROM HERE...

RIM

LAYOUT LINES

1"R.

...TO HERE.

TRAY RIM DETAIL

ATTACHING THE RIM

keep the rims in place as the glue dries. Clean up any excess glue before it has a chance to set. Repeat the process with the other rims.

5 **Cut the tray rims.** Each tray has two rim pieces. Before cutting the rims, measure the lengths needed. Start by laying out the positions of the two handles on each tray bottom, as shown in the *Top View*. Then extend two lines across the tray bottom and down the edges, as shown in the *Tray Rim Detail*. Measure from one line around the edge to the other end of the same line. Your measurement should be fairly close to 22¼ inches. Saw the rims from clear, straight-grain poplar. Make them the length that you just measured. Saw the ends to the shape shown in the *Tray Rim Detail*.

6 **Bend the tray rims.** Sand the rims and tray bottoms, but don't sand away the marks on the edges that show the rim locations. Spread glue around the portion of the tray edge that holds the rim. Line up one end of a rim with its mark and tack it in place with a small brad. Bend the rim into place and tack it down every 1½ inches, as shown in *Attaching the Rim*. The brads will

7 **Apply the finish.** Fill the nail holes around the tray and sand them smooth. Apply a coat of primer to the cart. When the primer dries, sand lightly. Clean up the dust and apply two coats of semigloss enamel.

If you choose to stain the cart, fill the nail holes with a filler that matches the stain. Sand the filler flush and apply a polyurethane varnish to protect the tray from moisture.

8 **Attach the hardware.** Follow the manufacturer's instructions to install a caster on the bottom of each leg. Drill the holes for the tray handles and screw them in position. To test the cart, load it with your favorite snacks and beverages and wheel it to your favorite chair.

FOLDING TRAY TABLE

If you have ever tried to serve guests (or yourself) and had no place to put things, you'll appreciate this folding tray. It can be set up anywhere to serve anything. It's lightweight and highly portable. The generously sized tray offers a large serving area and, when you are finished, the whole unit folds flat for storage. You may want to make two or three of these tray tables to have on hand for your next party.

The construction is straightforward. The tray bottom is a piece of ¼-inch cabinet-grade plywood with a rim around three sides. The legs pivot on a ¾-inch dowel. Two cloth straps keep the legs from opening too far. The tray hinges on two easily made metal strips.

1 Select the stock and cut the parts. Lay out the parts on your stock. Make the tray bottom from a high-quality plywood and the rest of the parts from the hardwood of your choice. Look for clear, straight-grain stock. Cut the parts to the sizes specified by the Cutting List.

2 Make the legs. Mark the midpoint of the length of each leg before you miter the ends of the legs. Set the miter gauge on the table saw to 60 degrees. Cut the ends of the legs, as shown in the *Top Stretcher Detail* and *Bottom Stretcher Detail*. Saw the notches in the ends of the legs for the stretchers.

3 Drill the pivot holes. Extend the midpoint marks you made on each

leg across one face and mark the center of this line. Choose two legs to be the inside legs and two to be the outside legs. Drill a ¾-inch hole through the inside legs at the center point.

Drill a ¾-inch hole ⅜ inch deep at the center point of the outside legs, as shown in the *Pivot Detail*. To be sure you make a left and a right outside leg,

EXPLODED VIEW

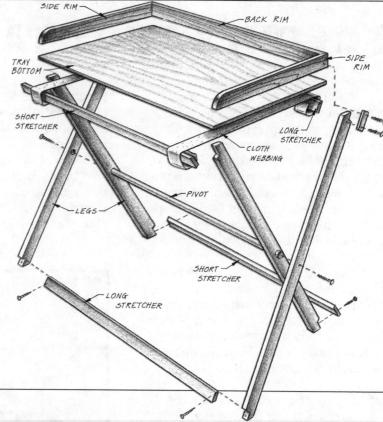

SIDE RIM

BACK RIM

TRAY BOTTOM

SIDE RIM

SHORT STRETCHER

LONG STRETCHER

CLOTH WEBBING

PIVOT

LEGS

SHORT STRETCHER

LONG STRETCHER

CUTTING LIST

Part	Quantity	Dimensions	Comments
Legs	4	¾″ × 1½″ × 36″	
Pivot	1	¾″ dia. × 30¾″	Hardwood dowel
Short stretchers	2	⅜″ × 1¼″ × 29⅞″	
Long stretchers	2	⅜″ × 1¼″ × 31½″	
Back rim	1	⅝″ × 1¾″ × 31½″	
Side rims	2	⅝″ × 1¾″ × 19¾″	
Tray bottom	1	¼″ × 19¾″ × 31½″	Hardwood plywood

Hardware

2 drywall screws, #8 × 1½″
4 drywall screws, #6 × 1″
#17 × 1″ wire brads
5′ cloth webbing, 2″ wide
Upholstery tacks
2 steel or aluminum strips, ⅛″ × ¾″ × 2¾″
4 roundhead wood screws, #10 × ¾″, with washers

put the legs side by side so that the angles at the top form a peak. Drill the stopped holes in the surfaces that face up. Drill and countersink a $\frac{5}{32}$-inch screw shank hole through the center of each stopped hole.

4 Install the pivot. Finish sand the legs and the pivot. Slide the two inside legs onto the pivot. If necessary,

enlarge the inside of the holes slightly with a round file so that the legs move freely. Be sure the angles at the top of the legs face the same direction.

Apply glue to the pivot holes in the outside legs and slide them onto the ends of the pivot. Be sure the angles at the tops of the legs are opposite those on the inside legs. Drill $\frac{3}{32}$-inch pilot holes through the shank holes in the legs into the ends of the pivot. Check that

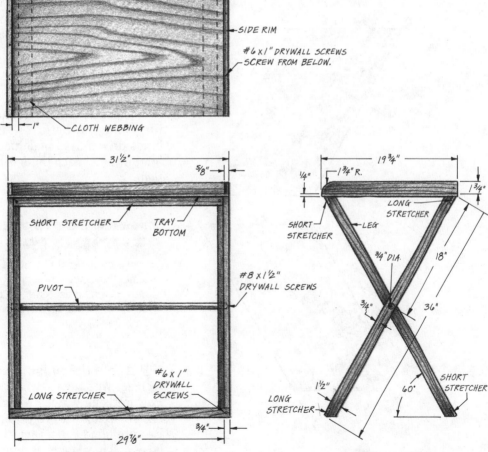

TOP VIEW

BACK RIM

SIDE RIM

#6 x 1" DRYWALL SCREWS
SCREW FROM BELOW.

1"

CLOTH WEBBING

FRONT VIEW

31½"

⅝"

SHORT STRETCHER

TRAY BOTTOM

PIVOT

#8 x 1½" DRYWALL SCREWS

#6 x 1" DRYWALL SCREWS

LONG STRETCHER

29⅛"

¾"

SIDE VIEW

19¾"

1¾" R.

¼"

1¾"

LONG STRETCHER

SHORT STRETCHER

LEG

¾" DIA.

18"

¾"

36"

1½"

LONG STRETCHER

60°

SHORT STRETCHER

21

the outside legs are parallel and not skewed by laying the assembly on a flat surface. Screw the outside legs to the pivot with #8 × 1½-inch drywall screws.

5 **Add the stretchers.** Drill and countersink 5/32-inch holes in the

ends of the stretchers, as shown in the *Top Stretcher Detail* and *Bottom Stretcher Detail.* Tilt the table saw blade to 30 degrees and rip the bevel on the top of one long and one short stretcher, as shown. Finish sand the stretchers. Attach the short stretchers to the inside legs and the long ones to the outside legs with glue and #6 × 1-inch drywall screws.

TOP STRETCHER DETAIL

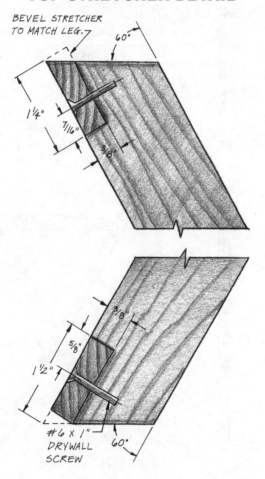

BEVEL STRETCHER
TO MATCH LEG.

60°

1 1/4"

7/16"

3/8"

3/8"

5/8"

1 1/2"

#6 X 1"
DRYWALL
SCREW

60°

BOTTOM STRETCHER DETAIL

6 **Make the tray.** The tray has a rim around three sides. The corners of the rim are mitered together. Set the table saw blade to 45 degrees and bevel both ends of the back rim and one end of each side rim. Radius the other ends of the side rims, as shown in the *Side View.*

Sand the tray bottom and the rim pieces. Apply glue to the bottom and mitered ends of the rim pieces. Nail the rim to the tray bottom with 1-inch wire brads driven from underneath. Drive a brad through each miter joint to keep it tight.

SHOP TIP: You can improve the strength of end grain glue joints by letting a coating of glue soak into the end grain for a few minutes, scraping off the excess, then recoating with fresh glue.

7 **Apply the finish.** Finish the project with your favorite wood finish. Polyurethane varnish would be a good choice because it protects against spills. Be careful not to get finish in the pivot holes—this will interfere with the legs' movement.

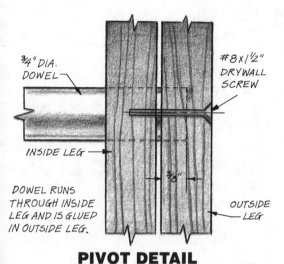

¾" DIA. DOWEL

INSIDE LEG

#8x½" DRYWALL SCREW

⅜"

OUTSIDE LEG

DOWEL RUNS THROUGH INSIDE LEG AND IS GLUED IN OUTSIDE LEG.

PIVOT DETAIL

length and tack them to the front stretcher with upholstery tacks.

8 **Attach the cloth webbing.** Locate the webbing strips, as shown in the *Top View*. Attach the strips with upholstery tacks to the inside of the stretchers, as shown in the *Webbing Detail*. Start by attaching the strips to the back stretcher. Then spread the legs and put the tray in place to determine the exact opening. The tray should overhang the legs by ½ inch in front and be flush with them in back. Cut the strips to

9 **Make and attach the tray hinge.** Cut two strips of metal to the shape shown in the *Hinge Detail*. Cut the metal with a hacksaw and clean up the edges with a file. Be sure to remove any burrs and gently round all the edges.

Drill the strips as shown. File the holes to remove any burrs. Drill pilot holes in the legs and side rims and screw the strips in position. Use roundhead wood screws and place a washer between the screws and the strips. Tighten the screws to remove any play, but leave the strips free to pivot at both ends. Once the hinges are in place and working properly, remove them and give them a coat of paint. When the paint dries, put the hinges back on and have a party.

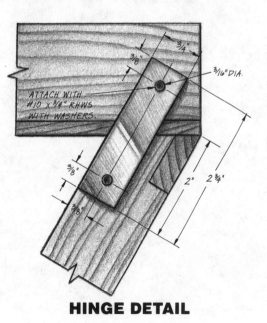

¾"

⅜"

³⁄₁₆" DIA.

ATTACH WITH #10 x ¾" RHWS WITH WASHERS.

⅜"

⅜"

2"

2¾"

HINGE DETAIL

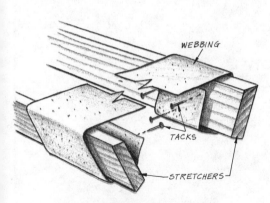

WEBBING

TACKS

STRETCHERS

WEBBING DETAIL

TOWEL SHELF

This towel shelf is so straightforward and so useful you'll be tempted to make several. It consists of four boards screwed and glued together with a dowel for the towel bar.

This would be a good project for starting a youngster in woodworking. The techniques are very basic and the project won't take more than a few hours. With careful guidance, a ten-year-old can do a good job of it.

1 **Select the stock and cut the parts.** Lay out the parts on your stock, then cut them to the sizes specified by the Cutting List.

2 **Join the shelf and back.** Cut mortises in the back for two keyhole hangers. (Don't forget to cut recesses for the mounting screws.) Edge-glue the back to the underside of the

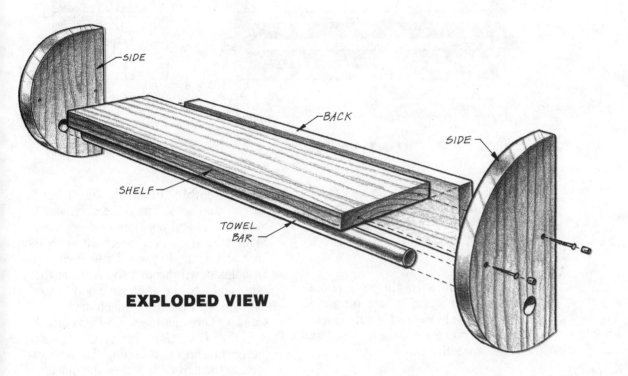

EXPLODED VIEW

CUTTING LIST

Part	Quantity	Dimensions	Comments
Shelf	1	¾″ × 4¾″ × 16″	Pine
Back	1	¾″ × 3⅝″ × 16″	Pine
Sides	2	¾″ × 4¾″ × 8″	Pine
Towel bar	1	¾″ dia. × 19″	Hardwood dowel

Hardware

6 drywall screws, #6 × 1½″
2 keyhole hangers. Available from The Woodworkers' Store, 21801 Industrial Blvd., Rogers, MN 55374–9514. Part #26302.
4 cup hooks or L hooks (optional)
6 wood plugs, ⅜″

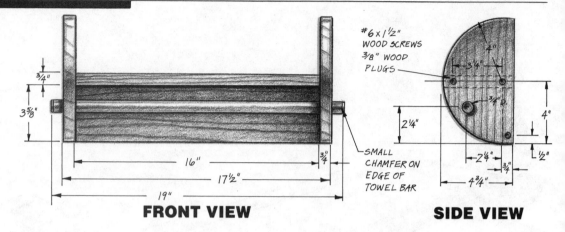

FRONT VIEW **SIDE VIEW**

shelf. Make sure the two pieces are flush along the back, then clamp them. Pad your clamps with scraps of wood to avoid denting the wood.

3 **Cut the sides to shape.** Lay out the circular shape shown in the *Side View* on each side piece. Cut the sides out with a band saw or coping saw. Sand the edges smooth.

SHOP TIP: When cutting two or more pieces to the same shape, clamp them together and do the final shaping on all the pieces at once. Their shapes will be identical.

4 **Drill the sides.** Lay out the locations for the screw holes and the towel bar hole on the sides, as shown in the *Side View*. Drill the ¾-inch holes for the towel bar. Drill ⁵⁄₃₂-inch holes for the screws and then counterbore these holes with a ³⁄₈-inch bit for the plugs. Be sure to counterbore the *outside faces* so that you have a left and a right side.

5 **Assemble the shelf.** Finish sand all the parts. Stand the shelf and back on end and position a side on top. Make sure the pieces are flush along the back and at the bottom. Drill ³⁄₃₂-inch pilot holes down through the holes in the sides and into the shelf assembly. Attach the side with #6 × 1½-inch drywall screws. Turn the piece over and attach the other side. Glue the wood plugs into the counterbores, orienting the grain direction to align with that of the sides. Pare them flush with the surface of the side.

Lightly chamfer the ends of the towel bar and slide it into position. If it slides in snugly, you won't need to fasten it further; your finish will effectively "glue" it. If it's loose, a 1-inch finishing nail driven into the dowel from the edge of a side will anchor it.

6 **Finish the shelf.** Do any touch-up sanding necessary. Choose and apply a finish that's appropriate for the room where you intend to hang the rack. Install the keyhole hangers and hang the rack on the wall. Add cup hooks along the bottom edge if you like.

JELLY CUPBOARD

While you may not have enough jelly to fill a cupboard, you probably have plenty of other stuff needing a place of its own. Rick Wright of Schnecksville, Pennsylvania, designed this cupboard with a slate top, which makes it particularly handy. You can put hot or wet things on it without concern for the finish. The cabinet is small enough to fit in a tight space, yet has plenty of room inside.

A jelly cupboard is a very traditional, country, farm-kitchen piece of furniture. The farmer himself, or a neighbor, often built simple furniture during the winter as an off-season trade. Easy-to-work woods like pine, basswood, and poplar are appropriate for its clean lines and straightforward construction.

To find a merchant who can supply the slate top, check the Yellow Pages under "Slate" or "Stone, Natural." If you have trouble, ask for advice from local masons, ceramic tile dealers, or contractors who build custom kitchens. If slate isn't your style, substitute a top of marble, granite, or wood.

1 **Select the stock and cut the parts.** This cupboard is simple to construct. The shelves fit dadoes in the sides; screws hold them. If you can't get full-width boards for the shelves, sides, and panels, edge-glue narrower boards before planing the stock to final thickness. Then, to get a good fit in the dadoes, joint and plane your stock to fit a sample dado routed into a piece of scrap. Cut the parts to the dimensions specified by the Cutting List.

2 **Cut the dadoes and rabbets in the cupboard sides.** Rout the four dadoes for the shelves in each side. On pieces this size, routing dadoes is safer than cutting them on the table saw with a dado blade. The router also gives more uniform results. Clamp a straightedge firmly across the sides to guide the rou-

ter, and rout each dado in several passes of increasing depth.

Cut the ⅜ × ¼-inch rabbets for the cabinet back. You'll probably find it easiest to set up the table saw to cut the rabbets as two side-by-side saw kerfs with the side flat on the saw.

3 **Shape the sides to make the feet.** Lay out the cutouts in the bottom of the sides, as shown in the *Side View,* and saw them out. Clean up the sawed edges with files and sandpaper.

4 **Drill and counterbore the cabinet sides for screws.** Lay out the screw locations in the sides, as shown in the *Side View.* Bore ⅜-inch-diameter × ³⁄₁₆-inch-deep counterbores in the sides with a brad-point bit. Then bore ⁵⁄₃₂-inch shank holes in the center of each counterbore.

Test assemble the sides and shelves without glue. Drill pilot holes into the shelves through the shank holes in the cabinet sides. Disassemble the cabinet.

5 **Assemble the cabinet sides and shelves.** Sand the inside of the sides and both sides of the shelves. Avoid oversanding the edges of the shelves that fit the dadoes. Lay one cabinet side on sawhorses. Glue the shelves

CUTTING LIST

Part	Quantity	Dimensions	Comments
Sides	2	¾″ × 11¼″ × 49½″	Pine
Shelves	4	¾″ × 11″ × 21¼″	Pine
Face stiles	2	¾″ × 3″ × 49½″	Pine
Back	1	¼″ × 21¼″ × 49″	Plywood
Door stiles	2	¾″ × 2″ × 46⅜″	Pine
Door rail stock	1	¾″ × 6½″ × 12¾″	Pine; rip later into 3 rails.
Door panels	2	¾″ × 12⅝″ × 20¾″	Pine
Turn button	1	⅜″ × ½″ × 2″	Maple
Top	1	½″ × 13″ × 24″	Slate, stone, or wood
Cleats	2	½″ × ½″ × 10¾″	Pine

Hardware

1 maple doorknob, 1″ dia. × 1″
2 brass cabinet hinges, 1½″ × 2″
#8 × 1¼″ flathead wood screws
⅜″ wood plugs
1 brass flathead wood screw, #6 × 1″
1″ wire-gauge nails

EXPLODED VIEW

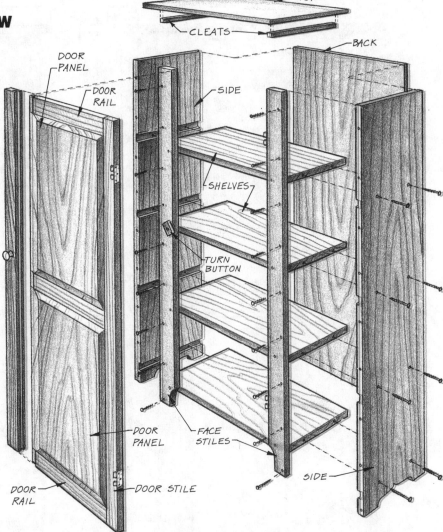

TOP

CLEATS

BACK

DOOR PANEL

DOOR RAIL

SIDE

SHELVES

TURN BUTTON

DOOR PANEL

FACE STILES

SIDE

DOOR RAIL

DOOR STILE

into the dadoes of that side. Glue the second side onto the shelves and clamp the cabinet. Make sure that it's square by measuring diagonally across the corners. Sight along the front edges of the sides to make sure the assembly isn't twisted.

With the cabinet still clamped, screw the sides to the shelves with #8 × 1¼-inch screws.

6 **Shape the face stiles.** The two face stiles are shaped to create the front feet. Rick calls the shape a bootjack end. Lay out the shape, cut it, and clean up the edges as you did for the edges of the side cutouts.

Lay out and prepare the screw holes the same way you did on the sides. The screw locations are given in the *Front View.*

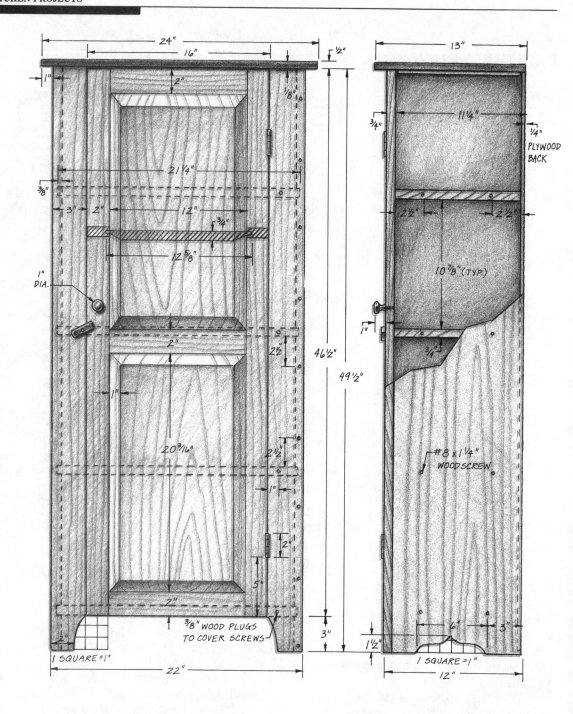

FRONT VIEW

SIDE VIEW (SECTION)

7 **Glue and screw the face stiles to the cabinet.** First, test clamp the face stiles to the cabinet. Drill pilot holes for the screws. Remove the stiles to apply glue, then clamp and screw them to the front of the cabinet.

8 **Plug the screw holes in the cabinet.** If you have a drill press, cut ⅜-inch plugs from scraps of the cabinet wood with a plug cutter. Otherwise, buy plugs that match as closely as possible. Glue and gently hammer the plugs into the counterbored screw holes in the cupboard sides and face stiles. Align the grain of the plugs with the grain of the cabinet. When the glue is dry, trim the plugs flush with the surface of the cabinet. A small backsaw or block plane and a sharp chisel are handy for this job.

SHOP TIP: You can drill counterbore, shank, and pilot holes in one step with a special drill bit. The assembly consists of a drill bit for the screw holes, a countersink for the head of the screw, and a cutter for the plug counterbore. The better sets have tapered drill bits for greater screw grip and stop collars for depth adjustment. If you use this type of tool, you can drill all the holes *in one pass* after the parts have been clamped together.

9 **Cut and attach the back.** The back is ¼-inch plywood. If you're building out of pine, you may be able to get plywood with pine face veneer; otherwise, use birch plywood. Cut the back to size and sand the inside surface. Glue and clamp it into the rabbets that you cut in the back edges of the sides. Nail it in place with 1-inch wire-gauge nails. Angle the nails in the sides toward the center of the sides. Position the nails carefully so they don't graze the side or miss it entirely.

10 **Tongue and groove the door stiles and rails.** Tongues on the rails fit into grooves in the stiles. These grooves also receive the door panels. A ¼-inch slot cutter in a table-mounted router makes quick work of both the tongues and grooves. The *Door Detail* shows how the parts come together.

Begin by cutting a sample groove in a piece of scrap. To make a matching tongue, lower the bit to cut a ¼-inch-wide × ⅜-inch-deep rabbet in both sides of a piece of scrap. Test fit this tongue in the sample groove and adjust the cutter height as necessary to get a good fit. When you've got it right, cut the tongues on the ends of the 6½-inch-wide rail stock, then rip and joint the rail stock to make three 2-inch-wide rails.

Lay a rail on the router table and raise the cutter to the exact height of the tongue on the rail. Cut full-length grooves on one edge of both stiles and two of the rails. Rout both edges of the third rail.

11 **Make the raised door panels.** Cut the bevel on the raised panels on the table saw. Screw a tall plywood auxiliary fence to the table saw fence. Tilt the blade 25 degrees away from the fence. The beveled edge must extend 5⁄16 inch into the grooves in the stiles and rails. Adjust the fence and make test cuts in scrap until your test piece fits the groove. Saw the bevels with the panels on edge against the tall fence.

12 **Glue the door together.** Sand all the door parts. Sand the bevel on the door panel carefully to remove the saw marks but keep the edges crisp. Avoid sanding the sections of the stiles that meet the rails.

Glue and clamp the rail tongues into the stile grooves, sliding the panels into place as you do so. Don't glue the panel; it must be free to expand and contract with humidity changes. Wax on the cor-

ners of the panels will prevent excess glue from bonding the panel to the frame. Apply it carefully, as it will also interfere with finishing materials if it's on an exposed part of the panel.

Make sure the door is square and perfectly flat while the glue dries.

SHOP TIP: If you need to saw an identical pattern on several parts for a project, stack them, clamp them, and saw them together. If clamps get in the way, hold the pieces together with small brads, dabs of hot-melt glue, or double-faced tape. Leave the stacked parts together until after you have cleaned up the edges of the cut.

13 **Hang the door.** The door can open left or right. Lay the cupboard on its back and position the door on the cupboard. Be sure to allow clearance at the top, as shown in the *Front View.* You should have about $3/32$ to $1/8$ inch total clearance for the door from side to side. Mark the hinge locations on the door and face stiles.

Remove the door and lay out the hinge mortises at the marks. Mortise the hinges into the edges of the stiles. Gauge the depth of the mortises to leave $1/32$ inch clearance between the door and the stile after assembly. For more information, see "Mortising Hinges" on the opposite page.

Set the hinges in the mortises and mark the screw locations. Drill pilot holes for the screws and install the door. Check for adequate clearance at the top and both sides, then remove the door.

DOOR DETAIL

14 Add the knob and turn button. The simple wood knob can be turned on a lathe or purchased ready-made. Drill and countersink a hole in the door stile for the knob screw. Drill a pilot hole in the knob and screw it to the door.

Ease the edges and corners of the turn button and drill it for the screw that holds it. Since it will show, a brass screw would be a nice touch here. Make the shank hole a bit oversize so the turn button rotates easily, and countersink it deeply so the edges of the screw don't snag your shirt as you walk past.

15 Fit the slate top to the cupboard. The slate is heavy enough to stay put with just a pair of cleats glued on the bottom to keep it from sliding around. Set the slate in place on the cupboard and trace the inside surface of the sides and face stiles on the bottom of the slate. Glue two ½ × ½ × 10¾-inch wooden cleats to the slate just inside the pencil lines with construction adhesive.

16 Finish the jelly cupboard. Rick's technique for finishing began with a coat of paint. He then sanded the cabinet until the grain of the wood showed again. This colored the wood and created a nice effect when he put on his top coat of polyurethane. Seal the slate with two coats of boiled linseed oil.

MORTISING HINGES

Traditional cabinet butt hinges require mortises in the door and stile. While the fit of the mortise to the hinge is not highly visible, well-fitted mortises are a sign of skilled craftsmanship. Here are some tips for getting that fit.

1 Lay out the mortise on the door. Position the hinge on the edge of the door, as indicated in your project plans. Scribe around the hinge lightly with a utility knife. Adjust a marking gauge to the mortise depth—usually the thickness of the hinge leaves. Scribe this depth on the face of the door.

If you'd like to know what the space between the door and stile will be, close a hinge and adjust it so the leaves are parallel to each other. The space between the leaves will be the door clearance if the mortises are the depth of the leaf thickness. You can increase the clearance by decreasing the mortise depth and vice versa. Make sure there is at least some clearance, or you will pull out the hinge screws when you try to close the door.

2 Deepen the layout lines. One of the secrets of tight-fitting hinge mortises is deepening the layout lines without enlarging the mortise. Unfortunately, pushing a chisel, or even a utility knife, into the wood to the full depth of a hinge mortise inevitably enlarges the mortise. To avoid this, deepen the layout lines

(continued)

MORTISING HINGES—CONTINUED

with a utility knife held at a slight angle, as shown in *Deepening Layout Lines.* The purpose of the angle is not to undercut the edge of the mortise but to make a straight cut in spite of the bevel on the edge of the knife. Deepen the lines no more than 1/64 inch and then cut away waste on the inside of the lines by making a second angled cut alongside the first. Removing the waste will make room for the thickness of the blade as you deepen the lines another 1/64 inch. Continue as necessary to the depth of the mortise.

① DEEPEN SCRIBE MARK.

UTILITY KNIFE AT ANGLE

② REMOVE WASTE.

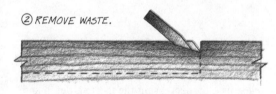

③ REPEAT.

DEEPENING LAYOUT LINES

3 **Score the waste.** The bulk of the waste can be removed quickly in big chunks if you chop across the grain, inside the V-grooves that now outline the mortise, as shown in *Scoring the Waste.* A sharp chisel and a mallet work well for this.

SCORING THE WASTE

4 **Remove the waste.** Pare away the waste with a chisel, starting the chisel on the face of the door. Begin the final paring cuts with the chisel in the scribed depth line, as shown in *Removing the Waste.*

REMOVING THE WASTE

5 **Mortise the stiles.** Position the door in its opening. Insert shims around the edges to hold the door with the proper clearance around the edges. Mark the locations of the mortises on the stiles. Remove the door, position a hinge at the marks on the stile, trace around the hinge, and cut the stile mortise just as you did the door mortise.

If you install a lot of cabinet hinges that require mortises, it will be worth your while to buy a No. 271 router plane or equivalent. You can use it instead of the marking gauge for scribing the depth of the mortise, then use it for paring the mortise to its precise depth.

STACKED SHELF

You can build this shelf unit from a couple of boards in one day. It's perfect for filling a narrow wall space. And it's useful: six shelves and two small drawers will hold all sorts of treasures. The dimensions for the shelves in the photo are given here, but feel free to change them to fit your needs. You can even change the entire shape of the project, making it wider or shorter—build it to suit you.

1 **Select the stock and cut the parts.** This entire project can be made from 10 feet of 1 × 6. Cut the back, shelves, and drawer case sides to the sizes specified by the Cutting List. Set the remaining wood aside for the drawers.

2 **Cut the dadoes in the back.** Lay out the dadoes, as shown in the *Front View.* Adjust a dado blade on the table saw to make a ¾-inch-wide × ⅜-inch-deep cut. Make a test cut in a piece of scrap. Adjust the cutting width as necessary so the shelves fit snugly in the dado. If you have a stacked dado blade, you can adjust the width by putting paper shims over the arbor between the chippers.

Guide the shelf stock across the blade with a miter gauge to cut the dadoes. The spacing for the dadoes is not critical, except for the dadoes that will hold the drawer cases. These must be exactly 2 inches apart.

EXPLODED VIEW

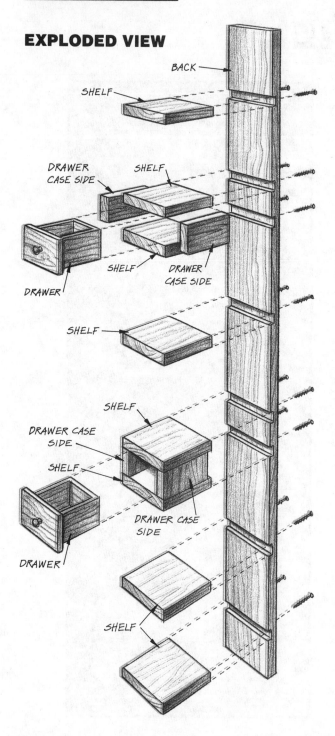

BACK

SHELF

DRAWER CASE SIDE

SHELF

SHELF

DRAWER CASE SIDE

DRAWER

SHELF

SHELF

DRAWER CASE SIDE

SHELF

DRAWER CASE SIDE

DRAWER

SHELF

SHELF

3 Mortise for the hangers. The keyhole hangers are mortised into the back. Position them, as shown in the *Front View,* and trace around them with a pencil. Cut the mortises with a ¼-inch straight bit in a hand-held router. Rout close to the lines, then clean up the mortises with a chisel. Rout slightly deeper into the stock to create a recess for the head of a hanging screw.

4 Make the drawer cases. Build and install the drawer cases as units. Select shelves to be the tops and bottoms. Glue the sides between them, as shown in the *Drawer Case Detail.* Make sure the assemblies are flush in front and along the sides. The shelves should overhang the sides by ⅜ inch in the back.

5 Attach the shelves. Finish sand the back, shelves, and drawer cases. Drill and countersink two 5/32-inch holes through each dado, as shown in the *Front View.* Fit the shelves into the dadoes. Drill 3/32-inch pilot holes in the shelves through the holes in the back. Screw the shelves and drawer cases in place with #6 × 1½-inch drywall screws.

6 Make the drawer fronts. Cut the drawer fronts to the size specified by the Cutting List. Cut ⅜-inch-deep rabbets around the inside of the drawer fronts, as shown in the *Drawer Front Detail.* Note the three different widths. Cut the rabbets with a ¾-inch-diameter straight bit in a table-mounted router. If your router table doesn't have a miter gauge, guide the drawer fronts along the fence with a square scrap.

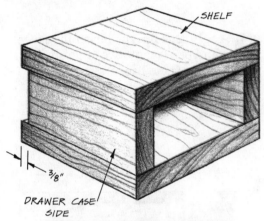

DRAWER CASE DETAIL

7 **Make the drawers.** Resaw the remaining stock to just over ¼ inch thick, then plane it to ¼ inch. For more information, see "Resawing on the Table Saw" on page 13. Saw the drawer sides and backs to the sizes specified by the Cutting List. Plane the leftover piece to ⅛ inch thick for the drawer bottoms and saw them to size. Nail and glue the drawers together, as shown in the *Drawer Exploded View.* Use wire brads and predrill the holes to avoid splitting the wood. Set the brads with a nail set.

SHOP TIP: Traditionally, only drawer fronts were finished. If you would like to finish the insides of drawers, use shellac. It will seal the wood and keep the insides of the drawers smelling sweet. Rub paraffin on the outside of the sides so that the drawer will run smoothly.

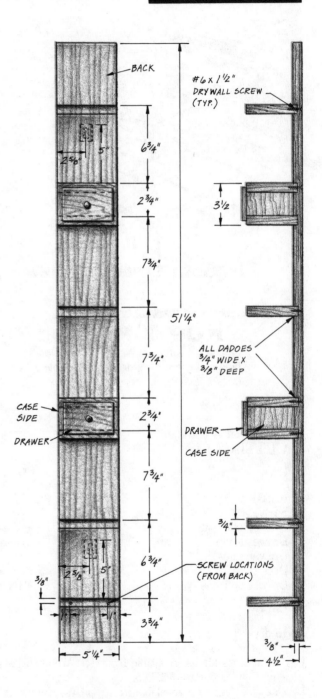

FRONT VIEW   **SIDE VIEW**

37

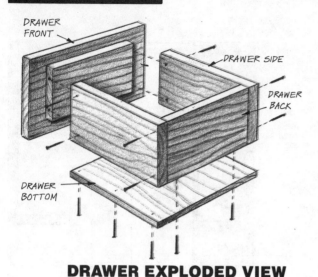

DRAWER FRONT

DRAWER SIDE

DRAWER BACK

DRAWER BOTTOM

DRAWER EXPLODED VIEW

8 **Fit the drawers.** Try the drawers in their cases. If they don't slide in smoothly, sand the sides until they do.

9 **Apply the finish.** Finish the piece with your favorite wood finish, then install the keyhole hangers and drawer knobs.

SHOP TIP: When pre-drilling holes for brads, cut the head off a brad and use it for a drill bit. The hole it drills is exactly the correct diameter.

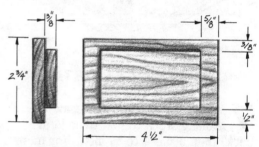

DRAWER FRONT DETAIL

CUTTING LIST

Part	Quantity	Dimensions	Comments
Back	1	$3/4'' \times 5\frac{1}{4}'' \times 51\frac{1}{4}''$	Pine
Shelves	8	$3/4'' \times 5\frac{1}{4}'' \times 4\frac{1}{2}''$	Pine
Drawer case sides	4	$3/4'' \times 4\frac{1}{8}'' \times 2''$	Pine
Drawer fronts	2	$3/4'' \times 2\frac{3}{4}'' \times 4\frac{1}{2}''$	Pine
Drawer sides	4	$1/4'' \times 1\frac{7}{8}'' \times 3\frac{3}{4}''$	Pine
Drawer backs	2	$1/4'' \times 1\frac{7}{8}'' \times 3\frac{1}{4}''$	Pine
Drawer bottoms	2	$1/8'' \times 3\frac{3}{4}'' \times 3\frac{3}{4}''$	Pine

Hardware

16 drywall screws, #6 × 1½"

#18 × ¾" wire brads

2 solid brass knobs. Available from The Woodworkers' Store, 21801 Industrial Blvd., Rogers, MN 55374–9514. Part #35295.

2 keyhole hangers. Available from The Woodworkers' Store. Part #26302.

PART
TWO

ACCENTS

QUILT OR DRYING RACK

Look at this quilt rack, then look at it again. At first look it's a reasonable, if somewhat plain, quilt rack. On the second look, it's a towel rack in a bathroom shared by Mom, Pop, and two teenagers. Or is it in the laundry room drying the jeans that didn't get entirely dry in the time it took to dry everything else in that load? It seems to be a pretty simple, straightforward project. But then there are those eight wedged mortise-and-tenon joints. This is a project that shows off some easy but impressive joints, is appreciated by the family for its genuine utility, and doesn't use much wood. The combination is tough to beat.

Phil Gehret of the Rodale Design Center built it mostly out of poplar, with commercially available oak dowels for two of the bars. The thicknesses listed in the Cutting List are the actual measurements of Phil's rack. If you make it

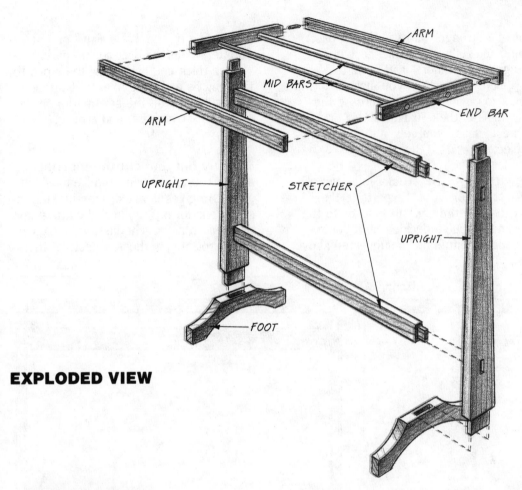

Labels on the exploded view: ARM, MID BARS, END BAR, ARM, UPRIGHT, STRETCHER, UPRIGHT, FOOT

EXPLODED VIEW

CUTTING LIST

Part	Quantity	Dimensions	Comments
Uprights	2	1″ × 3″ × 33½″	Poplar
Arms	2	1″ × 1¼″ × 14″	Poplar
Feet	2	1¼″ × 4″ × 15″	Poplar
Stretchers	2	1″ × 2″ × 32″	Poplar
Mid bars	2	½″ dia. × 32″	Oak dowel
End bars	2	⅜″ × 1¼″ × 32″	Poplar

Hardware

4 dowels, ¼″ dia. × 1¼″

out of a stronger hardwood, like oak, you could reduce the thickness of the uprights, stretchers, and arms to ¾ or ¹³⁄₁₆ inch. Similarly, if you make it out of pine, you might want to increase the thickness of these parts to 1¹⁄₁₆ or 1⅛ inches. Please yourself; it's a versatile project.

1 Prepare the stock. Joint and plane stock for all of the parts to the thickness in the Cutting List, or to the thickness you've decided on if you're making adjustments as suggested above.

"Resawing on the Table Saw" on page 13 offers helpful advice for preparing the ⅜-inch-thick end bars. Saw the stock to the lengths and widths in the Cutting List and plane off the saw marks on the end bars, stretchers, and arms.

2 Lay out and cut the mortises. "Cutting Mortises and Tenons" on page 145 gives detailed, step-by-step instructions for laying out and cutting mortises and tenons. The instructions given here explain only those aspects of the

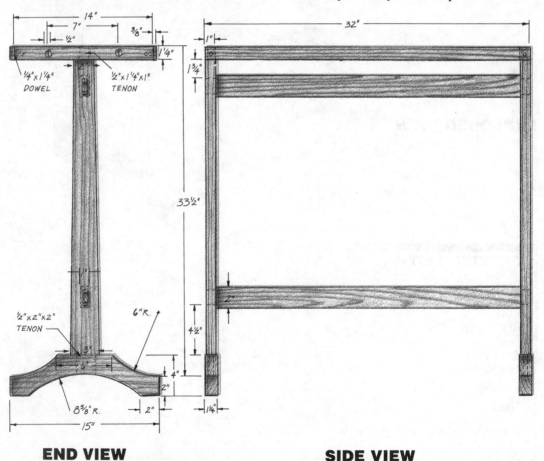

END VIEW   **SIDE VIEW**

joinery that are unique to this and similar projects.

The mortises will be easier to lay out and cut if you do it before tapering the uprights or shaping the feet. The same will be true for cutting the tenons on the uprights. Lay out the mortises in the arms, uprights, and feet.

Cutting the arm and upright mortises is straightforward. However, even though the foot mortises are not blind in the finished feet, cutting them before shaping the feet is similar to cutting blind mortises. Cut them about ⅛ inch deeper than the required 2 inches and keep the undercutting of the mortise length to a minimum; wedging the tenons can take up a little undercutting but not more than ¹⁄₃₂ to ¹⁄₁₆ inch on each end.

Drill the holes in the arms for the mid bars.

3 **Shape the feet.** The *End View* gives the radii for the curved cuts on the feet. Using the same center, draw both arcs on a piece of paper, one inside the other. Ninety degrees of arc is enough. Lay out the end points of the arcs on both feet, as shown in the drawing. Cut out the larger radius on the paper, line it up with the end points of the bottom curve, and trace it onto both feet. Then cut out the smaller radius and trace the two upper curves on both feet. Saw to the lines with a band saw or coping saw and clean up the saw marks with a spokeshave or sandpaper. Cutting the bottom curve opens up the mortise for the upright. Check that the ends of the mortise are square; if they aren't, square them with a chisel.

4 **Cut the tenons.** The uprights and stretchers have tenons on each end. Both of these parts are the same thickness and all of the tenons are the same thickness. Phil knows how to make life easy; cut all of the tenons with the same setup, varying only the tenon widths. Since all of the tenons fit into through mortises, make the tenons ¹⁄₃₂ inch longer than specified in the drawings so you can trim them perfectly flush after assembly. If you haven't developed a favorite tenon-cutting routine, see "Cutting Mortises and Tenons" on page 145. Cut the tenons, then kerf the ends for wedges, as shown in the *Tenon Detail*. Also kerf the ends of the mid bars.

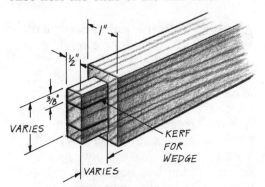

TENON DETAIL

SHOP TIP: Sawing out tiny tapered wedges to wedge tenons can be frustrating, not to mention dangerous. To do it safely, rip out a *long* strip equal in thickness to the thick end of the wedges and equal in width to the width of the wedges. Hand plane the end to a wedge, then saw it off. Repeat until the strip is too short to hold, then toss the remainder.

5 Taper the uprights. Taper the edges of the two uprights from 3 inches wide at the bottom to 2 inches wide at the top, a loss of ½ inch from each edge at the top. See "Tapering Legs" on page 124 for help in making taper cuts on the table saw.

SHOP TIP: When tapering opposite edges of stock with a tapering jig, you can sometimes avoid readjusting the tapering jig for the second cut by taping the wedge-shaped cutoff back onto the stock with masking tape.

---

6 Assemble the ends. Sand all of the parts, then draw a lightly penciled centerline down each of the uprights. Assemble the rack without glue to check that everything fits properly. Check that the arms and feet are square with the centerline on the uprights. Saw 24 tenon wedges out of scrap so you have 4 to spare. Make the wedges ½ inch wide, 2 inches long, tapered from a feather edge at one end to twice the wedge kerf width at the other end. Insert the wedges by hand but don't tap them in during the trial assembly. Note any corrections indicated by the trial assembly, then disassemble the rack and make the corrections.

Brush a thin film of glue onto the surfaces of the mortises in the arms and the corresponding tenons on the uprights, including the tenon shoulders. Work some glue into the wedge kerfs with a toothpick. Insert the tenons into the arms, check that the arms are square with the centerline on the up-

rights, then wedge the tenons, driving the wedges firmly into place.

7 Assemble the stretchers. If you work carefully to avoid banging or jarring the end assemblies, you can assemble the stretchers without waiting for the previous glue to dry. Apply glue to the mortises, holes for the mid bars, and stretcher tenons. Lay an end assembly flat and fit both stretchers and the mid bars to it. Make sure the kerfs in the mid bars are perpendicular to the length of the arms. Fit on the second end assembly. Stand the assembly upright on a flat surface. Use a framing square to check that the uprights are perpendicular to the stretchers. Measure from the ends of the arms and feet on one end of the assembly to the corresponding points on the other end to make sure the end assemblies are parallel. Wedge the tenons and mid bars as you did before, then let the glue cure well overnight.

8 Assemble the end bars. Saw off all of the protruding wedges, then pare the wedges, mid bars, and tenons flush with the surrounding wood. A razor-sharp block plane or chisel does a nice job of this kind of paring, but you can also sand them flush. However you pare down the tenons, finish by sanding off the lightly penciled centerline on the uprights.

Apply glue to the ends of the arms, let it soak in for a couple of minutes, then scrape it off. Apply a thin film of fresh glue to the ends of the arms and to the matching surfaces of the end bars and clamp the end bars in place. Let the glue dry, then dowel the end bars to the arms, as shown in the drawings.

9 Apply a finish. This is really an optional step. If you intend to use the rack routinely for drying swimwear, towels, or laundry, you may find that it's difficult to keep a finish looking good. For this kind of use, wet the rack down to raise the grain, then let it dry and give it a final hand sanding. Left without any further finish it will gray but not look unattractive in a utilitarian setting.

For less severe use, give it your favorite natural finish. If your favorite happens to be Danish oil, let the finish cure for 28 days—yes, four full weeks—before hanging damp things or your favorite quilt or comforter on it. If your finish is an unmodified boiled linseed or tung oil, let it cure for 28 days; then, before hanging your quilts on it, clamp an old white T-shirt around a bar with a spring clamp. Let it stay clamped for a day before checking it for stains. If you're really antsy to press the stand into service, use one of the more modern high-tech clear finishes and follow the instructions on the label.

SHELF AND PEGS

This shelf is about as simple as projects get, yet it is every bit as useful as more complicated projects. Use it in an entryway, in a hall closet, by the back door, or in a bedroom. It will quickly become indispensable. You can change the layout and number of pegs to accommodate a collection of anything that hangs, from scarves to kitchen mugs.

1 **Select the stock and cut the parts.** Most woods are quite suitable for this shelf. If you want to paint or stain the shelf, a less expensive wood such as poplar is a good choice. If you do not have a lathe to turn your own pegs, you can buy similar pegs at wood-

worker supply houses and hardware stores.

Cut the stock to the dimensions specified by the Cutting List. Edge-glue boards to form the shelf and back if necessary.

2 **Turn the pegs.** Cut two pieces of wood $^{13}/_{16}$ inch square × 8 inches long. Each of these blanks will yield three pegs. Mount the blanks on your lathe between centers. Turn the pegs to the shape shown in the *Peg Detail*. Sand the pegs right on the lathe, then saw them apart. Sand the ends by hand once the pegs are separated.

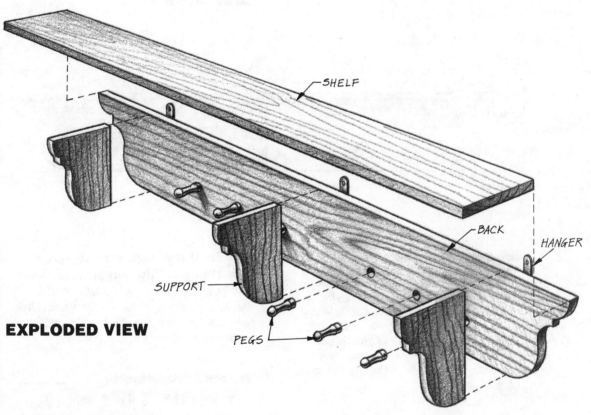

EXPLODED VIEW

CUTTING LIST

Part	Quantity	Dimensions	Comments
Shelf	1	¾″ × 8⅝″ × 71″	
Back	1	¾″ × 9⅞″ × 71″	
Supports	3	¾″ × 7⅞″ × 9⅞″	
Peg blanks	2	¹³⁄₁₆″ × ¹³⁄₁₆″ × 2¼″	Saw into 3 each after turning or buy 6 total.

Hardware

3 brass hangers, ¹⁄₁₆″ × ⅝″ × 2⅛″
6 wood screws, #8 × 1½″
6 brass wood screws, #6 × ¾″

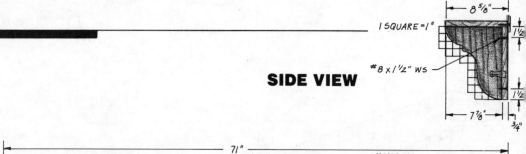

SIDE VIEW

1 SQUARE = 1"

8 5/8"

#8 x 1 1/2" WS

1 1/2

1 1/2

7 7/8"

3/4"

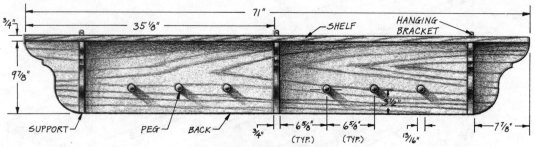

FRONT VIEW

71"

35 1/8"

3/4"

9 7/8"

SHELF

HANGING BRACKET

SUPPORT

PEG

BACK

3 1/2"

3/4"

6 5/8" (TYP.)

6 5/8" (TYP.)

13/16"

7 7/8"

SHOP TIP: To check the diameter of a round tenon as you turn it, drill the appropriate-size hole in a small piece of ¼-inch plywood. Slip this gauge over the tailstock of your lathe. Stop the lathe and slide the gauge out onto the tenon to check the size of the tenon.

3 Drill holes in the back for the pegs. Lay out and drill ¹³/₁₆-inch holes for the pegs, as shown in the *Front View*. Drill the holes ½ inch deep.

4 Saw out the shapes on the ends of the back and the shelf supports. Make a posterboard or ¼-inch plywood template of the curved profile shown in the *Side View*. Cut it to shape with a coping saw or band saw. File or sand the sawed edges to smooth the curves. Trace the pattern onto the back and supports. Saw and smooth the parts as you did the pattern.

5 Drill the back for the screws that hold the supports. Lay out the positions of the supports on the back, as shown in the *Front View*. Drill and countersink for #8 by 1½-inch wood screws, as shown in the *Side View*.

SHOP TIP: When shaping identical parts, you can save steps by cutting several at once. Draw the pattern on one blank and stack several blanks together. Hold them in place with double-faced tape or a couple of dabs of hot-melt glue. Saw out the stack of pieces on the band saw and smooth the edges before separating them. The wide edge surface makes cleaning up the curves easier.

6 Assemble the shelf. Sand the shelf, back, and supports. Place the back on edge on your workbench with the top edge down and the back surface facing you. Hold the supports in position behind the back and drill ³/₃₂-inch pilot holes through the shank holes in the back. Glue and screw the supports to the back. Make sure they are flush along the top edge. Glue and clamp the shelf to the back and the supports.

Glue the pegs into the holes in the back. If the fit is very snug, saw a small groove along the peg tenons to release the air and glue trapped at the bottom of the hole.

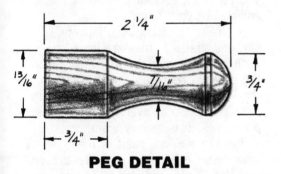

PEG DETAIL

7 Make and attach the hangers. The hangers on this peg shelf are shop-made. You may find a suitable substitute at the hardware store. If you want to make your own, it's very simple. Begin with a piece of $\frac{1}{16}$-inch-thick brass, available at most hardware stores. Lay out a $\frac{5}{8} \times 7$-inch strip by scribing it right into the metal. Cut along the line with metal shears, then file or sand the cut edge clean. Lay out three hangers, as shown in the *Hanger Detail*. Lightly

mark the center of each hole by striking it with an awl or center punch. Bore these holes on the drill press and countersink them with regular twist drills. Clamp the strip down as you drill and countersink it, otherwise the hangers may catch on the drill bit and whirl out of control. Once you've countersunk the holes, cut the metal hangers from the strip. File the radius on the end that has the larger hole.

Position the hangers on the shelf and mark for the screw holes. Drill $\frac{5}{64}$-inch pilot holes in the wood, then screw the hangers to the shelf with #6 $\times$ $\frac{3}{4}$-inch brass flathead wood screws.

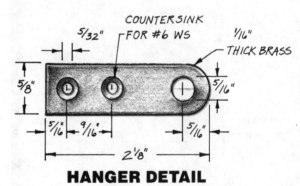

HANGER DETAIL

8 Apply the finish. Finish sand the shelf unit. Choose a finish to suit the intended location of the shelf and apply it.

RICE PAPER SCREEN

Traditionally, the Japanese separate one room from another with rice paper screens called *shoji*. This simple rice paper screen is similar to a *shoji*. The screens provide a sense of privacy without isolating the room from the rest of the house. The translucent screens allow outside light to filter through gently.

Their mobility makes it easy to change the room arrangement for other uses.

You can use this screen as a room divider or dressing screen. Or you can set it up in front of a window to reduce the glare from the sun without eliminating all the incoming light. Whatever use you put it to, it is sure to be an elegant addition to your home.

Unlike the traditional Japanese screens, these frames are joined together with screwed butt joints. Since the screens receive very little stress, the screws provide adequate strength.

Rice paper is available from art supply stores. It is usually white or off-white, but you can paint or dye it to suit your taste, even after the screen is assembled. You could also fill the frames with fabric instead of rice paper and create a totally different look.

1 Select the stock and cut the parts. Almost any wood will work for this screen. If you plan to use a natural finish on the wood, choose a fine hardwood like cherry or oak. If you plan to paint or stain the screen, then a wood like poplar or basswood will do. Cut the parts to the dimensions specified by the Cutting List. To cut all the crosspieces to the same length, butt them against a stop block clamped to a miter gauge extension fence on the table saw.

2 Drill and counterbore the uprights. Lay out the positions of the crosspieces on the uprights, as shown in

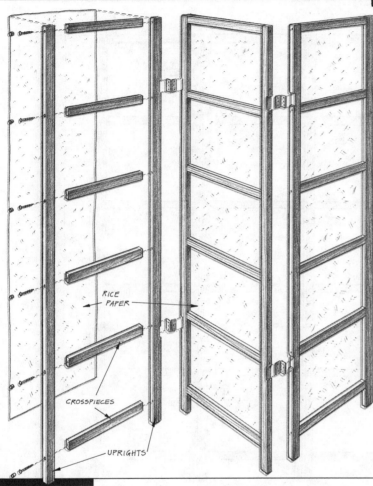

EXPLODED VIEW

RICE
PAPER

CROSSPIECES

UPRIGHTS

CUTTING LIST

Part	Quantity	Dimensions	Comments
Uprights	6	¾" × 1⁵⁄₁₆" × 74¾"	Hardwood
Crosspieces	18	¾" × 1⁵⁄₁₆" × 15"	Hardwood

Hardware

4 pairs brass butt hinges, 1½" × 2"
or
4 pairs double action hinges, ¾" × 2⅛". Available from The Woodworkers' Store, 21801 Industrial Blvd., Rogers, MN 55347–9514. Part #29033.
36 flathead wood screws, #8 × 2¼"
36 wood plugs, ⅜"
1 roll of rice paper, 18" wide × 18' long

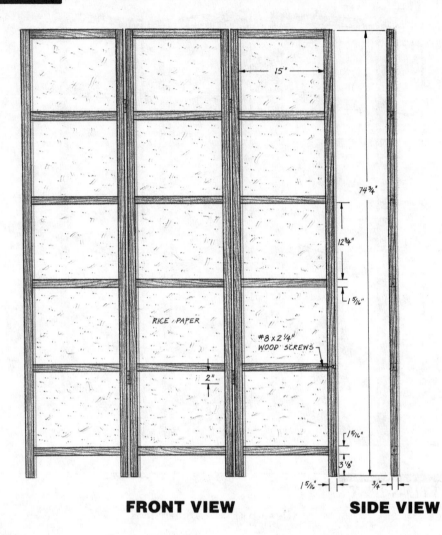

FRONT VIEW

SIDE VIEW

the *Front View*. Mark where both the top and bottom edges of the crosspieces meet the uprights. Mark the screw locations halfway between these marks. Drill shank holes for the screws, then counterbore them, as shown in the *Screw Joint Detail*.

3 **Assemble the screen sections.** Lay out one screen frame section on your bench. Clamp the crosspieces in place. Using the shank holes for a guide, drill pilot holes for the screws into the ends of the crosspieces.

Sand all the parts, but avoid sanding the mating surfaces. Glue and reclamp the screen frame together on your bench, making sure it is square and flat. Screw the screen together with #8 × 2¼-inch wood screws.

Repeat this process with the remaining two screen sections.

SHOP TIP:
You can improve the strength of end grain glue joints by letting a coating of glue soak into the end grain for a few minutes, scraping off the excess, then recoating with fresh glue.

4 **Plug the screw holes.** Chuck a ⅜-inch plug cutter in your drill press. Cut plugs for the counterbores from matching scrap wood. Brush some glue in the counterbores and tap the plugs in place with a mallet. Orient the grain of the plugs to match the grain of the uprights. Trim the plugs flush with a block plane or a chisel.

If you don't have a plug cutter, precut plugs are available from hardware stores and mail-order supply houses.

5 **Cut the hinge mortises.** Cut the hinge mortises on the two outside frames first. If you use conventional hinges, the hinge barrels on one section must be on one side of the assembled screen while the barrels on the other section must be on the other side. The two-way hinges listed in the Cutting List allow the sections to fold in either direction. See "Mortising Hinges" on page 33 for detailed instructions.

Lay the three screen frames beside each other on your bench or on the floor. Lay out the mortises for the center frame by transferring the location of the outer frame mortises. Cut the mortises, set the hinges in place in their mortises, and mark and drill for the hinge screws.

6 **Apply your finish to the screen frames.** Finish sand the frames. Apply your chosen wood finish to the front and sides of each frame. Do *not* get any finish on the back of the frames. This is where you will glue the rice paper. The finishing materials may interfere with the glue. Allow the finish to dry completely.

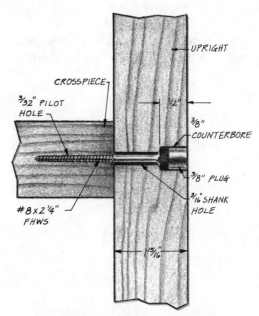

Labels: UPRIGHT, CROSSPIECE, 3/32" PILOT HOLE, 1/2", 3/8" COUNTERBORE, 3/8" PLUG, 3/16" SHANK HOLE, #8 x 2 1/4" FHWS, 1 5/16"

SCREW JOINT DETAIL

7 **Glue the rice paper to the screen sections.** Each frame is covered with a single piece of rice paper. Cut it to length, leaving 1 inch extra on each end. The paper from your roll should be wider than the frames. Don't cut the paper to width yet.

Use regular white glue to attach the rice paper. With a small brush, spread the glue thinly on the unfinished back of a frame. Lay out the rice paper on the frame with all the edges overhanging. Smooth the paper with your hands to remove wrinkles, pressing the paper into the glue. Spray the paper with a fine mist of water from a plant mister or old hand-pump spray bottle. Smooth the paper again. As the paper dries, it will shrink slightly and pull tight. Set the whole frame aside to dry. Repeat for the other two frames.

8 **Trim off the excess rice paper.** When the glue is dry, trim the paper to fit the frame by sanding through the paper along the outside edges. Use fine sandpaper and a sanding block as though you were chamfering the edges. Use a razor-sharp knife to trim the paper across the legs in line with the bottom crosspiece.

9 **Assemble the screen.** Screw the hinges in place in their mortises. Fold the screen in a slight accordion to get it to stand on its own.

SPOON HOLDER

About 15 years ago a spoon rack in Virginia's Colonial Williamsburg caught the eye of woodworker Rick Wright. He didn't have a camera, but he sketched the rack and took some notes. Since then he's made about one a year. Rick adapted the design and substituted the shelves you see here for the small drawers that appeared in the original. He also varies the wood and finish of his spoon racks. Some are made out of traditional cabinet woods and left with a natural finish, while others are made of pine or poplar and painted.

Although this rack has shelves for other little treasures, its real purpose is to showcase a collection of spoons. The scrollwork on the back and sides is quite traditional. Feel free to adjust the spacing of the shelves and the size of the spoon slots to suit your collection.

1 Select the stock and cut the parts. Choose a stable wood like cherry, butternut, or chestnut since the shelves prevent seasonal movement of the back. Make sure it is well-seasoned and select quarter-sawn boards if you can. Joint the lumber to flatten it, then plane it to thickness. Edge-glue the boards you selected to make up the 20-inch width of the back. Saw the parts to the dimensions specified by the Cutting List.

2 Lay out the back. Make a pattern for the back, as shown in the *Front View*. Note that the back has a lower, straight-sided portion that is 15½ inches wide. Cut out the pattern and transfer

the shape to the back. Lay out the star and 1-inch hole, as shown in the carving detail.

3 Drill the hole and carve the star. Bore the 1-inch hole at the center of the star with a brad-point bit or Forstner bit. You can carve the star with a veining tool or bench chisel. If you use a chisel, first cut with a sharp knife down

EXPLODED VIEW

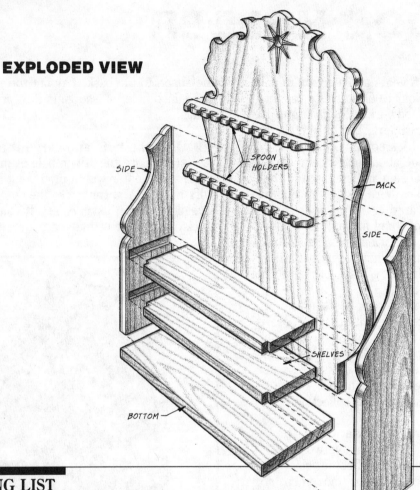

SPOON HOLDERS

SIDE

BACK

SIDE

SHELVES

BOTTOM

CUTTING LIST

Part	Quantity	Dimensions	Comments
Back	1	¾″ × 20″ × 30¼″	Follow pattern.
Sides	2	¾″ × 5¼″ × 18″	Follow pattern.
Shelves	2	¾″ × 5¼″ × 14¾″	
Bottom	1	¾″ × 7″ × 17″	
Spoon holders	2	½″ × 1½″ × 14″	Drill and saw spoon slots.

Hardware

10 flathead wood screws, #10 × 1¾″
10 wood plugs, ½″

the center of a ray. Then cut from the sides of the ray toward the knife line with the chisel, releasing the chip and forming a valley. Deepen the center cut and repeat the side cuts until the sides of the valley are at 90 degrees to each other. Repeat the process for all eight rays.

4 Cut out the back. You can cut out the pattern with a scroll saw, a ¼-inch blade on a band saw, or a coping saw. When you saw out the straight part at the bottom of the back, be sure to cut just outside the line—you'll trim it to size later. Clean up the decorative sawed edges with files and sandpaper.

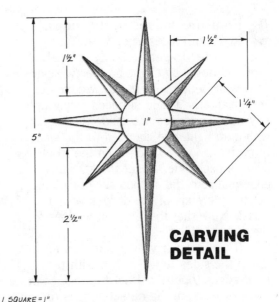

CARVING DETAIL

FRONT VIEW

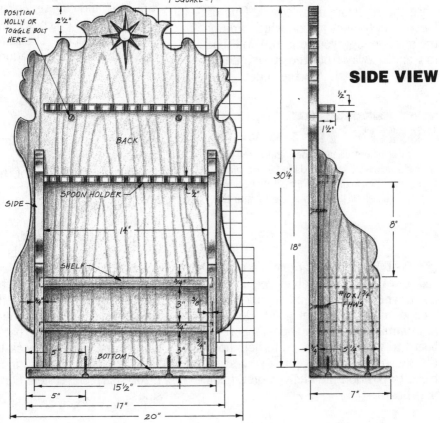

SIDE VIEW

5 Rout the dadoes in the sides. Rout both sides at once with a plunge router to get perfectly parallel shelves. Begin by clamping the two sides onto your bench with the *back* edges together and the inside surfaces facing up. Lay out the dadoes and guide the router with a straightedge clamped to the sides. Stop the dadoes ½ inch from the front edge of each side. Reset the straightedge and rout the second set of dadoes. Square the ends of the dadoes with a chisel. Note that there are no dadoes for the spoon holder.

If you don't have a plunge router, clamp the sides to the bench with the *front* edges together. Rout the dadoes in two passes from the outside edges toward the adjoining front edges. One of these cuts (depending on which side of the straightedge you're using) will tend to wander away from the straightedge, so keep a tight grip on the router.

SHOP TIP: To get a perfect fit between a shelf and the dado that houses it, cut the dado before planing the shelf to final thickness. Then hand plane the shelf until it fits snugly into the dado.

6 Notch the front corners of the shelves. The shelves require a notch where they extend beyond the stopped dadoes. To get good, clean, uniform notches, screw a wide support board to your miter gauge to help hold the shelves during the cut. Use a stop block to position the shelves on the support board.

Test fit the shelves in the sides and clamp the assembly. Check that it isn't too wide for the back. Trim the shelves if necessary. With the shelves in place, trace their locations onto the back edges of the sides.

7 Cut the sides to shape. Lay out the shape of the sides directly onto the stock, as shown in the *Side View*. Stick the two sides together with double-faced tape and cut to the line. Clean up the sawed edges as you did for the back.

8 Drill screw holes in the back. Drill and countersink shank holes for the #10 × 1¾-inch screws that hold the back to the sides. The *Side View* and your penciled shelf locations show where these screws should go.

9 Assemble the shelf unit and attach it to the back. Sand the sides, shelves, and back. Be sure not to round-over the edges of the back as you sand. Glue and clamp the shelves into the side dadoes. Make sure that the unit is square.

When the glue is dry, glue and screw the shelf unit to the back. Make certain the bottom edges of the shelf unit are flush with the bottom edge of the back. Drill pilot holes through the shank holes and into the sides. Glue and screw the sides to the back. When the glue is dry, pare the back flush with the sides along the lower 3 inches. Use a razor-sharp chisel held flat against the sides.

10 **Attach the bottom to the shelf unit.** Drill and counterbore screw shank holes in the bottom, as shown in the *Front View* and *Side View*. Sand the bottom. Drill pilot holes, then glue and screw the bottom to the shelf unit and back.

Make plugs for the counterbored holes with a plug cutter on the drill press. Make them from the same wood as the bottom. Glue the plugs into the screw holes to hide the screw heads. Sand the plugs flush.

11 **Make and attach the spoon holders.** Lay out the spoon slots in the spoon holders, as shown in the *Spoon Holder Detail*. Drill the ends of each slot with a ¼-inch bit in the drill press. Cut out the rest of each slot and the end detail with a scroll saw or coping saw. Clean up and shape each slot with files and sandpaper.

Sand the top and bottom of each spoon holder, then glue and clamp them both to the back. Clamp as far in as you can reach with deep-throat clamps or

hand screws. You can also drill and screw the spoon holders from behind if necessary.

12 **Finish the spoon holder.** To approximate an antique appearance on the spoon holder, first paint it a solid color. When the paint is dry, sand off the paint in places that would get a lot of wear in normal use, then stain the entire project. Finally, finish in a traditional manner with oil, varnish, or lacquer.

13 **Hang the spoon holder.** You can hang the spoon holder on your wall with toggle or molly bolts, or you can rout two keyhole slots in the back to accept screws you place in the wall. The heads of toggle or molly bolts are not obvious behind the spoons. You can paint them to match the wood if you like. To make keyhole slots in the back, you need a keyhole bit for your router, available from The Woodworkers' Store, 21801 Industrial Boulevard, Rogers, MN 55374-9514.

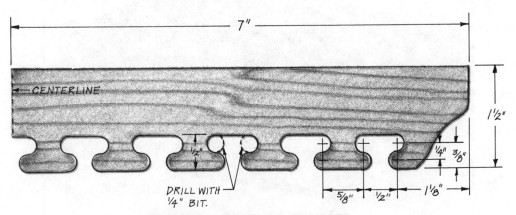

SPOON HOLDER DETAIL

OPEN WALL BOX

A wall box is a traditional household furnishing that hangs from a nail and can keep a variety of things handy. These were originally hung near the fireplace where they held candles or matches, but they can be used for outgoing mail or keys near a door, spices near the stove, medicine chest overflow in the bathroom, or a dried flower arrangement. This particular example was made by Brent and Linda Kahl of Kahl's Furniture Refinishing in Richland, Pennsylvania. A nice feature of this box is the ample size, which makes it quite versatile.

Made of pine, rabbeted and nailed together with fine cut finish nails, the box is an easy one-evening project. Make several and give them as gifts, perhaps with a flower arrangement or spices already in the box.

1 Select the stock and cut the parts. If necessary, edge-glue narrower pieces for the back. Plane the stock for all of the parts to ⅝ inch thick and cut the parts to the dimensions specified by the Cutting List.

EXPLODED VIEW

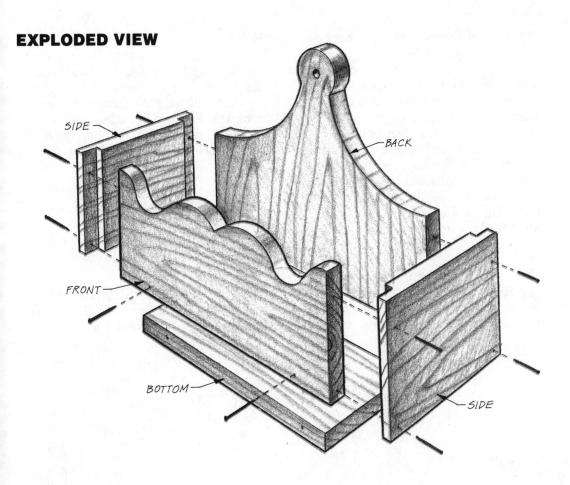

SIDE

BACK

FRONT

BOTTOM

SIDE

CUTTING LIST

Part	Quantity	Dimensions	Comments
Sides	2	$5/8'' \times 4'' \times 5\frac{1}{4}''$	Pine
Front	1	$5/8'' \times 4'' \times 10\frac{1}{2}''$	Pine
Back	1	$5/8'' \times 10\frac{1}{2}'' \times 8\frac{1}{2}''$	Pine; grain in $8\frac{1}{2}''$ direction
Bottom	1	$5/8'' \times 4'' \times 9\frac{3}{4}''$	Pine

Hardware

12 fine cut finish nails, 4d. Available from many lumber dealers and from Tremont Nail Company, P.O. Box 111, Wareham, MA 02571. Part #CE-4.

2 **Rabbet the box sides.** Chuck a ¾-inch straight bit in your table-mounted router. Adjust the fence to expose ⅝ inch of the bit and adjust the height to cut ⅜ inch deep. Since the sides are relatively small, make sure your fingers are well clear of the bit as you slide them along the fence to make the cuts. Hold them against the fence with your left hand and push them past the bit with a separate block of wood in your right hand in order to avoid tear-out when the bit exits.

3 **Cut the patterns on the box front and back.** Lay out the curve on the front of the box, as shown in the *Front View.* Begin the curve at least

½ inch from the ends. Cut out the shape with a coping saw or band saw and clean up the sawed edge with files and sandpaper.

Lay out the back pattern with a compass. Saw out the shape and clean up the edges. Be sure to keep the back a full 4 inches high where it joins the sides.

4 **Drill the hanging hole.** Drill a ¼-inch hole in the center of the circle in the back, as shown in the *Front View.*

5 **Glue and nail the box together.** Assemble the box with glue and fine cut finish nails. Drill pilot holes slightly

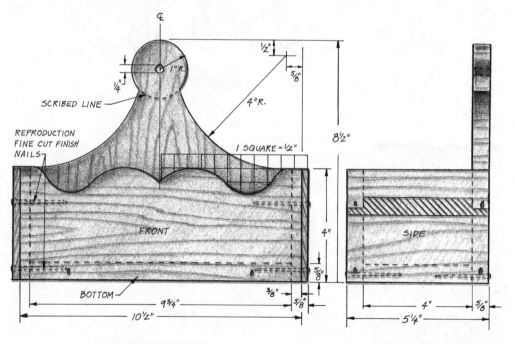

FRONT VIEW **SIDE VIEW**

smaller than the nails themselves to prevent the possibility of the nails splitting the wood. Glue and nail a side to the back. Then glue and nail the bottom to the side and back. Add the front, then the remaining side.

6 **Finish the wall box.** A nice detail that you may notice in the photo is a scribe line that completes the circle at the top of the back. To reproduce that line, hold a 2-inch-diameter object, like a 6-ounce juice can, in place on the back of the box and scribe around it with a sharp awl.

To get the antique crackled-paint finish shown in the photo, use milk paint with a gelatin coating under the top coat (both available from the Old Fashioned Milk Paint Company, P.O. Box 222, Groton, MA 01450). If you don't like the crackled look, you can still paint the box with milk paint or give it a natural finish like linseed or Danish oil.

CANDLE BOX

This traditional sliding-lid box stored the household candles during the colonial period, a time when candles held a much more important role than they do now. Candles were made of tallow, and mice loved to eat them; hence the box. You can still keep candles in the box, of course, but it will also hold a recipe file. You could adapt a toilet-paper holder spindle to prevent the recipe cards from falling over.

Brent and Linda Kahl of Kahl's Furniture Refinishing in Richland, Pennsylvania, make this particular design for sale at craft fairs. Black cherry, walnut, and maple are appropriate traditional Ameri-can woods for the box. The dovetails that the Kahls use to join the corners are strong, attractive, and traditional. Feel free to change the dimensions of the box, especially if you have something particular in mind to keep in it.

1 Select the stock and cut the parts. About the only requirement for the wood in this project is that you avoid knots, which should be easy with parts this small. Choose whatever wood you like to work with. If this is your first hand-cut dovetail project, choose an easily worked wood like basswood, pine, or

EXPLODED VIEW

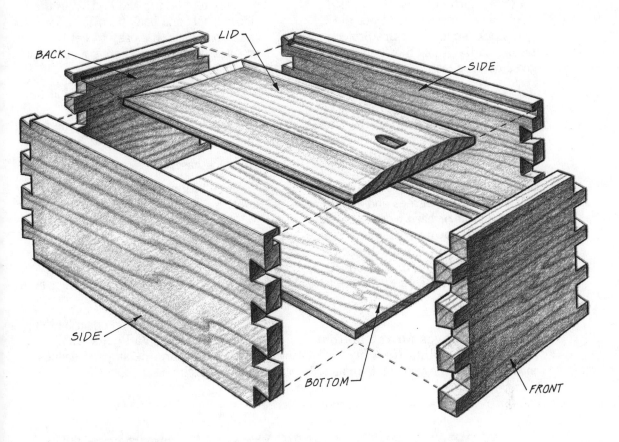

BACK

LID

SIDE

SIDE

BOTTOM

FRONT

CUTTING LIST

Part	Quantity	Dimensions
Sides	2	$\frac{1}{2}'' \times 4\frac{3}{4}'' \times 10''$
Back	1	$\frac{1}{2}'' \times 4\frac{3}{4}'' \times 6\frac{1}{4}''$
Front	1	$\frac{1}{2}'' \times 4\frac{3}{16}'' \times 6\frac{1}{4}''$
Lid	1	$\frac{1}{2}'' \times 5\frac{9}{16}'' \times 9\frac{11}{16}''$
Bottom	1	$\frac{1}{2}'' \times 5\frac{9}{16}'' \times 9\frac{9}{16}''$

poplar. Plane all the stock to ½ inch thick and cut the parts to the dimensions specified by the Cutting List. If you have 5/4 (five-quarter) or 6/4 (six-quarter) stock, you can resaw it to get the ½-inch stock required for this project. "Resawing on the Table Saw" on page 13 gives detailed instructions.

2 **Cut the dovetails in the box.** Dovetail angles range from a shallow 7 degrees sometimes used on hardwoods to about 14 degrees, more often used on the softer woods. These dovetails angle at 10 degrees and are suitable for either soft or hard woods. Lay out the pins, as shown in the *Front View,* and cut the dovetail joints. Refer to "Cutting Through Dovetails" on the opposite page if you need further help.

3 **Rout grooves for the bottom and the sliding lid.** Chuck a ⁵⁄₁₆-inch straight bit in your table-mounted router. Adjust the height of the router to cut ⁵⁄₁₆ inch deep. Position the fence ¼ inch from the bit. Lay out the required grooves for the top and bottom in the sides, front, and back from the *Side View* and *Front View.* It's easy to get the grooves confused, so here's a checklist. The sides have:

• a bottom groove, stopped at the back and front.
• a lid groove, stopped at the back, open at the front.

The back has:

• a bottom groove, stopped at both sides.
• a lid groove, stopped at both sides.

The front has:

• a bottom groove, stopped at both sides.

Rout the grooves as described in "Plunge Routing on a Router Table" on page 120. Square the stopped dadoes with a ¼-inch chisel.

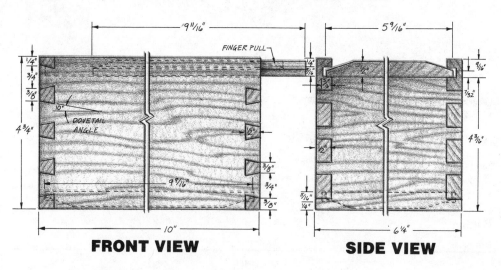

FRONT VIEW   **SIDE VIEW**

CUTTING THROUGH DOVETAILS

Much of the mystique of cutting dovetails comes from the mystique of hand woodworking tools. Those of us who grew up with machines are more comfortable with a table saw than with the far simpler handsaw. While books and magazines often remind us that it takes time to become skilled with hand tools, they overlook the fact that it takes time to become skilled with machines, too. The only real difference between hand and machine skills is that many of us have already invested the time in machines.

If you get more pleasure from working with machines than working with hand tools, use 'em. After all, you're doing it for your own satisfaction, not to please some purist. If you prefer to work with machines, get a dovetail jig to go with your router and follow the instructions.

If you do want to cut dovetails by hand, the most important thing to learn is that you can. If it took a lifetime to learn to cut dovetails by hand, we wouldn't see them all over the antique markets. If you botch the job the first time around, there's no great loss; good kindling is hard to come by.

1 **Lay out the length of the pins and tails.** For through dovetails, the length of a pin or tail equals the thickness of the adjoining board. That is, the length of a pin equals the thickness of the tail board, and vice versa. The traditional way to lay out these lengths on the stock is with a marking gauge. If you don't have a marking gauge, lay them out carefully with a straightedge. Most woodworkers protect

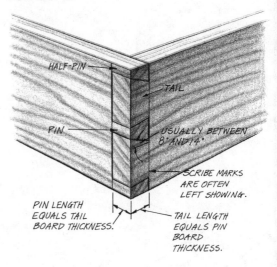

themselves from minor errors by making the error in their own favor: They cut the tails and pins slightly long, then trim them after the joint is assembled.

Lay out the length of both the pins and the tails on each side of their respective boards. These lines marking the lengths are called the base lines because they mark the bases of the pins and tails. If you're laying out the base lines with a straightedge, use a knife or a very sharp, hard pencil.

2 **Lay out the tails.** Lay out the width of the tails along the end of the tail board. Scribe a line square across the end grain at

(continued)

CUTTING THROUGH DOVETAILS—CONTINUED

STEP 2

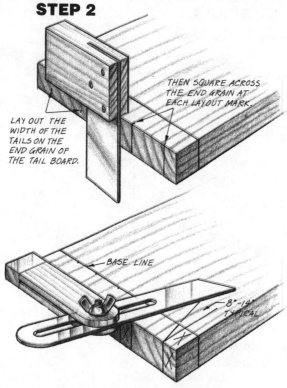

LAY OUT THE WIDTH OF THE TAILS ON THE END GRAIN OF THE TAIL BOARD.

THEN SQUARE ACROSS THE END GRAIN AT EACH LAYOUT MARK.

BASE LINE

8°-14° TYPICAL

STEP 3

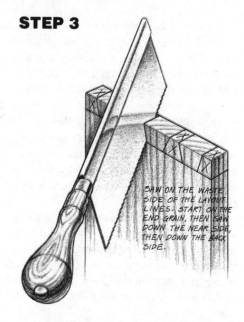

SAW ON THE WASTE SIDE OF THE LAYOUT LINES. START ON THE END GRAIN, THEN SAW DOWN THE NEAR SIDE, THEN DOWN THE BACK SIDE.

each layout mark, as shown. Set a sliding T-bevel to the angle required by your project—usually between 8 and 14 degrees. (Hardwoods compress less, so they can use the more elegant, shallow angle.) With the T-bevel, scribe from the end grain layout lines to the base lines on both faces of the board. Mark the waste areas between the tails and at the ends. Mark both faces and the end grain.

3 **Saw the sides of the tails.** Clamp the board vertically in a vise with the tails at

about elbow height. Start with the end grain line. Put a fine-tooth gent's saw or dovetail saw on the waste side of an end grain line. Cut a shallow kerf in the end grain. Then gradually angle the saw as you cut and follow the layout line on the face of the board. Cut along this line, as shown, staying on the waste side of the layout lines. When you reach the base line, extend the kerf down the back side of the board. The kerf you've cut on the front will guide the saw down the back.

4 **Chop out the waste between the tails.** Joint and plane a piece of hardwood to about 2 inches square × 1 foot long. Make sure the sides are straight and flat and the faces are square with each other. Place the

STEP 4

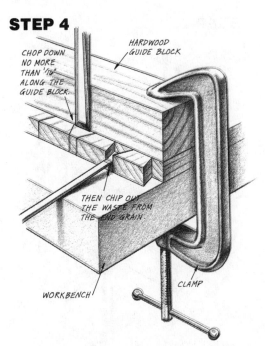

CHOP DOWN NO MORE THAN 1/16" ALONG THE GUIDE BLOCK.

HARDWOOD GUIDE BLOCK

THEN CHIP OUT THE WASTE FROM THE END GRAIN.

WORKBENCH

CLAMP

stock on a solid workbench so the tails are close to the near edge of the bench. Line up the hardwood 2 × 2 on the tail board precisely on the base line and clamp the 2 × 2 and board securely to the bench, as shown.

Hold a sharp chisel flat against the 2 × 2 in one of the waste areas. Tap it into the waste—no more than 1/16 inch—with a mallet. Repeat for all of the waste areas. Now hold the chisel horizontally against the end grain and chip out the top 1/16 inch of each waste area. Repeat the vertical and horizontal cuts. As you make the vertical cuts, angle the chisel very slightly. Keep the chisel against the bottom edge of the 2 × 2, but angle it so that it's about 1/16 inch from the top edge. This very

slight undercut is another case of making the error in your favor and is one of the secrets of tight-fitting dovetails. Any unevenness caused by the chisel will be below the surface of the joint, where it won't interfere with assembling the joint.

Continue until you've removed the waste halfway through the tail piece. Then turn the board over, line up and clamp the 2 × 2, and chop out the remaining half of the waste in the same manner.

STEP 5

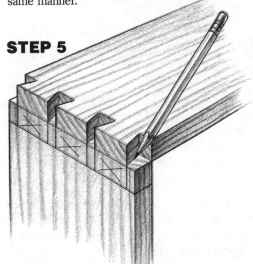

5 **Lay out the pins.** Scribe the pins directly from the tails. Clamp the pin board vertically in a vise. Hold the tail board in position on the end of the pin board. Make sure the base line is lined up with the edge of the pin board. Trace the tails onto the pins with a very sharp, hard pencil. (Many experienced woodworkers advise scribing with an awl, but beginners

(continued)

CUTTING THROUGH DOVETAILS—CONTINUED

sometimes find that the awl tends to push aside the tail piece. The pencil does the job with less pressure.)

Square down from the ends of the tail tracings to the base lines. Mark the waste areas between the pins.

STEP 6

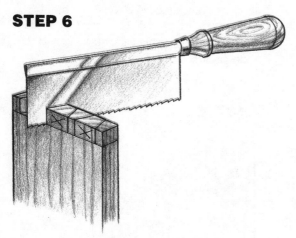

STEP 7

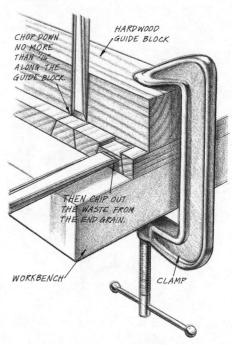

CHOP DOWN NO MORE THAN 1/16" ALONG THE GUIDE BLOCK

HARDWOOD GUIDE BLOCK

THEN CHIP OUT THE WASTE FROM THE END GRAIN.

WORKBENCH

CLAMP

6 Saw the sides of the pins. Saw down the sides of the pins the same way that you sawed the sides of the tails. Be sure to saw on the waste side of the layout lines and leave the entire pencil line—don't split the line.

7 Chop out the waste between the pins. Place the hardwood 2 × 2 on the pin board, line it up with the base line, and clamp the two to the bench as before. Chop out the waste between the pins, but keep in mind that the socket you are creating is tapered. When chopping from the narrow side of the pins—the

wide side of the waste—be careful that you don't chop into the pins, weakening them.

Once you've cut a dozen dovetail joints, you'll find that they fit like a glove without any further work. The first few joints may require some paring. Try fitting the tails to the pins. If they don't go together, carefully examine the entire joint. Paring the wrong side of a pin may allow it to fit between the tails, but may make it impossible to fit the remainder of the joint. When you have a good idea of where you need to remove material, take it off in small increments. Pare off a shaving or two with a sharp chisel and then try the joint again.

4 **Bevel the lid and the bottom.**
The beveled edges of the lid and
the bottom are shaped like the edges of
a raised panel. Tilt the table saw blade
17 degrees from vertical, away from the
fence. Depending on your saw, you may
have to put the fence on the left side of
the blade to do this. Position the fence
¼ inch from the blade. Cut bevels on

both sides and one end of the lid, and on
all four edges of the bottom.

Smooth the bevels with a block
plane and sandpaper, reducing the edge
thickness to about ⁷⁄₃₂ inch.

SHOP TIP: When bevel-
ing the edges of panels on the table saw,
add a tall auxiliary fence to your saw
fence for safety. Screw a scrap piece of
½ or ¾ × 12 × 24-inch plywood or particleboard to your fence. When beveling
the ends of narrow boards, push the
stock through the blade with an 8 × 8-
inch scrap with square corners.

5 **Glue together the box.** Finish
sand the inside surfaces of the box
pieces. Don't sand the mating surfaces of
joints. Glue the two ends to one of the
sides, insert the bottom with the beveled
side down, and glue the second side in
place. Clamp the box and check that it
lies flat on a flat surface.

If necessary, smooth the outside of
the dovetails with a very sharp hand
plane and sandpaper. Work from the
edges toward the middle of the box to
avoid splintering the end grain. Finish
sand the box.

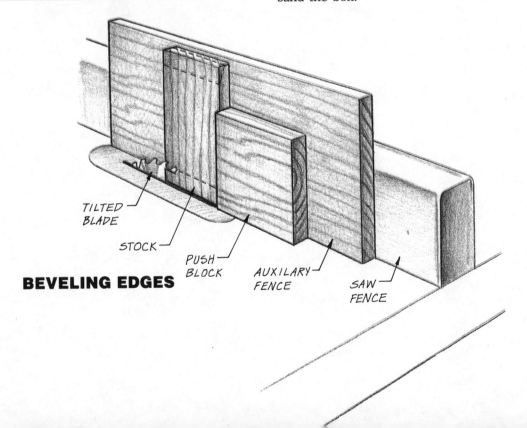

TILTED
BLADE

STOCK

PUSH
BLOCK

AUXILARY
FENCE

SAW
FENCE

BEVELING EDGES

6 **Carve the finger pull in the box lid.** Carve the finger pull with a ½-inch gouge and a shop knife. First, score the deep end of the finger pull with the shop knife, ¾ inch from the square end of the lid, as shown in the *Finger Pull Detail*. Then, remove a shaving with the gouge, cutting toward the score mark. The shaving will pop out as the gouge approaches the score mark. Deepen the score mark, remove another shaving, and repeat until the finger pull is configured as shown.

7 **Finish the candle box.** If you made your candle box from a fine hardwood, it is easy to finish with a pen-

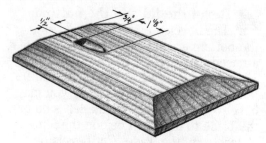

FINGER PULL DETAIL

etrating oil finish. A spray finish in an aerosol can also gives good results with a project this small. Several different kinds of finish come in aerosols, including lacquer and shellac.

CONTEMPORARY JEWELRY BOX

A jewelry box is really a treasure chest. It should look solid and secure to guard its precious contents. An air of mystery is appropriate. Joe Kovecses of Coopersburg, Pennsylvania, has managed to include these features in this contemporary jewelry box.

His unusual hasp/latch gives the box the appearance of securely locking away the contents, while the splined corners give the look of solid, impossible-to-broach construction. It all comes together with a look that is both exotic and contemporary.

Make the box from an attractive wood, such as cherry or walnut. You can make the hasps and inserts from a complementary decorative wood. The total quantity of wood is small, so the materials cost should remain modest.

DOWELS

BRASS
HINGE
PIN

TOP

LONG
HASP ARM

EXPLODED VIEW

SPLINES

SIDE

END

BRASS
HINGE PI.

SHORT
HASP
ARM

END

BOTTOM

CUTTING LIST

Part	Quantity	Dimensions	Comments
Sides	2	$7/16'' \times 2\ 1/16'' \times 9\ 1/8''$	Cherry, walnut, or exotic wood
Bottom	1	$3/4'' \times 3\ 7/8'' \times 9\ 1/8''$	Hardwood
Ends	2	$7/16'' \times 2\ 1/2'' \times 4\ 3/4''$	Cherry, walnut, or exotic wood
Splines	12	$1/8'' \times 3/4'' \times 1\ 1/2''$	Complementary wood
Top	1	$7/16'' \times 4\ 3/4'' \times 9\ 1/8''$	Cherry, walnut, or exotic wood
Long hasp arms	2	$5/16'' \times 7/8'' \times 5''$	Complementary wood
Short hasp arms	2	$5/16'' \times 7/8'' \times 2\ 3/8''$	Complementary wood
Dowel stock	1	$1/8''$ dia. $\times 6''$	Contrasting wood

Hardware

2 brass hinge pins, $1/8''$ dia. $\times 1''$ (brazing rod works well)
2 brass hinge pins, $1/16''$ dia. $\times 7/8''$ (brazing rod works well)

1 Prepare the stock and cut the parts. Joint your stock and plane it to thickness. Cut it to the dimensions specified by the Cutting List. Make certain the sides and bottom are exactly the same length. Prepare the spline material later, after you cut the spline kerfs.

SHOP TIP: Jointing and planing highly figured wood can be a challenge. It doesn't take long to find out if the grain tends to tear out. With cherry, you can often solve tear-out problems by planing at about a 30 degree angle to the grain direction. With other woods, final surfacing with a cabinet scraper is the best way to avoid tear-out.

2 Assemble the box. Sand the faces of the box parts. Glue and clamp the sides of the box to the bottom. Make sure the ends of the pieces are flush. When the glue is dry, glue and clamp the ends of the box to the sides and bottom.

Sand the edges of the box ends flush with the sides and bottom.

3 Make the first corner spline kerfs. Make a corner kerfing jig, as shown in the *Spline Jig Detail*. Make the V-block by ripping a V-groove in a 2 × 4 × 12-inch piece of scrap wood.

Set the miter gauge to 90 degrees and tilt the saw blade 15 degrees. Adjust the height of the blade to extend ¾ inch

TOP VIEW

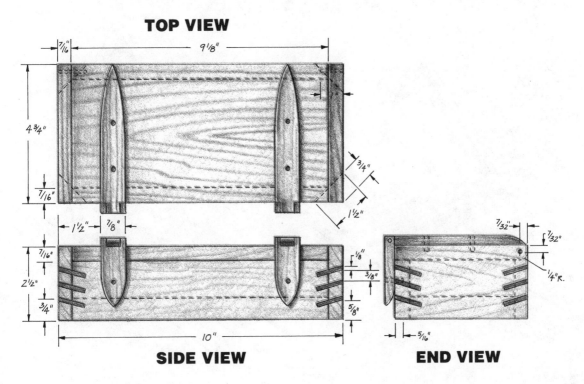

SIDE VIEW

END VIEW

above the bottom of the V in the V-block. Clamp the V-block to the miter gauge, as shown in the drawing. Cut a kerf in the V-block.

Screw a stop block inside the V ⅝ inch from the deepest end of this kerf. Set a corner of the box in the jig with the bottom of the box against the stop block. Pass it through the saw, making the first spline kerf. Kerf the remaining three corners in the same way.

4 **Prepare the spline stock.** Plane the spline stock or rip it on the table saw so it slides snugly into the spline kerfs. Plane enough material to make all of the splines and a few extras.

5 **Complete the corner spline kerfs.** Remove the stop block from the V-block and remove the V-block from the miter gauge. Glue a piece of spline stock in the kerf in the V-block, as shown in the *Spline Jig Detail*. Position the V-block on the miter gauge to cut a kerf ⅜ inch from the first kerf. Clamp the block in place.

To cut the second spline kerf, set the box in the jig. Put the kerf you've already cut in the box over the spline in the jig. Cut the second kerf as you did the first. Move the box over so the spline is in the second kerf and cut the third kerf. Repeat for the remaining three corners to complete the kerf cutting.

SPLINE JIG DETAIL

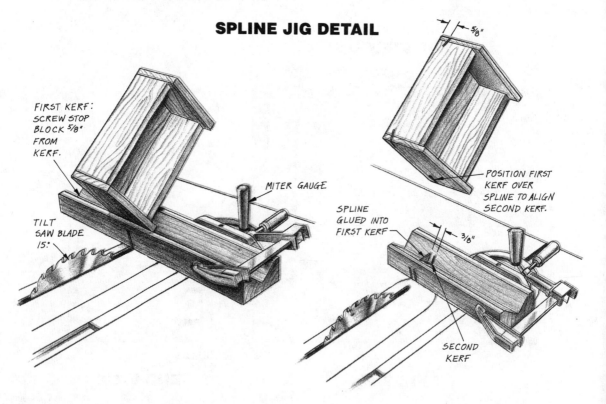

FIRST KERF: SCREW STOP BLOCK ⅝" FROM KERF.

TILT SAW BLADE 15°

MITER GAUGE

⅝"

POSITION FIRST KERF OVER SPLINE TO ALIGN SECOND KERF.

SPLINE GLUED INTO FIRST KERF

⅜"

SECOND KERF

6 **Glue the splines into the corners.** Saw out a dozen slightly oversize splines. Glue the splines into the kerfs, seating them firmly in the kerf bottoms. When the glue is dry, trim the splines with a block plane and sand them flush with the sides of the box.

7 **Fit the box top and drill for the top hinge pins.** Trim the top to fit the box with about 1/32-inch total clearance at the ends. Round-over the bottom back edge of the top with a 1/4-inch-radius roundover bit in a table-mounted router. This roundover provides clearance for the top to lift up without interfering with the back. Clamp the top in place on the box.

Lay out the centers of the hinge pins on the box ends, as shown in the *End View.* Lay the pins out as precisely as you can. Mark the positions with an awl and drill the holes with a small brad-point bit. Drilling them on the drill press

will help you get the holes positioned correctly and perpendicular to the ends. Drill through the box ends and into the top, as shown in the *Top View.* Remove and sand the top.

8 **Make the latch hasps.** The long hasp arms attach to the box top. The short hasp arms provide both handles to open the box and latches to keep it closed.

Lay out the hinge on the short hasp arm, as shown in the *Hasp Detail.* Cut the hinge much as you would make a dovetail. Saw and chisel out the center section. Chisel from both sides to avoid splitting out the grain. Lay the short arms on the long arms and scribe the second half of the hinge directly from the first with a sharp knife. Saw the waste from the long arms and check the fit of the hinges. Pare away excess wood with a sharp chisel for a free fit that's not too loose.

HASP DETAIL

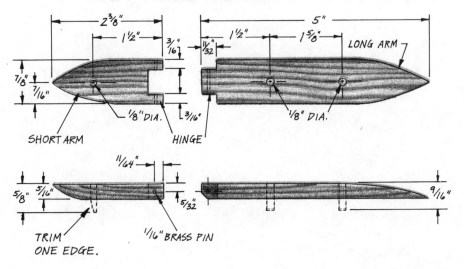

9 **Drill and shape the hasp pieces.** Lay out the holes for the 1/16-inch-diameter hinge pins and mark the spots with an awl. Fit the two arms of the hasps together and clamp them to backup scraps to hold them in position. Drill the pin holes through the hinges. Separate the hasps and make the 45 degree relief cuts on the ends of the long arms, as shown in the *Hasp Detail*. Round the ends slightly, if necessary, to allow the hasps to pivot 90 degrees.

Lay out the shaped ends of the hasps. Saw to the layout lines, then file and sand the edges smooth.

10 **Assemble the hasp.** Slide the 1/16-inch hinge pins through the holes in the hasp. Before pushing the pin entirely in, work the hasp to make sure it doesn't bind. Make any necessary adjustments.

The hasp is doweled onto the box top. Lay out the dowel holes on the hasps, then clamp the hasps in position on the box top. Drill the two 1/8-inch dowel holes through the long arms and 1/4 inch into the box top. Glue and dowel the hasps to the box top.

11 **Attach the top.** Install the top by inserting the 1/8-inch brass hinge pins through the sides and into the top. Check the swing as you did for the hasps. With the top closed, drill through the hasp and 5/16 inch into the front of the box. Glue the dowels in the hasps, then shape the protruding dowels so they can enter the holes in the box. The final fit should be a bit snug so the dowels can keep the box closed.

12 **Finish the box.** Select your finishing materials to suit the woods you've chosen for the box. If you chose a nice hardwood, no stain is necessary. The jewelry box is small enough to spray with an aerosol finish, or you can rub it with a penetrating oil. These oils give an attractive luster on fine woods and they're easy to apply.

PART THREE

OUTDOOR PROJECTS

GARDEN TRELLIS

No garden is complete without a trellis to add height and interest to an otherwise flat plot. Flowering or fruiting vines planted at the base will climb right to the top. Put a trellis in your vegetable garden for cucumbers or squash. With a little coaxing, you'll be able to harvest the vegetables without even bending over. If you grow scarlet runner beans on a trellis, you'll add a splash of color as well as a tasty crop.

This trellis is really four individual trellises joined at the corners. Unlike most trellises, it stands on its own. If you separate the four sides, each can lean individually against a wall.

The trellis will last longer if you paint it. You can make it from an inexpensive wood, or you can use a rot-resistant wood, such as Western cedar, to further prolong its life.

1 **Select the stock and cut the parts.** Note that the uprights are triangular in cross section, as shown in the *Exploded View* and the *Cross Section at Bottom*. You can cut them from either 5/4 (five-quarter) or 4/4 (four-quarter) stock, as shown in *Cutting Parts from 5/4 Stock* and *Cutting Parts from 4/4 Stock*. Use whichever thickness is available at your local supplier.

If you use 5/4 stock (dressed thickness 1⅛ to 1⁵⁄₃₂ inches), you'll be able to resaw it into three lattice pieces, as shown in *Cutting Parts from 5/4 Stock*. If you get 4/4 stock (dressed thickness ¾ to ¹³⁄₁₆ inch), you can only resaw it into two lattice pieces, as shown in *Cutting Parts from 4/4 Stock*.

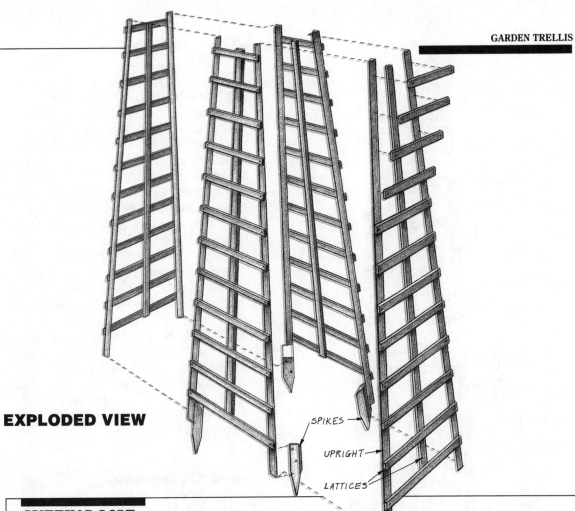

EXPLODED VIEW

SPIKES

UPRIGHT

LATTICES

CUTTING LIST

Part	Quantity	Dimensions	Comments
Uprights	8	$1\frac{1}{8}'' \times 1\frac{1}{8}'' \times 79''$	Cedar; triangular cross section
Lattice stock	84'	$\frac{1}{4}'' \times \frac{7}{8}'' \times$ (variable)	Cedar; purchase extra for waste.
Spikes	4	$1\frac{1}{2}'' \times 1\frac{3}{4}'' \times 10''$	Cedar
Hardware			

16 brass flathead wood screws, #8 × 1″
8 brass flathead wood screws, #8 × 2″
¾″ coated nails
½″ coated nails

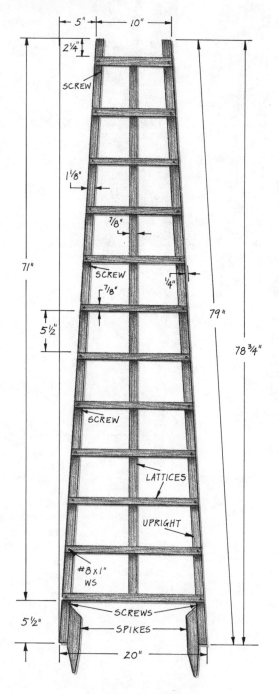

FRONT VIEW

2 **Attach the top and bottom lattices to the uprights.** Because the uprights are triangular in cross section, you'll need V-blocks to hold them while you work. Make a set of four V-blocks like those shown in the *Support Block Detail*. Cradle two uprights in the support blocks, wide side up, on the floor. Arrange them in the position shown in the *Front View*.

Lay out the position of the top and bottom lattices on each upright. Lay lengths of lattice in place across the uprights at the top and bottom marks and mark them for length. Cut them to length at an 86 degree angle to match the tilt of the legs. Cut four top and four bottom lattices to these lengths.

Glue and nail one set of top and bottom lattices to the uprights on the floor. Assemble the remaining three sides of the trellis.

SHOP TIP: Driving nails through thin pieces of wood will often cause the wood to split. You can prevent this by blunting the point of the nail and driving the nail near the edge of the board. If the wood still tends to split, clip the head off one of the nails and use it like a drill bit to drill pilot holes for the nails.

3 **Attach the remaining lattices to the uprights.** Lay out the location of the remaining lattices. Cut them to fit, then glue and nail them in place. To save time, cut four of each size lattice at once, one for each side.

Position the lattices with the help of a spacer 5½ inches wide × 20 inches long. Put one edge of the spacer against an installed lattice. Put the new lattice against the other edge and nail the lattice in place.

4 **Add the center vertical lattice strips.** Each side of the trellis has a vertical strip of lattice running down the center. Cut these pieces to length on the table saw. With the trellis sides face down, glue and nail the vertical strips in place.

SHOP TIP: While yellow (aliphatic resin) carpenter's glue works fine for most woodworking projects, it is not the best choice for outdoor exposure. Powdered urea formaldehyde resin glues are much more water resistant and don't deteriorate as quickly as yellow glue. Wear a dust mask when mixing the glue to prevent breathing the powder.

5 **Drill and countersink the uprights for brass screws.** The trellis sides are joined together with

CUTTING PARTS FROM 5/4 STOCK

LATTICE
LATTICE

⅞"

ADJUST THICKNESS TO GET 3 EQUAL LATTICES WITH YOUR SAW KERF.

UPRIGHT

UPRIGHT

1⅛"

SAW KERF

VARIES WITH KERF WIDTH

LATTICE
LATTICE

⅞"

UPRIGHT

UPRIGHT

¾"

CUTTING PARTS FROM 4/4 STOCK

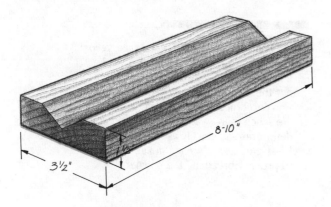

SUPPORT BLOCK DETAIL

#8 × 1-inch wood screws, as shown in the *Exploded View* and *Cross Section at Bottom*. Drill and countersink shank holes through both uprights of two of the four sides.

6 Paint or varnish the trellis. Before you assemble the trellis, finish each side with an exterior paint or varnish. Apply several coats to all surfaces.

7 Assemble the trellis. When the finish has thoroughly dried, screw the trellis together. Brass or stainless steel screws are best because they don't rust.

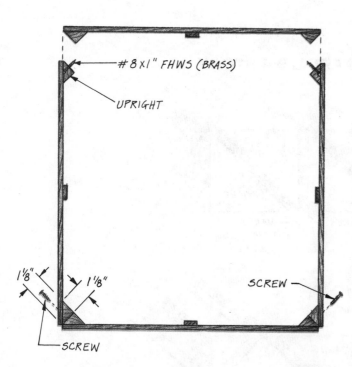

CROSS SECTION AT BOTTOM

8 Attach the ground spikes to the uprights. The ground spikes secure the completed trellis to the ground. Sharpen one end of each spike, as shown in the *Ground Spike Detail*. Bevel the other end at a 45 degree angle so it will shed water. Drill and countersink screw shank holes in each spike and screw a spike to each corner of the trellis with two #8 × 2-inch brass flathead wood screws. About 4 to 5 inches of the spike should extend below the upright.

If you prefer, you can wire the spikes to the bottoms of the uprights. Wrap two lengths of wire around each spike and upright, and twist them tight with pliers. Any wire that you can twist without breaking will do. Paint the spikes or treat them with a wood preservative to make them last longer.

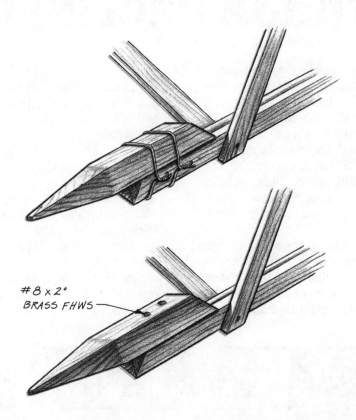

#8 x 2"
BRASS FHWS

GROUND SPIKE DETAIL

OUTDOOR RECLINER

This chair is made for quiet evenings on the deck or sunny afternoons by the pool. The backrest adjusts to different angles, allowing comfortable relaxation or sunbathing. A small tray pulls out from beneath the chair to hold your drink or your suntan lotion. During the winter you could put the chair outside the mudroom door—it makes a good place to sit when removing your snowy boots.

Since the chair is meant to be kept outdoors, make it from a wood that weathers well, such as Western cedar. Redwood is also a good choice, but is more expensive. Avoid treated lumber since your skin will frequently contact the chair. To make the chair portable, attach wheels to the legs on the backrest end. The rails at the other end can serve as handles.

1 Select the stock and cut the parts. Joint and plane the stock to thickness, then cut it to length. If you buy dimensioned lumber and $^{13}/_{16}$-inch-thick stock is not available, you can substitute ¾-inch-thick stock without having to make further adjustments to the dimensions.

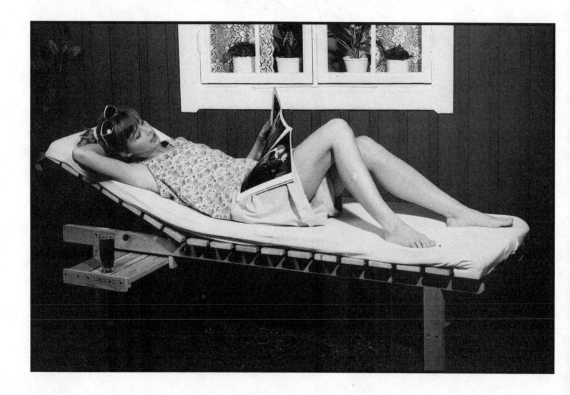

2 **Cut the leg-to-rail lap joints.**
Lay out the lap joints on the rails
and legs, as shown in the *Lap Joint Detail*. Scribe the depth of the joint with a
marking gauge set for one-half the thickness of the rail. Raise the dado head on
the table saw to cut to the scribe line,
then cut the notches in the rails. Make
the first cut in the middle of the waste
area and work out to the edges of the
joint. Guide the pieces through the dado
head with a miter gauge.

Cut the notches in the tops of the

legs in the same manner. Start the cut at
the top of the leg and work back to the
layout line.

3 **Notch the legs for the long
cross supports.** While the dado
head is still on the saw, notch the legs
for the long cross supports. Be sure to
lay out the notch on the side of the leg
opposite the main rail joint. Adjust the
height of the dado head to cut the notch
1 inch deep.

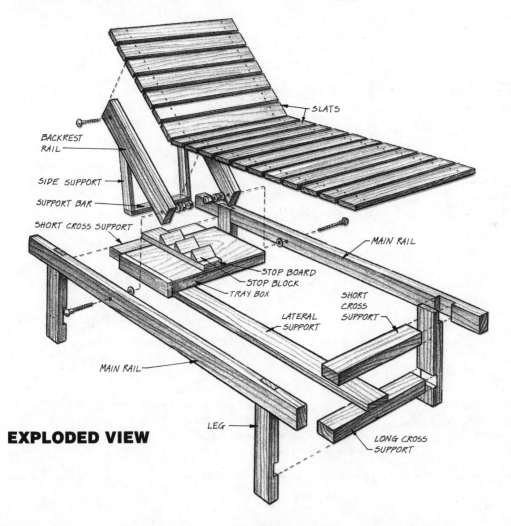

SLATS

BACKREST
RAIL

SIDE SUPPORT

SUPPORT BAR

SHORT CROSS SUPPORT

MAIN RAIL

STOP BOARD
STOP BLOCK
TRAY BOX

SHORT
CROSS
SUPPORT

LATERAL
SUPPORT

MAIN RAIL

LEG

LONG CROSS
SUPPORT

EXPLODED VIEW

4 **Drill and countersink for the screws.** This chair relies on screws as well as glue to hold it together. Lay out the screw holes on the legs, main rails, and slats, as shown in the *Top View, Side View,* and *Drilling the Slats.* Drill ⁵⁄₃₂-inch shank holes and countersinks for #8 screws on the drill press. To make drilling the slats easier, set up stop blocks on the drill press, as shown in *Drilling the Slats.* Reposition the rear stop block to drill the backrest slats.

5 **Drill the holes for the hinge bolts.** Lay out and drill the ⁹⁄₃₂-inch bolt holes in the rails and side supports, as shown in the *Side View* and *Support Arm Detail.*

CUTTING LIST

Part	Quantity	Dimensions	Comments
Main rails	2	1¾" × 2¾" × 72⅞"	Cedar
Legs	4	1¾" × 2¾" × 15¾"	Cedar
Slats	18	¹³⁄₁₆" × 3¾" × 23⅝"	Cedar
Side supports	2	¹³⁄₁₆" × 1⁷⁄₁₆" × 21"	Cedar
Support bar	1	¹³⁄₁₆" × 1⁷⁄₁₆" × 12¼"	Cedar
Long cross supports	2	1¾" × 2¾" × 18⅛"	Cedar
Lateral support	1	¹³⁄₁₆" × 3¾" × 60⅝"	Cedar
Short cross supports	2	1¾" × 2¾" × 16⅛"	Cedar
Backrest rails	2	1¾" × 2¾" × 30⅞"	Cedar
Tray box sides	2	¹³⁄₁₆" × 1¹¹⁄₁₆" × 18¹³⁄₁₆"	Cedar
Tray box back	1	¹³⁄₁₆" × 1¹¹⁄₁₆" × 12⅛"	Cedar
Tray box brace	1	¹³⁄₁₆" × 2¾" × 12⅛"	Cedar
Tray runners	2	¹³⁄₁₆" × ¾" × 14⅜"	Cedar
Tray front batten	1	¹³⁄₁₆" × ¾" × 12"	Cedar
Tray face	1	¹³⁄₁₆" × 2¾" × 13¾"	Cedar
Tray slats	3	¹³⁄₁₆" × 3¾" × 17⅞"	Cedar
Tray back batten	1	¹³⁄₁₆" × 2¾" × 10⁹⁄₁₆"	Cedar
Tray top	1	⅜" × 13¾" × 18¹³⁄₁₆"	Plywood
Stop board	1	¹³⁄₁₆" × 3¾" × 16½"	Cedar
Stop blocks	3	1" × 1" × 3¾"	Cedar

Hardware

2 carriage bolts, ¼" × 4"
2 carriage bolts, ¼" × 3"
8 flat washers, ¼"
8 nuts, ¼"

#8 × 1¼" galvanized flathead wood screws
#8 × 1¾" galvanized flathead wood screws
12 galvanized flathead wood screws, #8 × 3"
4d galvanized finish nails

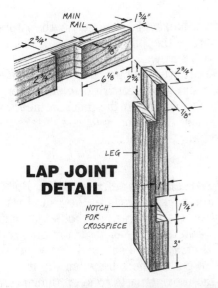

MAIN RAIL

1¾"

2¾"

2¼"

⅞"

6⅛" 2¾"

2¾"

⅞"

LEG

1¾"

3"

NOTCH FOR CROSSPIECE

LAP JOINT DETAIL

6 **Assemble the frame.** Join the legs and main rails first. Clamp the pieces temporarily as you drill ³⁄₃₂-inch pilot holes for the #8 screws. Apply a water-resistant glue, such as Titebond II,

TOP VIEW (BACKREST DOWN; 5 SLATS REMOVED FOR CLARITY)

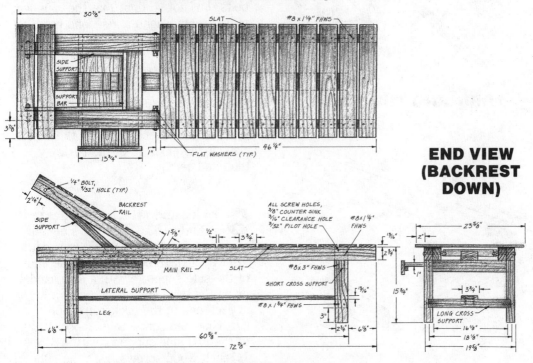

30⅞"

SLAT

#8 x 1¼" FHWS

SIDE SUPPORT

SUPPORT BAR

3⅜"

13¾"

1"

FLAT WASHERS (TYP.)

46¼"

END VIEW (BACKREST DOWN)

¼" BOLT, ⁵⁄₃₂" HOLE (TYP.)

2¼"

BACKREST RAIL

SIDE SUPPORT

ALL SCREW HOLES, ⅜" COUNTER SINK ³⁄₁₆" CLEARANCE HOLE ³⁄₃₂" PILOT HOLE

#8 x 1¼" FHWS

13⁄₁₆"

2¾"

15⅜"

1⅝"

½"

3¾"

MAIN RAIL

SLAT

#8 x 3" FHWS

SHORT CROSS SUPPORT

13⁄₁₆"

LATERAL SUPPORT

#8 x 1¾" FHWS

LEG

3"

6⅛"

2¾"

6⅛"

60⅝"

72⅞"

23⅝"

2"

1"

3¾"

LONG CROSS SUPPORT

16⅛"

18⅛"

19⅝"

SIDE VIEW (BACKREST UP)

to the joining surfaces and assemble them. Drive in the 1¼-inch galvanized screws to assemble the frame permanently. Then, using the same procedure, glue and screw the long cross supports into their leg notches with 1¾-inch

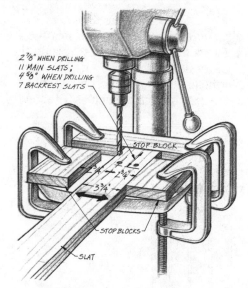

2⅞" WHEN DRILLING 11 MAIN SLATS; 4⅝" WHEN DRILLING 7 BACKREST SLATS

STOP BLOCK

¾" 1¾"

3¾"

STOP BLOCKS

SLAT

DRILLING THE SLATS

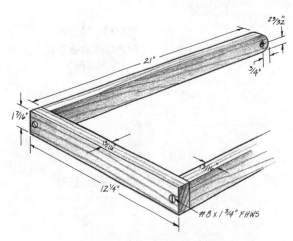

2³/₃₂"

21"

¾"

1⁷/₁₆"

1³/₁₆"

1³/₁₆"

12¼"

#8 × 1¾" FHWS

SUPPORT ARM DETAIL

screws. Next, glue and screw the lateral support to the long cross supports with 1¾-inch screws. Finally, glue and screw the short cross supports to the legs with 3-inch screws. Measure diagonally from corner to corner. If the measurements are equal, the frame is square. Make any necessary adjustments.

7 Attach the backrest rails. Bolt the backrest rails to the main rails with ¼ × 4-inch carriage bolts with nuts and washers to fit, as shown in the *Exploded View, Side View,* and *Top View.* Be sure to put washers between the frame and the moving parts to keep things running smoothly. Slip a washer on the end of the bolt and snug the nuts on the bolts, but not so tight that the rails won't move freely. Tighten a second nut against the first nut to lock it.

8 Screw the slats to the rails. Line up the slats on the rails, as shown in the *Side View.* Be sure to leave 1⅝ inches of space between the two slats at the juncture of the backrest and the fixed seat.

9 Make and attach the backrest support. The backrest side supports attach to the backrest rails with ¼-inch carriage bolts. Round the ends of the side supports with a disk sander or on the band saw. Drill a shank hole in each end of the backrest support bar. Glue and screw the support bar to the two side supports with #8 × 1¾-inch wood screws. Bolt the support in position under the backrest.

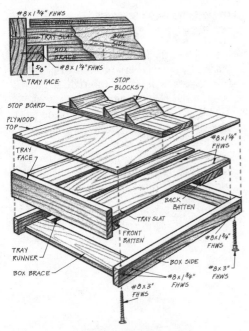

TRAY DETAIL

10 **Make the tray box.** The tray slides in and out of a box that attaches to the chaise. Drill and countersink 3/16-inch shank holes in the box sides to attach the box back and brace, as shown in the *Tray Detail*. Drill matching pilot holes in the ends of the back and brace, then glue and screw the box together with #8 × 1 3/4-inch wood screws. Glue and nail the tray runners in place with 4d galvanized finish nails, as shown in the drawing.

11 **Make the tray.** Center the front batten on the tray face 5/8 inch from the bottom edge. Glue and screw it in place with #8 × 1 1/4-inch screws.

Next, drill the shank holes, countersinks, and pilot holes for the #8 × 1 3/4-inch screws that attach the tray face to

the slats, as shown in the *Tray Detail*. Glue and screw the tray face to the slats. Center the middle slat on the front batten. Align the edges of the other two slats with the ends of the batten. Center the back batten from side to side at the back edge of the slats. Glue and screw it in place with #8 × 1 1/4-inch screws.

Place the tray in the tray box. Run it in and out a time or two to check its operation. If it seems to bind, remove a little wood from the offending parts with a hand plane. When you are satisfied with the operation of the tray, leave it in place and nail the plywood tray top to the tray box with 4d galvanized finish nails, as shown. This will lock the tray in the box so it won't pull out entirely and dump your drink on the ground. Turn the whole unit over, then drill and countersink 3/16-inch holes in the edges of the box sides, as shown, to attach the tray box to the chair frame.

12 **Attach the tray box to the chair frame.** You can position the tray unit so the tray pulls out to either the right or the left. The face of the tray should be flush with the outside surface of the chair's main rail and leg. Glue and screw the box to the main rails with #8 × 3-inch screws.

13 **Attach the stop board and stop blocks.** Lift the backrest and position the stop board across the short cross support and tray box. Screw it in place with #8 × 1 1/4-inch screws but don't glue it.

Experiment to find comfortable backrest positions. Prop up the backrest with well-clamped braces to try out the positions. When you find a comfortable position, mark where a stop block must go to support the backrest in that position. When you've marked three positions, remove the stop board. Rip the stop blocks to a triangular cross section, as shown in the *Tray Detail*, and glue and screw them to the stop board with #8 × 1¼-inch screws. Put the stop board in position on the recliner and glue and screw it to the cross brace and tray top.

14 **Finish the chaise.** Sand the chaise thoroughly to remove splinters and ease edges. Further finishing is optional. Left to weather, the chaise will acquire a silver-gray color. Any other finish will require periodic refinishing. If you decide to apply a finish, use materials intended for exterior use. Avoid chalking house paints and natural finishes that contain wood preservatives or fungicides that would get on your skin.

SHOP TIP: Avoid kickback when ripping bevels. Most right-handed woodworkers prefer to rip with the table saw fence on the right-hand side of the blade. Unfortunately, most tilting-arbor table saws tilt the blade to the right for bevel cuts. If the blade tilts toward the fence, kickback is almost inevitable. Unless you have one of the few saws that tilt the blade to the left, always rip bevels with the fence to the left of the blade.

TWO-WHEEL WAGON

If you ever had a wagon when you were a kid, you know how much fun it is to cart stuff around. This wagon is a gem. Solid wood gives it an appeal that you can't find in a hardware store wagon. You probably won't even have to pull it. Any youngsters in the neighborhood will be delighted to haul your apples or pumpkins or kindling if you let them use your wagon. The only problem you might have is getting it back.

The 14-inch-diameter wheels are made by the Gleason Wheel Company and are readily available from local hardware stores. They are big enough to make the wagon easy to pull over yard and garden terrain. The wheels are attached to a steel axle that fits in a groove cut in the cross brace. If you don't want to buy wheels, you can make a pair from plywood. Simply cut out two discs on the band saw. Have the wheels on hand before you make the rest of the wagon. Then if you decide to use different wheels, you can modify the rest of the design to suit.

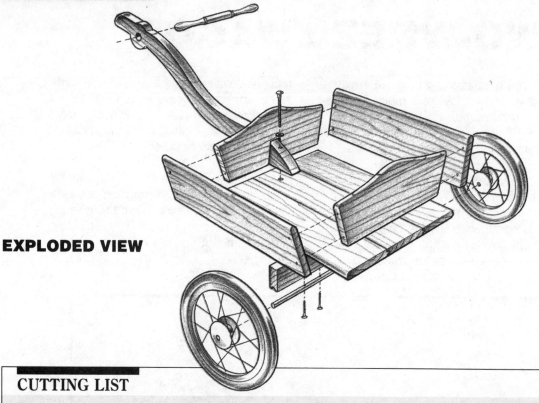

EXPLODED VIEW

CUTTING LIST

Part	Quantity	Dimensions	Comments
Bottom	1	$\frac{3}{4}'' \times 14\frac{1}{4}'' \times 19\frac{7}{8}''$	Use several tongue-and-groove boards.
Cross brace	1	$1\frac{1}{2}'' \times 2\frac{3}{4}'' \times 15\frac{1}{8}''$	
Ends	2	$\frac{7}{8}'' \times 6\frac{1}{8}'' \times 13\frac{3}{4}''$	
Sides	2	$\frac{7}{8}'' \times 5'' \times 19\frac{1}{8}''$	
Draw bar stock	1	$1\frac{3}{8}'' \times 4\frac{1}{2}'' \times 39\frac{3}{8}''$	
Handle	1	$1\frac{1}{4}''$ dia. $\times 11''$	Turn to shape.

Hardware

1 steel rod, $1\frac{1}{2}''$ dia. $\times 20''$

2 wheels, $1\frac{3}{4}'' \times 14''$ dia., spoked, ball bearing, 100-lb. load rating. Available from local hardware stores. Gleason Wheel Co. part #14129. Ace Hardware part #74569.

2 cotter pins, $\frac{1}{8}'' \times 1\frac{1}{4}''$

4 flat washers, $\frac{1}{2}''$

1 bolt, $\frac{1}{4}'' \times 3\frac{1}{2}''$, with nut and 2 washers

Brass flathead wood screws, #8 $\times 2\frac{1}{2}''$

1 Select the stock and cut the parts.

Choose a species of wood that is suited to your intended use of the wagon. Oak will stand up to carting stones around but is on the heavy side. Cedar is lightweight and rot resistant but easily abraded and may split. Elm is moderate in weight, unlikely to split, and resists abrasion, but is not easy to find. The wagon shown in the photograph is made of fir, reasonably light and strong but prone to splitting. Cut the parts to the dimensions specified by the Cutting List. Cut tongue-and-groove joints in the bottom boards with matched molding head cutters on the table saw or with tongue-and-groove router bits on the router table. Don't glue them together; the tongues and grooves will keep the boards aligned while allowing them to expand and contract with moisture changes.

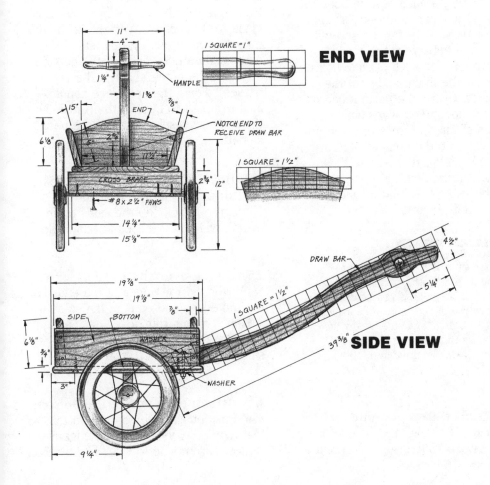

END VIEW

I SQUARE = I"

HANDLE

11"
4"
1¼"
1⅜"
⅞"
15°
END
NOTCH END TO RECEIVE DRAW BAR
6⅛"
2⅝"
5"
11½"
CROSS BRACE
#8 x 2½" FHWS
2¾"
12"
14¼"
15⅛"

I SQUARE = 1½"

DRAW BAR
4½"
5¼"
I SQUARE = 1½"
39⅜"   **SIDE VIEW**

19⅞"
19⅛"
⅞"
SIDE
BOTTOM
WASHER
6⅛"
¾"
WASHER
3"
9¼"

2 Rout the axle groove in the cross brace. Rout the axle groove in the bottom of the cross brace with a ½-inch core box bit in a table-mounted router. Position the router table fence so the groove is centered on the cross brace. Cut the groove in several shallow passes to avoid overstressing the bit. The final depth of the groove should be ¼ inch.

3 Screw the bottom to the cross brace. Round-over the outside edges of the two outside bottom boards. Draw a line across each bottom board at its center. Drill and countersink shank holes along these lines for the screws that attach the bottom to the cross brace—two holes in each outside board and one near the tongue edge of the other boards. Clamp the bottom boards together as though you were gluing them, then clamp the cross brace in position. Make sure the ends of the bottom boards are lined up, then screw the cross brace in place with #8 × 2½-inch brass wood screws. Round-over the ends of the bottom assembly.

SHOP TIP: When assembling projects with brass screws, it is very easy to break the screw or distort the slot as you drive it home. To avoid this problem, drive in a steel screw the same size as the brass screw, remove the steel screw, and drive in the brass screw.

4 Crosscut the wagon ends to 15 degrees. Set the miter gauge on the table saw to 15 degrees. Crosscut a bevel onto the ends of the front and back end pieces, as shown in the *End View*.

5 Cut the curves on the ends. Lay out the top curve on the ends, as shown in the *End View*. Cut the pieces to shape on the band saw. Clean up the sawed edges with spokeshaves and sandpaper.

6 Make the draw bar notch. Lay out the notch on one end, as shown in the *End View*. It should be centered from side to side. Raise the table saw blade to 2⅝ inches. With the blade and miter gauge at 90 degrees, stand the end piece on edge and cut the outside edges of the notch. Then make repeated passes, sliding the end piece about ⅛ inch per pass to cut out the remainder of the waste. Chisel the top of the notch smooth.

7 Bevel the bottom edges of the sides. Adjust the table saw to cut a 15 degree bevel. Rip the sides to an overall width of 5 inches at this angle.

8 Round-over the edges. Round-over the top edges of the ends and the top edges and ends of the sides with a ⅜-inch-radius roundover bit. Sand all the edges and corners until they're smooth and friendly to the touch.

9 Attach the ends to the bottom. Position the ends on the bottom so that they're ½ inch from the edge and centered from side to side. Lightly trace their positions on the bottom. Drill screw shank holes down through the bottom, centered in the traced outlines. Drill one hole in each bottom board, about 1 inch from the tongue edge. Turn the bottom over and countersink the holes. Put the ends in position again, drill pilot holes, and screw the ends to the bottom.

10 **Attach the sides.** Set the sides in place and trace, drill, and countersink as you did for the ends. This time, remember that the screws must angle outward at 15 degrees to match the angle of the sides. Drill pilot holes and screw the sides to the bottom. Drill, countersink, and screw the sides to the ends.

SHOP TIP: As an aid to drilling angled holes, cut the end of a ¾ × 2 × 4-inch scrap of wood at the angle for the hole. Position this next to the hole as a reference as you drill. Sight along the cut edge and hold your drill at this angle.

11 **Make the draw bar.** Make a paper pattern of the draw bar, as shown in the *Side View,* and trace it onto the draw bar blank. Saw out the draw bar. Clean up the sawed edges with spokeshaves, files, and sandpaper. Round-over the edges of the draw bar with a ⅜-inch roundover bit in your router. (Don't round-over the flat at the bottom where the bar will join the wagon.) Sand the bar to remove all the machine marks.

12 **Drill the mounting and handle holes.** Drill a shallow, 1-inch-diameter hole with a Forstner or spade bit where the bolt passes through the draw bar into the wagon bottom. This hole provides a flat seat for the washer. Drill a $\frac{9}{32}$-inch hole at the center of the 1-inch hole for the bolt. Hold the draw bar in position on the wagon and continue the $\frac{9}{32}$-inch hole through the bottom.

Mark the center of the handle hole on the draw bar. Drill a 1¼-inch hole through the bar for the handle.

13 **Turn and attach the handle.** Turn the handle to the shape shown in the *End View.* Sand the handle before removing it from the lathe, then hand sand the ends. If you don't have a lathe, make the handle from a 1¼-inch wooden closet pole.

Drill and countersink a screw shank hole in the bottom edge of the draw bar for the screw that locks the handle in place. Spread some glue in the draw bar hole and slide the handle through. Drill a pilot hole in the handle and screw it in place.

14 **Attach the wheels.** A cotter pin at each end holds the wheels on the axle. Wood screws hold the axle in the groove in the cross brace. Lay out the centers for the $\frac{3}{16}$-inch screw holes and ⅛-inch cotter pin holes on the axle, as shown in *Drilling the Axle.* Mark the centers by striking them with a center punch. Clamp the axle in a V-block on the table of the drill press. Make sure the point of the V is directly in line with the center of the drill. Drill the holes with standard twist drills at about 2,000 rpm. Use plenty of oil to lubricate and cool the bit and use firm pressure without excessive force. If the bit doesn't cut freely, replace it with a new one.

When you've drilled all of the holes, reduce the speed of the drill press to about 800 rpm and countersink the screw holes. If you don't have a metal-cutting countersink, use a ⅜-inch or larger twist drill.

Clean up any oil residue and file off the burrs around the edges of the holes. Install the washers and wheels on the axle, but open the cotter pins only enough to keep them from falling out. Place the axle in the groove in the cross brace. The wheels should have just enough side-to-side play to turn freely. If necessary, add washers between the wheels and cross brace to take up excessive play. Drill through the existing axle holes to drill pilot holes in the brace. Screw the axle in place.

15 Attach the draw bar to the wagon bottom. Slide the draw bar into the notch in the end of the wag-

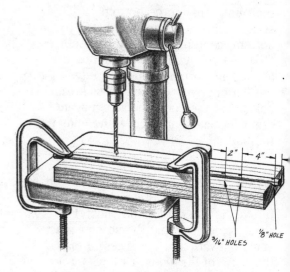

DRILLING THE AXLE

on. Bolt the draw bar in place on the wagon bottom.

16 Finish the wagon. The finish you put on the wagon should be durable, since it may be left outside. Either spar varnish or polyurethane is a good choice. You can also paint the wagon if you choose.

OUTDOOR BENCH

This outdoor bench is made from fairly substantial lumber, yet has refinement and style. Unlike a lot of bulky commercial outdoor furniture, the parts of this bench are shaped. The result is a durable piece of furniture that adds to the beauty of its setting.

The bench will give the longest service if you make it from rot-resistant wood. The commercially available choices include cedar and redwood. Excellent choices that may be available in your area include catalpa, chestnut, black locust, and Kentucky coffee tree.

If you're considering using pressure-treated lumber, keep in mind that the dust is bad for you, as is handling the wood itself. To protect yourself, wear a tight-fitting dust mask when cutting the wood. Wash your hands thoroughly whenever you take a break, and shower at the end of the day. When you are finished for the day, clean up all the sawdust and scraps very carefully and *don't burn them*. Finally, be sure to paint the bench to prevent skin contact.

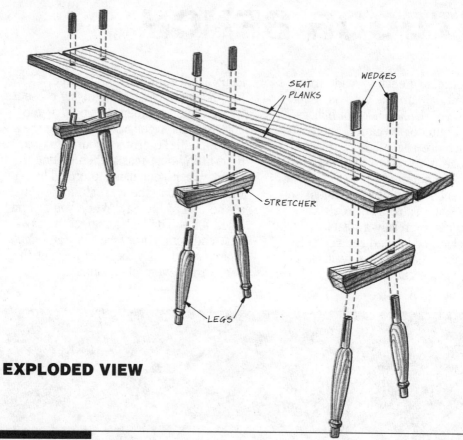

WEDGES

SEAT
PLANKS

STRETCHER

LEGS

EXPLODED VIEW

CUTTING LIST

Part	Quantity	Dimensions	Comments
Seat planks	2	1½″ × 6¾″ × 96″	Make all parts from rot-resistant wood.
Stretchers	3	2½″ × 3½″ × 12⅞″	Rip from 4 × 4s.
Legs	6	2½″ dia. × 18¼″	Rip from 4 × 4s; turn to shape.
Wedges	6	³⁄₁₆″ × 1½″ × 4″	Taper with a hand plane.

Hardware

3″ galvanized deck screws

1 Select the stock and cut the parts. For outside use, your wood doesn't have to be totally dry, but it shouldn't be tangibly wet. If it's green, let it dry indoors for a few weeks before you begin building.

When you buy the wood, avoid pieces that include the pith (the center of the tree). If the rings on the end grain form a bull's-eye, you've found the pith. Pieces that include the pith are more likely to split as they dry. If you can't avoid the pith, look for pieces where it is off to one side and cut around it as you work.

Once the wood has had a chance to dry a bit, cut the seat planks and stretchers to the sizes specified by the Cutting List. Cut 2⅝ × 2⅝ × 18¼-inch blanks for the legs. Cut the wedges later, from scrap.

2 Make the seat planks. Lightly chamfer all the edges and corners of the seat planks with a piloted chamfering bit in a router. The size of the chamfer is not important. Choose a profile that pleases your eye. Sand or plane the planks to remove any mill marks. If you

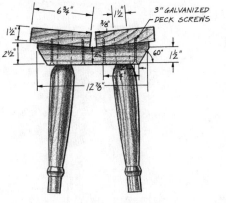

END VIEW

FRONT VIEW

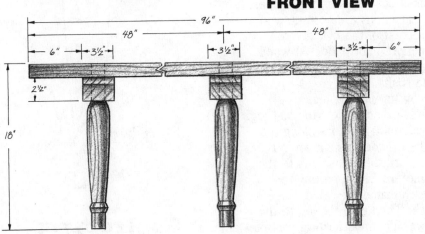

adjust a hand plane to remove a hefty shaving, it will leave a nice hewn appearance and raise no dust.

3 **Make the stretchers.** Saw the stretchers to the shape shown in the *End View.* Scrape, plane, or sand to eliminate the saw marks. Lightly chamfer the edges with a chamfering bit in a router.

4 **Join the stretchers to the seat planks.** Clamp the stretchers to the seat planks, as shown in the *Side View* and *End View.* Make sure you leave a ³⁄₈-inch gap between the seat planks. Turn the assembly upside down. Drill and countersink ⅛-inch pilot holes through the stretchers, as shown. Screw the stretchers to the planks with 3-inch galvanized deck screws.

5 **Turn the legs.** When turning duplicate parts, it is easiest to turn all the blanks to cylinders first. Then lay out the transitions between the shapes. When the transitions are correct, you can turn the rest of the cylinder to shape. For more information on woodturning, see the book *Creative Woodturning* by Dale Nish.

Begin by turning the legs to 2½-inch-diameter cylinders. On the last leg, mark the various transitions along the length of the cylinder, as shown in the *Leg Detail.* Turn the transitions to the proper diameters with a parting tool. Measure each diameter with a calipers as you work. Then turn the leg to the shape shown. The most critical part of

the leg is the tenon. Make it exactly 1½ inches in diameter. Turn all the legs to the same shape.

SHOP TIP: For tight-fitting tenons on outdoor furniture, turn the tenons slightly oversize. Then dry the turnings further by putting them in a warm, dry environment for a week or two. Just before final assembly, turn the tenons to a final, snug fit in their bores. When the finished furniture is moved outdoors, the tenons will absorb moisture, swelling in the bores.

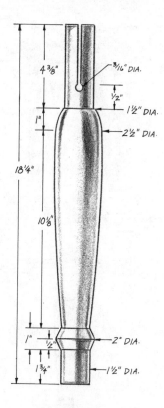

LEG DETAIL

6 **Cut the wedge slots.** On each
leg, saw a kerf down the middle of
the tenon, perpendicular to the growth
rings. Stop the cut ½ inch from the
tenon shoulder. At the bottom of the
cut, drill a ³⁄₁₆-inch-diameter hole through
the tenon. This hole helps keep the
wedge from splitting the leg.

7 **Drill the leg holes.** Locate the
center of each leg hole on the seat,
as shown in the *Hole Detail*. Drill the
1½-inch-diameter holes perpendicular to
the seat surfaces. The holes go all the
way through both the seat and the
stretcher. You can drill the holes with a
spade bit in an electric hand drill or with
an expansion bit in a brace.

8 **Assemble the bench.** Insert the
legs in their holes. The tenons
should extend slightly above the seat.
Turn the legs so the slots are perpendicular to the length of the bench. This way
the seat is less likely to split when you

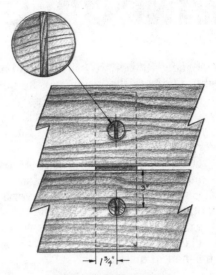

HOLE DETAIL

drive in the wedges. Saw the wedges to
size and taper them with a hand plane
from ³⁄₁₆ inch at one end to almost nothing at the other. Mix some epoxy and
work it into the slots in the leg tenons.
Drive the wedges into the slots with a
mallet. When the epoxy has hardened,
cut the tenons flush with the seat with a
backsaw or chisel. Sand away any saw
marks.

9 **Apply the finish.** The bench can
be left to weather without a finish,
or you can apply a waterproofing stain.
(If you built the bench out of pressure-
treated lumber, you should paint it.) If
your bench will be exposed to rain followed quickly by direct sunlight, waterproofing will minimize the formation of
fine cracks in the surface over time.
Whether or not you waterproof, soak the
bottom end grain of the legs with a wood
preservative.

WINDOW BOX

Window boxes are easy to build and brighten up both the inside and the outside of your home. In the country or the city, they add charm. You can build just one for a special window, or one for every window in your house.

Unlike many window box projects, this one is really a holder for a standard plastic window box. There are several advantages to this approach. The actual soil container is plastic and impervious to rot. The visible parts are wood and can be finished to match your house. The

plastic box can be removed for planting and soil improvement or replacement. You could even keep several of the plastic boxes planted with different flowers and put them in the window box on the house as they come into bloom.

The only part of this project that you can't finish in a day is raising the flowers, so start with a trip to the garden store. Buy the plastic boxes, seed, soil if you need it, and get the plants going. That way you'll have something to put in the box when you finish it.

EXPLODED VIEW

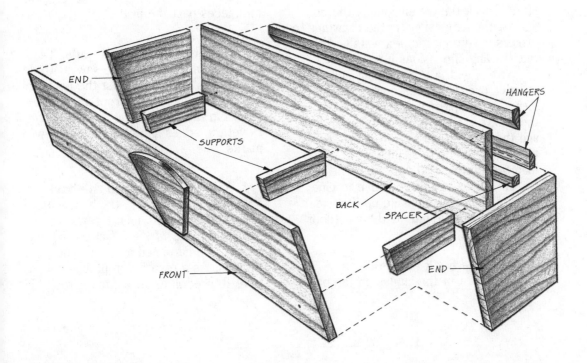

CUTTING LIST

Part	Quantity	Dimensions	Comments
Back	1	¾″ × 8″ × 32½″	Cedar
Ends	2	¾″ × 8⅝″ × 7⅞″	Cedar
Front	1	¾″ × 8⅝″ × 32½″	Cedar
Supports	3	¾″ × 2″ × 6⅜″	Cedar
Hangers	2	¾″ × 1¾″ × 28″	Cedar
Spacer	1	¾″ × ¾″ × 28″	Cedar
Medallion	1	¾″ × 7⁷⁄₁₆″ × 7¾″	Cedar; optional

Hardware

1¼″ galvanized deck screws
1½″ galvanized deck screws
2½″ galvanized deck screws
1 plastic window box, 6″ × 6″ × 30″

1 **Cut the parts to size.** Buy and measure the plastic box before you start. Check the dimensions of the box against the dimensions in the drawings to make sure the plastic box will fit. Adjust the drawing dimensions if necessary.

A box with a sloping front and ends, like this one, has some compound angles. The simplest way to deal with them is to start with the simpler joints and then scribe and saw the other parts to fit. Cut the parts ½ inch or so longer than the Cutting List specifies, but don't cut the angles yet. If you have to glue up narrow boards to make up the wider pieces, use a glue intended for outdoor use.

2 **Cut the back and ends to shape.** Cut the angles on the back and ends on the table saw. Set the miter gauge to 15 degrees and use it to guide the pieces past the blade.

3 **Bevel the front and ends.** Tilt the blade on the table saw to 15 degrees from vertical. Adjust the fence to bevel the edges of the front and ends, as shown in the *Front View* and *End View*. Bevel the edges and plane off the saw marks.

4 **Attach the ends to the back.** Screw the ends to the back with 1½-inch galvanized deck screws, as shown in the *End View*. Galvanized deck screws are hardened and have special threads. As a result, you probably won't have to predrill cedar for the screws. If

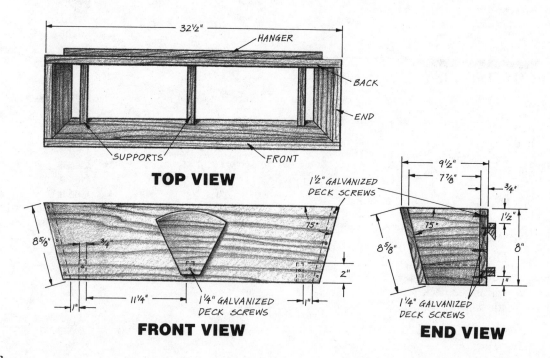

you're working in hardwood, however, it's a good idea to predrill.

5 **Cut and attach the front.** Place the front on your workbench. Position the end and back assembly on top of it. Make sure the ends are square to the back, then trace the outside of the ends onto the front to mark the angles. Adjust a sliding T-bevel to this angle and then set the miter gauge to match the angle on the T-bevel. Cut the angles on the front.

Hold the front in position on the end and back assembly. You may notice that the front does not join the ends perfectly; there is a slight gap along the inside. If the slight gap bothers you, plane a slight bevel on the front so the joint closes tightly.

Screw the front to the ends, predrilling if necessary.

6 **Cut and attach the supports.** Cut the supports to fit snugly inside the bottom of the box. Cut the supports on the table saw using the miter gauge set at 15 degrees from a square crosscut. Screw the supports in place with 1¼-inch galvanized deck screws, as shown in the *Front View.*

SHOP TIP: When cutting several pieces to the same length, screw an extension fence to your miter gauge. Then clamp a stop block to the fence at the necessary distance from the blade. As you cut, hold each piece against the stop block.

7 **Cut and attach the hanger and spacer.** The hanger interlocks with a similar hanger on the house to hold the box in place. The spacer keeps the box from tilting.

Set the table saw blade to a 45 degree angle. Bevel one edge of each hanger, as shown in the *End View.* Round-over the sharp edges slightly with a block plane or sandpaper. Glue and screw one of the hangers and the spacer to the back of the box, as shown in the *End View* and *Top View.* Use a screw every 4 inches for the hanger. Three screws are enough for the spacer.

8 **Cut and attach the medallion.** The medallion is a purely decorative feature. Feel free to modify the shape to suit your sense of design. You might even want to use two or more cutouts along the length of the box.

Lay out the shape of the medallion on the stock, as shown in the *Medallion Detail.* Cut it to shape on the band saw.

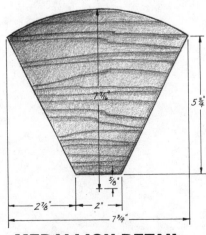

MEDALLION DETAIL

Center it on the front of the box, as shown in the *Front View*. Screw it in place from inside with 1¼-inch screws.

9 **Apply the finish.** Make the box an integrated part of your house exterior by finishing it to match. You can choose between your exterior wall color and your trim color.

10 **Hang the box.** Screw the remaining hanger to the side of your house so that it's about 2 inches down from the bottom of the windowsill. If your house has bevel siding, you'll need to create a flat area from which to hang the box. Cut a 28-inch-long shim from a piece of siding and screw it in place, as shown in the *Hanging Detail*. Drive a 2½-inch galvanized deck screw every 4 inches and make sure you get at least two screws into wall studs. Then slip the box over the hanger on the house so that the two hangers interlock.

If you're hanging the box at a second-story level, drive several 2½-inch screws from inside the box directly into the wall.

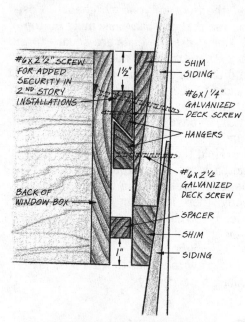

HANGING DETAIL

SEESAW

Wooden playground equipment has become quite popular in recent years. The rusty metal swingsets and jungle gyms are gone, replaced by wooden structures with towers, swinging bridges, and climbing nets. The wooden replacements are more friendly and aren't so hard and cold. This wooden seesaw is simple and compact enough for your own backyard. It is easy to build, portable, and relatively inexpensive. And a seesaw teaches cooperation rather than competition, a healthy balance in our society.

The seesaw pictured is made from standard sizes of construction lumber: 2 × 6s for the legs and gussets, 4 × 4s for the feet, 5/4 × 6-inch decking for the stretchers, and a 2 × 10 for the plank. (Note that 5/4 (five-quarter) lumber dresses out to 1⅛ inches.) Pressure-treated wood will last longer in contact with the ground but costs considerably more and is much less enjoyable to work with. Wear a mask while sawing it, wash regularly and thoroughly to keep the stuff off your skin, and then figure out how to dispose of the waste.

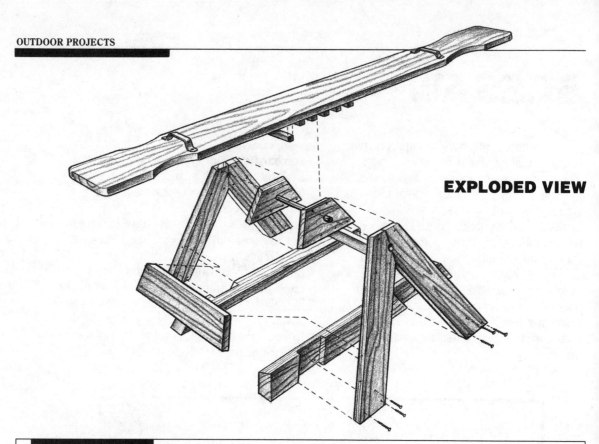

EXPLODED VIEW

CUTTING LIST

Part	Quantity	Dimensions	Comments
Legs	4	1½″ × 5½″ × 28⅜″	Construction lumber
Gussets	2	1½″ × 5½″ × 13″	Construction lumber
Feet	2	3½″ × 3½″ × 47″	Construction lumber
Stretchers	2	1″ × 5½″ × 27½″	Decking
Plank	1	1½″ × 9½″ × 12′	Avoid big knots and splintery pieces.
Cleats	6	1″ × 1¼″ × 8″	Rip from 1″ decking.

Hardware

Galvanized deck screws, #8 × 2½″
1 galvanized steel pipe, 1″ O.D. × 18″, threaded on one end
2 galvanized door handles with screws, 6½″

(Don't burn it. The fumes are toxic.) You certainly should not use pressure-treated wood for the plank, which will be in regular contact with the kids' skin. And unless you really expect it to be around for more than one generation, there's no need for the longer life expectancy. The kids will outgrow the seesaw before common construction lumber rots away.

You can build the seesaw with only a circular saw and a few hand tools. Access to a table saw and a jointer might make the task quicker.

1 **Cut the legs to shape.** Cut the legs from your stock at a 60 degree angle, 30 inches long overall, as shown in the *Front View*. Make the cut at the top of the leg with the blade at 90 degrees to the shoe of the saw, but tilt the blade to 75 degrees for the cut at the bottom, as shown in the *Side View*. Keep in mind that you need two right-hand legs and two left-hand legs and that the bevels on the left legs are the opposite of those on the right legs. Once you've cut the leg blanks to 30-inch lengths, you'll need to trim them to create the surface where the two legs join. Lay out the cut, as shown in the *Front View*. Cut as close as you can to the line and clean up the cut with a hand plane.

2 **Assemble the legs.** Cut the gussets slightly longer than specified by the Cutting List. Cut one end of each gusset at a 60 degree angle. Hold one pair of legs together in the position shown in the front view. Put the gusset in position on the legs. Trace along the leg at the other end to mark the gusset for length. Cut the gusset to length

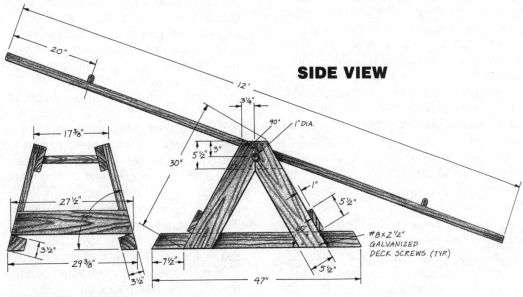

SIDE VIEW

FRONT VIEW

along this angled line. Screw the gusset to the legs, as shown in the *Front View*. Repeat with the other gusset and pair of legs.

3 **Cut the feet to length.** Mark the ends of the feet at a 60 degree angle and saw them to length. If you are working with a hand-held circular saw, you'll probably have to cut from both faces of the 4 × 4. Lay out and saw the first face, then transfer the layout lines to the other side with a square. Clearly mark which side of the line the kerf goes on, then finish the cut.

4 **Join the legs and feet.** The legs are notched into the feet. Lay out the notches by holding a pair of legs in place along one of the feet. Center the legs from end to end. Make sure legs and feet are flush at the bottom. Scribe along the legs to mark where the notches go on the foot. Adjust the depth of cut of the circular saw to the thickness of the legs. Saw just inside the scribe lines on the foot, then saw a kerf about every half-inch between the scribe lines. Chisel out the waste. The regular kerfs will make it easier to remove most of the waste in big blocks. Repeat with the other legs and foot.

5 **Bevel the feet.** The bottoms of the feet must be beveled, as shown in the *Side View*. This is easily done on a jointer or table saw if you have one. If you don't, you can cut the bevel with a portable circular saw. Tilt the shoe of the saw to cut a 75 degree bevel and adjust the depth of cut to about half of the maximum for your saw. Rip down the outside bottom corner of the foot, then increase the depth of cut to the maximum and repeat. Finish with a handsaw. It's good exercise and you'll deserve a break when you're done.

6 **Join the legs to the feet.** Put the legs back in their notches. Screw them to the feet with #8 × 2½-inch galvanized deck screws, as shown in the *Side View*.

7 **Attach the stretchers.** The cutoff pyramid shape of the seesaw base produces some oddball angles on the stretchers. Get them right by scribing the ends of the stretchers directly from the base. Find a good flat surface like a garage floor or sidewalk to work on. Lean the two leg assemblies against each other. Stick the 10-foot plank through the triangular opening in the two leg assemblies as they lean together. The plank will weigh them down enough for them to stand on their own without leaning against each other. Now spread them apart so they're 29⅜ inches apart at the bottom. If your bevel angles on the bottom of the feet were right on the money, you'll find that the two leg assemblies are now 17⅜ inches apart at the top. They probably won't be, so tack a scrap stick across the top to hold them that distance apart. Check that they're still 29⅜ inches apart at the bottom. Check that the two assemblies tilt at very nearly the same angle and provide some further propping if necessary.

Now hold one of the stretcher pieces in place and mark it for length and angle at both ends. Saw it to the marks and hold it back in position. You'll notice that it fits tightly at the outside surface of each leg but that there is a slight gap at the inside surface. A few strokes with a block plane on the ends of the stretcher will fit it to the leg without a gap. When you're happy with the fit, cut the other stretcher in the same way. Screw the stretchers in place.

8 **Drill the pipe holes.** Mark the center of the pipe hole on the outside of each leg, as shown in the *Side View*. Drill through each leg assembly with a 1-inch spade bit in an electric drill. These holes must be in line with each other but, since the leg assemblies are not parallel, the holes will not be perpendicular to the legs. To help aim the drill accurately, lay a straight stick across the top of the leg assembly, directly above the marked hole centers. Hold the drill so the bit is parallel to this stick as you bore. To avoid splitting out the back side of the holes, drill in from the outside until the pilot just begins to come through, then finish the hole from the inside.

9 **Cut the seats to shape.** Lay out the shape of the seats on each end of the plank, as shown in the *Seat Detail*. Cut the seats to shape with a saber saw or coping saw. Smooth the sawed edges with rasps and sandpaper. Round-over the edges with a large roundover bit in a router or with a rasp. Sand the seats thoroughly to remove all splinters.

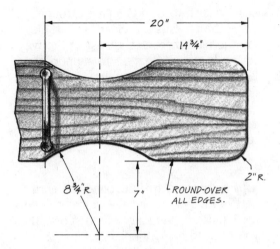

SEAT DETAIL

10 **Install the cleats.** The plank has six cleats screwed to the underside. These cleats let you adjust the balance point to help compensate for riders of different weights. Mark the center of the plank on its underside. From there, draw a line square across the plank 9/16 inch on each side of the center. Screw a cleat just outside this line, as shown in the *Pivot Detail*. Now use the pipe as a spacer to position the remaining five cleats as you screw them to the plank. Don't make the cleats too tight to the pipe. If you intend to paint the seesaw, allow room for the paint by using the pipe plus a piece of thin cardboard to space the cleats.

11 **Install the pipe.** Push the threaded end of the pipe through the hole in one of the leg assemblies from the outside. You may need to use a pipe wrench to turn the pipe through. Once the threads are clear of the hole, tap the pipe through the rest of the way with a hammer. Be sure to support the legs with your knee or a brace so you don't stress the joints too much. When the pipe reaches the other side, thread it into the hole by turning it with the pipe wrench.

12 **Apply a finish.** Sand the entire seesaw, rounding-over all the corners and removing any rough spots. If you want to apply a finish, choose a high-quality, non-chalking exterior or marine enamel or spar varnish. Make sure

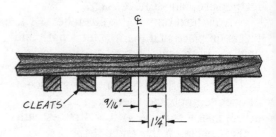

CLEATS 9/16" 1¼"

PIVOT DETAIL

the wood is quite dry and apply the finish according to the manufacturer's directions. Screw the handles in place, as shown in the *Seat Detail*.

PART FOUR

TABLES AND CHAIRS

STEP STOOL

Half of the population is below average height, but even if you're taller than average, a step stool can be the answer to your prayers. This one is a solid, stable, no-nonsense aid to seeing the rest of the world at eye level. Put it in the kitchen and you'll discover the half-box of birthday candles at the back of the top shelf. Put it in the bathroom and your children will wash their hands before dinner.

The step stool is fun to build and should provide years of service. Putting it together should take no more than an afternoon, or maybe two. The handle is handy and is a good excuse to get out the router you said you couldn't live without.

EXPLODED VIEW

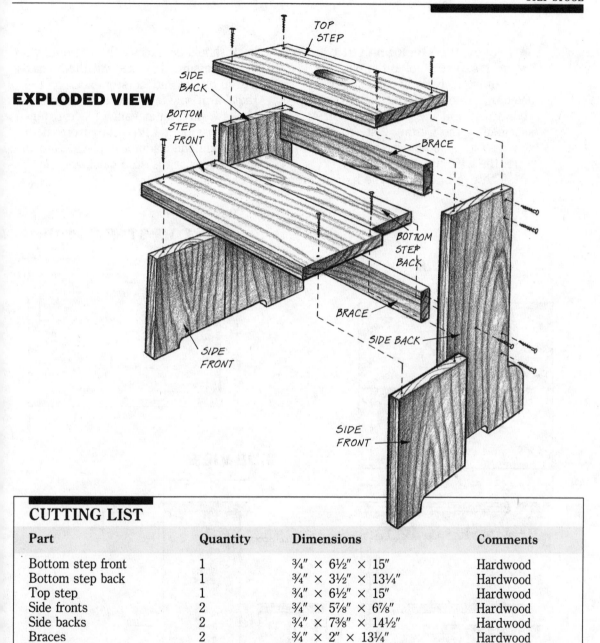

TOP STEP

SIDE BACK

BOTTOM STEP FRONT

BRACE

BOTTOM STEP BACK

BRACE

SIDE BACK

SIDE FRONT

SIDE FRONT

CUTTING LIST

Part	Quantity	Dimensions	Comments
Bottom step front	1	$\frac{3}{4}'' \times 6\frac{1}{2}'' \times 15''$	Hardwood
Bottom step back	1	$\frac{3}{4}'' \times 3\frac{1}{2}'' \times 13\frac{1}{4}''$	Hardwood
Top step	1	$\frac{3}{4}'' \times 6\frac{1}{2}'' \times 15''$	Hardwood
Side fronts	2	$\frac{3}{4}'' \times 5\frac{7}{8}'' \times 6\frac{7}{8}''$	Hardwood
Side backs	2	$\frac{3}{4}'' \times 7\frac{3}{8}'' \times 14\frac{1}{2}''$	Hardwood
Braces	2	$\frac{3}{4}'' \times 2'' \times 13\frac{1}{4}''$	Hardwood

Hardware

18 drywall screws, #6 $\times$ 1$\frac{1}{2}$"
18 wood plugs, $\frac{3}{8}$ inch

1 **Select the stock and cut the parts.** The stool in the photo is made of birch, but you can use just about any wood. Lay out the parts on your stock. Cut the parts to the sizes specified by the Cutting List. You'll probably have to glue up narrower boards to make the wide pieces.

The two braces and the bottom step back should be exactly the same length. To make sure they are, cut them against a stop block. Put the stop block on the radial arm saw fence or, if you use a table saw, on a miter gauge fence extension. Position it 13¼ inches from the saw blade and clamp it in place. Butt the pieces against the stop block and cut them to length.

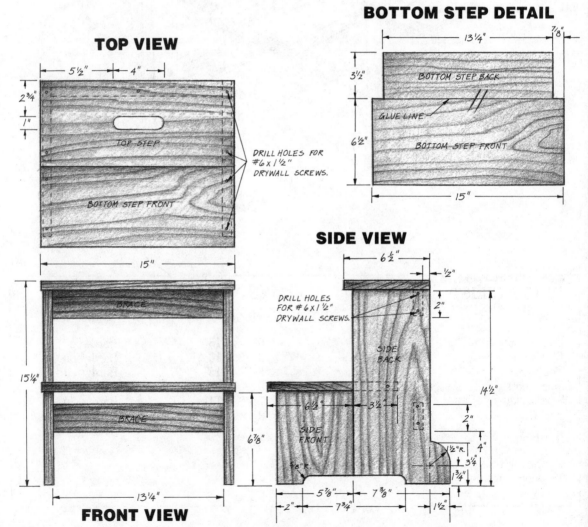

TOP VIEW

BOTTOM STEP DETAIL

SIDE VIEW

FRONT VIEW

2 **Glue up the bottom step.** The two parts of the bottom step are glued together, as shown in the *Bottom Step Detail*. Test fit the pieces, centering the shorter piece on the longer one. Check to be sure the overhangs at the ends are equal. When they are, draw a pencil mark across the joint. Apply glue and clamp the pieces together so that the two halves of the pencil mark align.

SHOP TIP: Boards often slip out of alignment when tightening clamps during glue-up. To prevent this, drive a couple of small nails partway into one of the gluing surfaces. Then cut the nails off with wire cutters. The slight projection of the cut-off nails will bite into the adjoining board and keep the two aligned.

3 **Rout the handle.** Mount a 1-inch-diameter straight bit in your table-mounted router and rout the handle in the top step, as explained in "Plunge Routing on a Router Table" on page 120. Round-over the edges of the handle with a ¼-inch roundover bit in a hand-held router.

4 **Glue up and shape the sides.** Glue the side fronts to the side backs the same way you glued up the bottom step. This time make the two parts flush at one end instead of one part centered on the other. Let the glue dry.

Lay out the back edge of the sides and the cutouts between the feet, as shown in the *Side View*. Make both cuts on a band saw if you have one, and clean up the marks. If you must make the curved cuts with a coping saw, you

may want to saw most of the straight portion of the back edge on the table saw and finish with the coping saw. In this case be sure to stop well short of the end of the straight line because the circular blade cuts further on the bottom where you can't see it than it does on the top. Sand the saw marks.

5 **Drill the screw holes.** Drill ⁵⁄₃₂-inch screw shank holes, as indicated in the *Top View* and *Side View*. Counterbore the holes ¼ inch deep with a ⅜-inch bit.

6 **Assemble the stool.** Finish sand all the parts but don't sand the tops of the steps with sandpaper finer than 100-grit. You want a bit of tooth there for safety. Position the bottom step on the sides. Drill ³⁄₃₂-inch pilot holes through the shank holes. Screw the step in place with #6 × 1½-inch drywall screws.

Position the braces, drill pilot holes, and screw them in place. Be sure the upper brace is flush with the top of the sides.

Center the top step on the sides. Drill pilot holes and screw it in place. Glue plugs in all the counterbores. When the glue is dry, pare the plugs flush with the surrounding wood with a razor-sharp chisel and sand them smooth.

7 **Apply a finish.** Finish the stool with your favorite wood finish. Consider using polyurethane for durability. For added traction on the steps, sprinkle a little very fine sand in the second-to-last coat of finish while it's still wet.

PLUNGE ROUTING ON A ROUTER TABLE

Sometimes it's easier to make an inside cut with a table-mounted router than it is to make it with a plunge router, especially if you don't *have* a plunge router. There are two keys to successful plunge routing on a router table:

• Limit the depth of cut of each pass to ⅛ inch or so.

• Lay out marks that tell you where the bit is cutting even when you can't see it.

1 **Install the bit.** Select a bit designed for end cutting, like a spiral upcut bit. Chuck it in the table-mounted router and adjust the depth of cut to about ⅛ inch. Clamp the router table fence the correct distance from the bit for the cut that you require.

2 **Mark the bit position on the fence.** Square over from the cutting circle of the bit to the fence, as shown in *Marking the Fence*. From there, square up along the face of the fence and mark the fence. Repeat for the other side of the cutting circle.

3 **Lay out the required cut on the stock.** Lay out the cut on the side of the stock that will be visible while making the cut, as shown in *Making the Plunge*. This will be on the side opposite a blind dado or mortise. Square over from the ends of the layout to the edge that will follow the router table fence and mark the stock.

4 **Make the cut.** Start the router. Hold the stock over the bit with the edge against the fence, the right end down on the table, and the left end suspended, as shown in *Making the Plunge*. Align the left mark on the stock with the left mark on the fence. Lower the stock onto the bit.

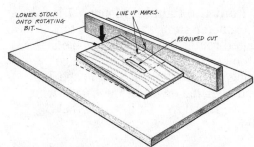

LOWER STOCK ONTO ROTATING BIT.

LINE UP MARKS.

REQUIRED CUT

MAKING THE PLUNGE

Guide the stock along the fence from right to left until the right mark on the stock aligns with the right mark on the fence. Carefully lift the right end until the stock clears the router bit, then lift the stock from the router table. Raise the bit about ⅛ inch and repeat. Continue until you've cut all the way through the stock or to the required depth.

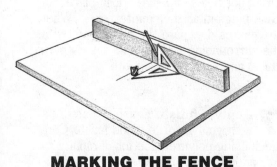

MARKING THE FENCE

HALL TABLE

A lot of activity goes on in a front hall or entry. Family members come and go. Guests arrive. Mail and packages arrive. It's a handy place for keys and outgoing mail, gloves and scarves, barrettes and hats. But space is usually limited, often too limited.

This hall table, designed by Steve Clerico of Free Union, Virginia, helps a front entry do its job. It is handsome enough to be the first piece of furniture that guests see but practical enough for daily family use. It is big enough to be useful but narrow enough to fit in a front entry. And this one is challenging enough to be fun to build but simple enough to build with common tools.

1 **Select the stock and cut the parts.** The table in the photo is oak. Make yours from whatever wood will go well in your entry. Try to find a single wide board for the top. You can use a less expensive secondary wood for the drawer sides, backs, and bottoms.

When your lumber is well-adjusted to the temperature and humidity of your

shop, choose the best-looking pieces for the top and drawer fronts. Lay out the drawer fronts so the grain runs from one to the other. Then lay out the rest of the parts. Resaw the drawer parts, as explained in "Resawing on the Table Saw" on page 13. Surface all of the stock, then cut the parts to the sizes specified by the Cutting List.

2 Cut the leg-to-apron mortise-and-tenon joints. The legs attach to the aprons with haunched mortises and tenons, as shown in the *Leg Joint Detail*. Cut the mortises with a ¼-inch-diameter straight bit. Cut the tenons to fit. For more information, see "Cutting Mortises and Tenons" on page 145.

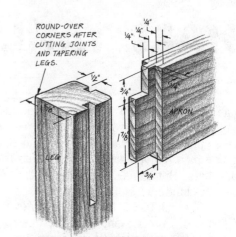

LEG JOINT DETAIL

On the table saw, rip the groove in the aprons for the tabletop fasteners, as shown in the *Interior Details*.

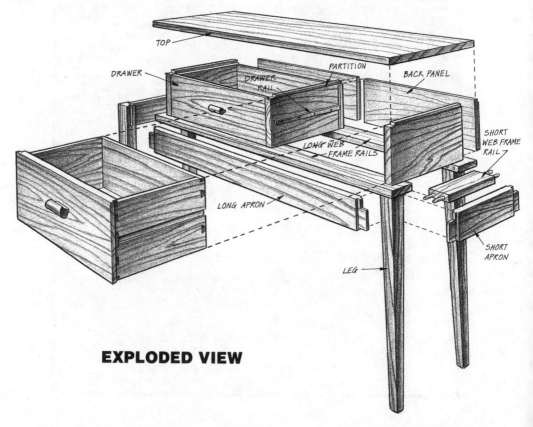

EXPLODED VIEW

3 **Taper and round-over the legs.**
The legs begin to taper just below
the aprons. If you don't have a manufac-
tured tapering jig, make one for this job,
as shown in "Tapering Legs" on page
124. Saw the taper slightly to the waste

side of the line, then plane down to the
line.
Round-over the corners of the legs
with a ¼-inch-radius roundover bit with
a ball-bearing guide mounted in your
router.

CUTTING LIST

Part	Quantity	Dimensions	Comments
Legs	4	1⅝″ × 1⅝″ × 23¼″	
Long aprons	2	¾″ × 2⅞″ × 38⅛″	
Short aprons	2	¾″ × 2⅞″ × 8″	
Top	1	¾″ × 11″ × 40″	
Partitions	3	¾″ × 5½″ × 9¾″	
Short web frame rails	2	¾″ × 3″ × 5″	
Long web frame rails	2	¾″ × 3″ × 40″	
Back panels	2	¾″ × 5½″ × 18¾″	
Drawer rails	4	⅜″ × ½″ × 8³⁄₁₆″	Resaw from 4/4 stock.
Drawer fronts	2	¾″ × 5¼″ × 18¼″	
Drawer sides	4	⅜″ × 5″ × 8¼″	Resaw from 4/4 stock.
Drawer backs	2	⅜″ × 4⅜″ × 18″	Resaw from 4/4 stock.
Drawer bottoms	2	⅜″ × 8½″ × 17½″	Resaw from 4/4 stock.
Stop blocks	2	¼″ × ¾″ × 1″	Cut from scrap.
Drawer stops	2	¼″ × ¾″ × 1″	Cut from scrap.
Drawer pull	1	¾″ × ¾″ × 12″	

Hardware

6 tabletop fasteners. Available from The Woodworkers' Store, 21801 Industrial Blvd., Rogers, MN
55374-9514. Part #34215 (pack of 10).
12 flathead wood screws, #8 × 1¼″
20 roundhead wood screws, #4 × ½″, with 12 washers
2 brass flathead wood screws, #8 × 1¼″
4 brass flathead wood screws, #4 × ½″
4 flathead wood screws, #6 × 1″
16 fluted dowels, ¼″ × 2½″

4 Groove the underside of the top.

The underside of the top is grooved for the back and partitions, as shown in the *Top Detail*. The partitions slide into grooves routed with a dovetail bit. They are not glued into these grooves. The back panels are glued into square-cornered grooves that are routed with a straight bit. The back panels lock the partitions in position in their dovetail grooves.

SHOP TIP: Lay out the centerline of routed grooves, then place a spacer half the width of the router base along the centerline. Clamp a fence along the other edge of the spacer. By guiding the router along the fence, the routed groove will be centered on the laid-out line, regardless of the width of the router bit. Save the spacer for future projects.

TAPERING LEGS

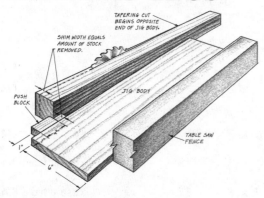

TAPERING CUT BEGINS OPPOSITE END OF JIG BODY.

SHIM WIDTH EQUALS AMOUNT OF STOCK REMOVED.

JIG BODY

PUSH BLOCK

TABLE SAW FENCE

1"

2"

6"

There are lots of fancy jigs for cutting tapered legs. Most of them are a lot of work to make and require a lot of math to calibrate. This one is simple, shop-made, and very easy to set up.

Begin by cutting the jig body shown in the drawing. You can make it from any ¾-inch-thick lumber, plywood, or particleboard. Saw it to about 6 inches wide and 3 inches longer than the tapered portion of the leg you want to make.

Next, saw a ¾ × 1 × 2-inch push block from a piece of scrap. Screw or glue it to the jig body, as shown.

The shim shown in the drawing determines how much wood will be cut from the leg blank. If you want to remove ⅝ inch of wood to create the narrowest part of the leg, make the shim ⅝ inch wide. Tack the shim to the jig with a small wire nail.

Cut the leg blanks to the untapered dimensions of the legs. Put the jig against the table saw fence. To set the fence, put a leg blank against the jig body but in front of the shim, not on it. Now slide the fence, jig, and leg blank up to the saw blade, then back away from the blade ⅟₃₂ inch or so. Lock the fence against the jig when it's in this position. This setting leaves the tapered leg ⅟₃₂ inch larger than final size so you have some stock to plane off when smoothing the legs.

To taper a leg, put a leg blank in the jig with one end alongside the shim and against the push block. Run the jig and leg through the saw. To taper an adjoining side of the leg, rotate the leg 90 degrees and run the jig and leg through the saw again.

To taper a leg on all four sides, make two adjoining tapers, then taper the remaining two sides using a shim that is twice as wide.

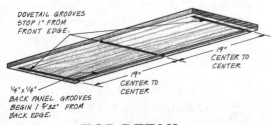

DOVETAIL GROOVES
STOP 1" FROM
FRONT EDGE.

19"
CENTER TO
CENTER

19"
CENTER TO
CENTER

¼" x ¼"
BACK PANEL GROOVES
BEGIN 1 ⁵⁄₃₂" FROM
BACK EDGE.

TOP DETAIL

Lay out the center of the dovetail grooves and rout them first. Use a ½-inch dovetail bit set to rout ½ inch deep. Rout the groove in a single pass.

Lay out the back panel grooves and rout them with a hand-held router guided by its fence attachment.

5 Cut the sliding dovetails. Rout the sliding dovetails on the partitions to fit in the dovetail groove. This involves some trial and error, so rout the tail on a test piece first.

Begin by setting up your router table, as shown in *Cutting Sliding Dovetails*. Use the same dovetail bit that you used for the grooves on the underside of the top.

Find or prepare a piece of scrap the exact thickness of the partitions. Place the scrap on edge against the auxiliary fence and rout the first side of the tail. Turn the scrap so the opposite face is against the fence and rout the second side of the tail. If the test dovetail is too big to fit the grooves in the top, move

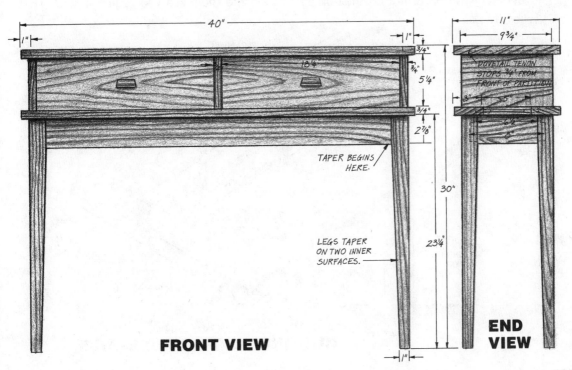

40"

1"

1"

18¼"

¾"

¾"

5¼"

¾"

2⅞"

TAPER BEGINS
HERE.

30"

23¼"

LEGS TAPER
ON TWO INNER
SURFACES.

1"

FRONT VIEW

11"

9¾"

DOVETAIL TENON
STOPS ¾" FROM
FRONT OF PARTITION.

3"

5"

6½"

END VIEW

the fence to expose more of the bit. If
the test dovetail is too loose, move the
fence to expose less of the bit.

When you're satisfied with the fit,
cut the sliding dovetail on the top edge
of each partition. Cut a dovetail on an
extra piece and set it aside. You'll use it
later to fill in a groove. The extra piece
need not be more than 2 inches wide ×
6 inches long.

6 **Dowel the web frame together.**
What looks in the photo like a wide
board below the drawers is really a
frame, as shown in the *Exploded View*.
This frame is called a web frame. It
saves wood and makes it easier to fit the
drawers because you can reach inside
the carcase from below.

The frame is doweled together, as
shown in the *Frame Joinery Detail*. First,
drill two holes in the ends of each short
web frame rail. To locate the holes in
the long web frame rails, put dowel centers, available at most hardware stores,
into the holes you've just drilled. Test

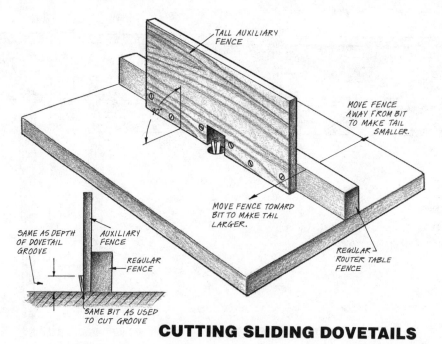

TALL AUXILIARY
FENCE

MOVE FENCE
AWAY FROM BIT
TO MAKE TAIL
SMALLER.

MOVE FENCE TOWARD
BIT TO MAKE TAIL
LARGER.

REGULAR
ROUTER TABLE
FENCE

SAME AS DEPTH
OF DOVETAIL
GROOVE

AUXILIARY
FENCE

REGULAR
FENCE

SAME BIT AS USED
TO CUT GROOVE

CUTTING SLIDING DOVETAILS

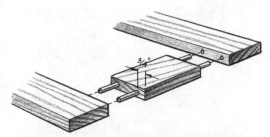

FRAME JOINERY DETAIL

assemble a joint, pressing the dowel centers into the long rails. Drill holes at the marks left by the dowel centers. Repeat for the remaining joints and glue the frame together. When the glue is dry, touch up any misalignment with a hand plane or sandpaper.

7 **Tongue and groove the partitions and back panels.** You have already cut grooves for the back panels in the underside of the top. Cut similar grooves in the partitions, as shown in the *Back Panel Detail*. The dimensions given will make the partitions project $1/32$ inch proud of the back panels, giving the back panels the appearance of drawers.

Cut the tongues on the ends and top edge of each back panel with a dado head on the table saw or with the router table. Later, you'll glue the tongues in the grooves. Make sure the fit is just barely snug, but not tight. A tight-fitting joint will bind during glue-up.

SHOP TIP: You can ease assembly of a project by chamfering the edges of tenons and tongues with a single stroke of a block plane.

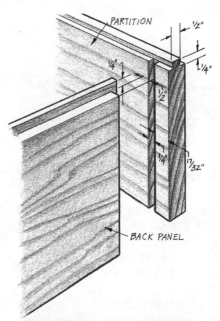

BACK PANEL DETAIL

8 **Assemble the carcase.** Begin the assembly of the carcase by screwing the drawer rails to the partitions, as shown in the *Interior Details*. They will need adjustment later, but it will be a lot easier to drive the screws if you do it now. The drawer rails are secured with #4 × $1/2$-inch roundhead wood screws with washers. Bore the counterbores and oversize shank holes, as shown in the *Drawer Rail Detail*. Position the rails *exactly* as shown in the *Interior Details*. Bore pilot holes in the *center* of the shank holes and screw the rails in place.

Cut away $3/4$ inch of the dovetail tenons at the front of the partitions. This will allow at least $1/4$ inch of empty groove in front of the tenon. The gap allows for shrinkage in the width of the top. Slide the dovetail joints together

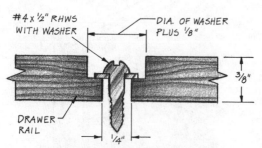

DRAWER RAIL DETAIL

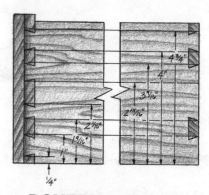

DOVETAIL DETAIL

without glue until the grooves in the partitions line up with the grooves in the top. Apply glue sparingly to the grooves for the back panels and to the back panel tongues, and slide the back panels in place.

Check that everything is correctly aligned and square and let the glue dry. Earlier, you routed a sliding dovetail on a piece of scrap. Carefully cut the tail off the scrap, positioning the cut so that you do not cut into the tail. Cut the tail to form three dovetail plugs, each about 1

inch long. Glue the plugs into the empty dovetail grooves in the rear overhang of the top. Saw them flush when the glue dries.

Put the top-and-partition assembly upside down on the workbench and place the web frame on it. Align the frame so it overhangs evenly on all sides. Clamp the whole works to the workbench. Make sure that the drawer openings are square. Drill and countersink for the #8 × 1¼-inch flathead wood screws that hold the frame to the upper assembly.

INTERIOR DETAILS

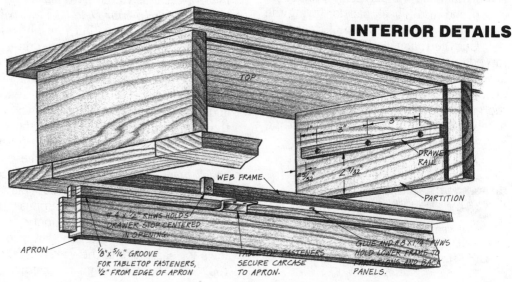

CUTTING HALF-BLIND DOVETAILS

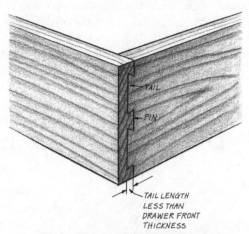

TAIL

PIN

TAIL LENGTH
LESS THAN
DRAWER FRONT
THICKNESS

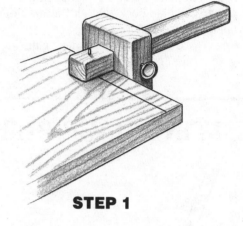

STEP 1

HALF-BLIND DOVETAILS

Half-blind dovetails allow you to join two parts with the strength of dovetails but with the joinery concealed on one side. They are commonly used to join the sides of a drawer to the front. In this case, the joint only shows on the side of the drawer so the joint is concealed when the drawer is closed.

The step-by-step instructions that follow assume you are making a drawer and that you know how to cut through dovetails. If you have never cut dovetails by hand before, read "Cutting Through Dovetails" on page 67 and cut the through dovetails at the back of your drawer first.

1 **Lay out the length of the pins and tails.** The length of the pins in a half-blind dovetail joint is equal to the thickness of the tails, just as it is with through dovetails. The layout is different, however. Use a marking gauge to scribe the *length* of the pins on the inside of the

drawer front only. This line is called the base line, as it marks the base of the pins.

The length of the tails must be less than the thickness of the drawer front. If the drawer side is thinner than the drawer front, as it usually is, make the tails the same length as the thickness of the drawer side. This makes the tails and pins the same length, so you can lay out the length without readjusting the marking gauge. If the drawer sides are the same thickness as the front you'll have to choose a tail length; ¾ of the stock thickness would do well. Scribe the tail length on both faces of the drawer side.

2 **Lay out and cut the tails.** Having scribed the tail length, the rest of the tail layout and the cutting of the tails is identical to laying out and cutting tails for through dove-

(continued)

Use two screws in the center partition, three in each outer partition, and two in each back panel. Remove the clamps. Apply glue to the edges of the partitions and back panels and screw the frame in place. Double-check that all the drawer openings are square.

While this assembly dries, glue together the aprons and legs.

9 **Dovetail the drawers.** The dovetail layout, as shown in the *Dovetail Detail* and *Drawer Details,* allows you to rout the drawer rail groove along the entire length of the drawer sides and front while still hiding the ends of the grooves in the assembled drawer.

Check the actual assembled dimensions of the carcase before you begin the

CUTTING HALF-BLIND DOVETAILS—continue

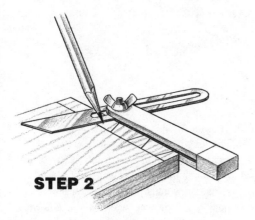

STEP 2

STEP 3

tails. Lay out the width of the tails on the end grain, drawing the lines across the end grain with the help of a square. With a T-bevel, lay out the angle of the tails by drawing a line from the end of the board to the base line.

Saw along the layout lines and chisel out the waste.

3 **Lay out the pins.** The depth of the pins is the same as the length of the tails. With the marking gauge still set for the length of the tails, scribe the depth of the pins on the end grain of the drawer front. Now trace the tails

onto the end of the drawer front just as you would for through dovetails. Square down from the end of each tracing to the base line. Mark the waste areas on the inside face and the end grain.

4 **Saw the sides of the pins.** When sawing the sides of through dovetail pins you are able to saw the entire side of the pins. With half-blind dovetails you can only saw half of the side of the pins. Saw from the end grain to the base line, following the layout lines. Be

drawers. If they are not as shown in the drawings, adjust the drawer dimensions to fit.

You can cut the dovetails by hand or with an adjustable dovetail jig and a router. For more information on cutting them by hand, see "Cutting Through Dovetails" on page 67 and "Cutting Half-Blind Dovetails" on page 129. If you use a jig, note that the drawer front, back, and sides are different widths. With some dovetail jigs it will be easier to cut the dovetails with all of the parts the same width, then rip the narrower parts to size. Rabbet the ends of the drawer fronts, as shown in the *Drawer Details,* before cutting the dovetails.

After cutting the dovetails, rout

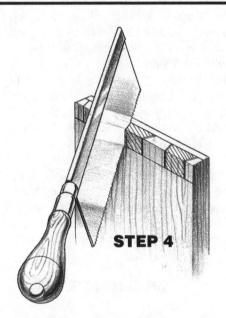

STEP 4

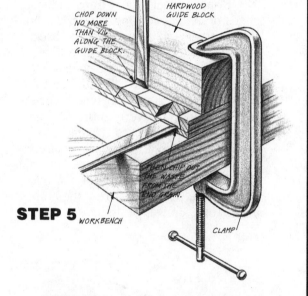

CHOP DOWN NO MORE THAN ⅛" ALONG THE GUIDE BLOCK.

HARDWOOD GUIDE BLOCK

THEN CHIP OUT THE WASTE FROM THE END GRAIN.

STEP 5 WORKBENCH

CLAMP

careful not to saw past either the base line or the pin-depth line.

5   Chop out the waste between the pins. Chop out the waste between the pins with the aid of a 2 × 2 hardwood block as you would for through dovetails. You can only chop from one side (the inside). Since you only need to go partway through the pin board, chopping out half-blind dovetail pins is very much like the first half of chopping out through dovetail pins.

Unfortunately, the saw never cuts along the entire edge of the pin when cutting half-blind dovetails. You need to chisel the sides of the pins where you were unable to saw. When chiseling this area it is very easy to let the socket get a bit narrower than it should be, so undercut slightly. As you approach the pin-depth line, proceed cautiously so you don't go beyond it.

Fit the joint, paring as necessary, just as you would with through dovetails.

¼-inch-wide grooves for the drawer bottoms in the drawer fronts and sides. Rout ½-inch-wide grooves for the drawer rails in the exact center of the sides.

10 **Assemble the drawers.** The drawer bottom grooves must align with the bottom of the back. Widen the grooves or trim the back as necessary.

Plane a bevel on the front and side edges of the drawer bottoms so the bottoms just slide in nicely from the back. Glue the dovetail joints and insert the bottoms to keep the drawers square. Place the drawers on a flat surface to check that they aren't twisted. If necessary, clamp the drawers to the flat surface while the glue dries. Double-check to make sure the drawers are square.

Cut slots in the bottom, as shown in the *Drawer Details,* and screw the bottom in place. Glue and screw the stop block to the drawer bottom.

SHOP TIP: Before assembling drawers, wax the corners of the drawer bottoms. This will prevent glue that squeezes out of the drawer joints from gluing the drawer bottom in place.

11 **Fit the drawers.** Plane the top, bottom, and ends of the drawer fronts so they fit the openings with a ¹⁄₃₂-inch clearance on all sides. Adjust the drawer rails so the drawers open without rubbing on the web frame. If they're too tight from side to side, plane the rails slightly thinner. It's okay if they don't seem to slide very easily at this point. Apply furniture wax after finishing the table to help the drawers slide smoothly.

Turn the carcase upside down on the bench and install the drawer stops, as shown in the *Interior Details.* With the carcase still upside down on the bench, put the leg-and-apron assembly in place. Fasten the web frame to the apron with tabletop fasteners.

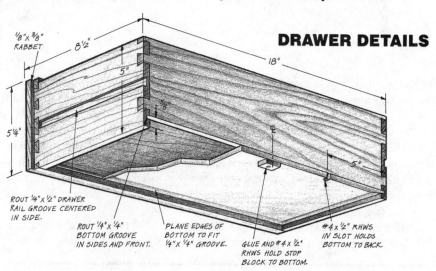

DRAWER DETAILS

⅛" x ⅜" RABBET

8½"

5"

18"

⅜"

5¼"

5"

ROUT ¼" x ½" DRAWER RAIL GROOVE CENTERED IN SIDE.

ROUT ¼" x ¼" BOTTOM GROOVE IN SIDES AND FRONT.

PLANE EDGES OF BOTTOM TO FIT ¼" x ¼" GROOVE.

GLUE AND #4 x ½" RHWS HOLD STOP BLOCK TO BOTTOM.

#4 x ½" RHWS IN SLOT HOLDS BOTTOM TO BACK.

12 **Make and install the drawer pulls.** Rout the drawer pulls from a piece of wood ¾ inch square by about 1 foot long. The extra length is necessary to shape the piece safely on the router table. Begin by rounding-over two adjoining edges with a ⅜-inch-radius roundover bit. Rout the remaining edges to the profile shown in the *Drawer Pull Detail* with a ⅜-inch-radius cove bit.

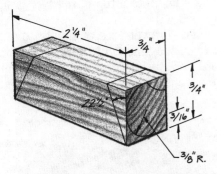

DRAWER PULL DETAIL

Cut the ends of the pulls at a 20 to 25 degree angle, cutting them to length in the process. Sand or file them to create a profile you like. When you're happy with the appearance, drill a pilot hole in each pull and a shank hole in the drawer fronts, and screw each pull in place with a #8 × 1¼-inch flathead wood screw.

SHOP TIP: To check the final appearance and position of a drawer knob, stick it to the drawer with double-faced tape.

13 **Apply the finish.** You can apply whatever finish will best fit the decor of your home. The table in the photo was finished with two coats of Danish oil. If you choose Danish oil, apply the first coat and wet sand with 400-grit wet/dry sandpaper. Apply the second coat and sand with 600-grit wet/dry sandpaper. A well-buffed coat of paste furniture wax after the oil is fully cured will give the table a soft sheen.

SHOP TIP: An ultrafine Scotch-Brite pad, available from auto-refinishing supply stores, makes a workable (if somewhat drippy) applicator for Danish oil. Dip the pad in oil and rub it on, wiping with the grain. It simultaneously applies oil and removes stray wood fibers sticking up.

SOFA TABLE

If you're wondering why this is a sofa table instead of a hall table, don't. If it would fit nicely in your hall, then it's a hall table. The slate top used by designer Rick Wright of Schnecksville, Pennsylvania, would go well in many entry halls.

The overall height of sofas has been decreasing for the past two decades. Sofa tables are also now lower, following the trend. If Rick's table is a bit high for your sofa, shorten the legs. The top of the table should be about the same height as the back of your sofa.

Slate makes an attractive and durable top for this table. It goes well with most hardwoods. To find a merchant who can supply the slate top, check the Yellow Pages under "Slate" or "Stone, Natural." If you have trouble, try masons, tile dealers, or contractors who build custom kitchens. If slate isn't your style, substitute a top of marble, granite, or wood.

The drawers are of simple construction but add function to this straightforward design. If you prefer, you can make the aprons without the ears at the ends.

1 Select the stock and cut the parts. Choose a hardwood for the color and grain pattern that you like. The table shown in the photo is made from oak. Select clear stock for the parts. Joint and plane the stock to the required thicknesses and cut the parts to the dimensions specified by the Cutting List. Edge-glue boards to get sufficient width if necessary. You can also glue up stock to get thicker material for the legs if necessary. Wait and cut the drawer kickers and kicker strips from the waste that will come from between the ears of the aprons.

2 Make the legs. Crosscut the legs to identical length. Lay out the tapers on two adjoining sides of each leg. Saw the taper just outside the line and joint the sawed surfaces. For detailed instructions on sawing tapers, see "Tapering Legs" on page 124. The jointed taper should end 8 inches from the top of the leg.

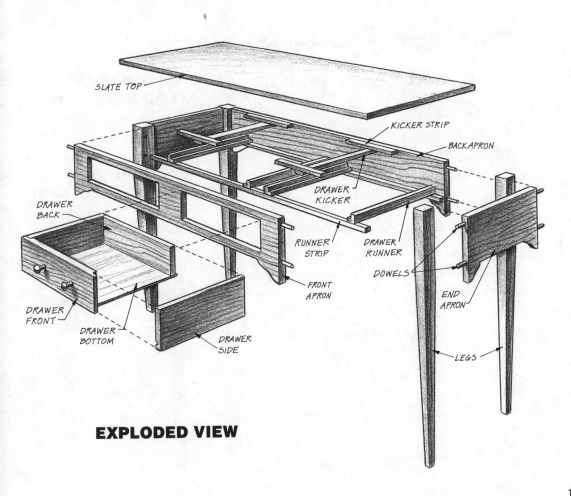

SLATE TOP

KICKER STRIP

BACK APRON

DRAWER KICKER

DRAWER BACK

RUNNER STRIP

DRAWER RUNNER

FRONT APRON

DRAWER FRONT

DRAWER BOTTOM

DRAWER SIDE

DOWELS

END APRON

LEGS

EXPLODED VIEW

3 Cut and glue the front apron.

The easiest way to cut neat, square-cornered drawer openings in an apron is to rip off the top and bottom of the apron, crosscut the drawer openings out of the middle piece, then glue the apron back together. With careful planning, you can make the drawer fronts out of the pieces that you cut out to make the openings. The *Front Apron Detail* shows the required cuts.

Start with a front apron piece that is the size specified by the Cutting List.

These dimensions allow for the saw cuts and jointing that will reduce the width. Rip off the top rail at a 1$\frac{1}{16}$-inch width, which allows $\frac{1}{16}$ inch extra so you can plane away the saw marks. Set your jointer to remove $\frac{1}{16}$ inch and joint the sawed edge of the rail.

Joint the sawed edge of the remaining piece. From this piece, rip a 4$\frac{1}{16}$-inch-wide piece for the drawers. Joint the sawed edge as before, reducing the width to 4 inches.

At this point, you have a top rail; a

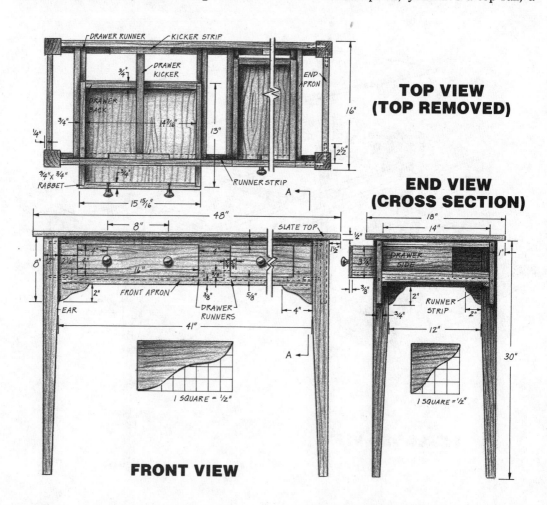

TOP VIEW (TOP REMOVED)

END VIEW (CROSS SECTION)

FRONT VIEW

piece that you will crosscut to make stiles, drawer openings, and drawer fronts; and a third piece. Joint the sawed edge of the third piece. Rip a 1¹⁄₁₆-inch-wide piece from it for the bottom rail. Joint the bottom rail, reducing it to 1 inch wide. Later you'll cut the ears and the drawer kickers from the last remaining piece.

Now cut the drawer openings in the 4-inch-wide piece. The pieces that you cut out to make the openings will be the drawer fronts. Cut the pieces in the order shown on the *Front Apron Detail* so the grain pattern will continue from part to part. Begin by cutting an end stile. Then cut a drawer, a center stile, another drawer, and the final end stile.

CUTTING LIST

Part	Quantity	Dimension	Comments
Legs	4	2″ × 2″ × 30″	Taper outside edges.
Front apron	1	⁷⁄₈″ × 9″ × 42″	Includes ears, drawer fronts, rails, and stiles.
Back apron	1	⁷⁄₈″ × 8¼″ × 41″	
End aprons	2	⁷⁄₈″ × 8¼″ × 12″	
Dowels	16	⁵⁄₁₆″ dia. × 2½″	
Runner strips	2	⅜″ × ¾″ × 41″	
Kicker strips	4	⅜″ × ¾″ × 8″	From waste from aprons; see text.
Drawer runners	4	1⅜″ × 1½″ × 14″	
Drawer kickers	2	⅝″ × 1″ × 14″	From waste from aprons; see text.
Drawer sides	4	¾″ × 3⅞″ × 13″	
Drawer backs	2	¾″ × 3″ × 14⁷⁄₁₆″	
Drawer bottoms	2	¼″ × 13″ × 14¹⁵⁄₁₆″	
Slate top	1	½″ × 18″ × 48″	
Cleats	4	½″ × ½″ × 8″	Optional; cut from scrap.

Hardware

6d finishing nails
2d common nails
4 drawer pulls, 1¼″ dia. × 1″. Available from Smith Woodworks & Design, R.R. 5, Box 42, Califon, NJ 07830.

Sand the end grain of the stiles smooth.

Glue and clamp the stiles in place between the top and bottom rails. Use the drawer fronts to check the spacing of the stiles but don't clamp the drawer fronts in the assembly—remove them so they don't accidentally get glued in place. Let the glue dry.

4 **Cut and glue the apron ears.** Rip off the ear piece from the bottom edge of the side and back aprons. Joint the sawed edges. Crosscut the ear blanks from these three pieces and from the remainder of the front apron. Remember that you want the grain to match after gluing the ears back on, so label each ear blank and where it came from. Set aside the waste from between the ears for the drawer kickers and kicker strips.

Make patterns in the shape of the ears, as shown on the *Front View* and

Side View, and lay out the shape on the eight ear blanks. Pay attention to whether each ear is a left or right ear when you lay out the curve.

Saw the ears to shape on the band saw. Stack them up, clamp them together, and smooth out the saw marks with rasps, scrapers, and sandpaper. By smoothing them all out at once they will be identical.

Glue the ears back in position on the aprons, each in the spot where it came from, so the grain matches.

Finally, plane all the aprons to ¾ inch thick and crosscut them to exact length. The glue lines should be nearly invisible. Plane the drawer fronts to thickness separately.

5 **Drill holes in the aprons and legs for dowels.** The aprons join the legs with 5⁄16-inch dowels. Commercially available grooved dowels are best.

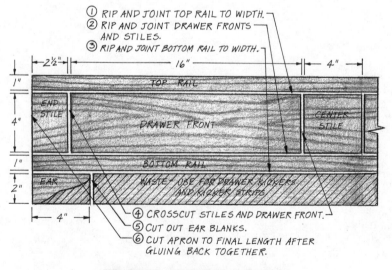

① RIP AND JOINT TOP RAIL TO WIDTH.
② RIP AND JOINT DRAWER FRONTS AND STILES.
③ RIP AND JOINT BOTTOM RAIL TO WIDTH.

④ CROSSCUT STILES AND DRAWER FRONT.
⑤ CUT OUT EAR BLANKS.
⑥ CUT APRON TO FINAL LENGTH AFTER GLUING BACK TOGETHER.

FRONT APRON DETAIL

The grooves allow air trapped at the bottom of the joint to escape instead of forcing the dowel out. Lay out and drill two 5/16 × 1¼-inch holes in each end of each apron with a doweling jig. Transfer the dowel locations to the legs with dowel centers and drill the matching dowel holes in the legs, setting the aprons ¼ inch in from the outside surface of the legs. Be sure to drill the dowel holes in the sides of the legs that are tapered.

SHOP TIP: If you get caught without grooved dowels, you can put grooves in an ordinary dowel by squeezing it in the pipe-gripping section of the jaws of ordinary pliers. Make sure the indentations line up in continuous grooves so excess glue can escape.

6 Assemble the sofa table. Sand the legs, except where they meet the aprons. Sand the aprons. Glue dowels into their holes in the aprons. Glue and clamp each end apron to one pair of legs. Let the glue dry. Then, on a flat surface, glue and clamp the front and back aprons to the assembled ends. Make sure the table is square by measuring diagonally across the corners. If necessary, make a tourniquet out of stout cord and a short stick. Attach the tourniquet to the legs in the long diagonal and pull the assembly square.

7 Install the runner strips and kicker strips. Glue and clamp the runner strips flush with the bottom of the front and back aprons. The drawer runners attach to these strips. Glue and clamp the kicker strips flush with the top of the front and back aprons. Center the kicker strips over the drawer openings. The drawer kickers attach to these strips.

8 Make and attach the drawer runners and kickers. Rip a ¾ × ¾-inch rabbet the length of each of the drawer runners. Scrape and sand the sawed surfaces clean.

Position the runners, as shown in the *Front View*. The surfaces of the rabbets must be flush with the corners of the drawer openings. Make sure the runners are square to the aprons and parallel to each other. Mark their positions on the runner strips. Remove each one in turn, apply glue, and clamp it back in position.

The drawer kickers keep the drawers from tipping when you pull them out. The bottom surfaces of the kickers must be flush with the top edges of the drawer openings. Glue and clamp the drawer kickers to the kicker strips at the center of the drawer openings.

9 Fit the drawer parts to the openings. The drawers should fit the openings with no more than 1/16 inch of clearance from side to side or top to bottom. Trim the drawer fronts, sides, and backs as necessary.

10 Rabbet the drawer fronts for the drawer sides. Saw a ⅜ × ¾-inch rabbet in each end of the drawer fronts. The rabbet receives the drawer sides. Begin the rabbet with a crosscut guided by the miter gauge. Then stand the drawer front upright in a tenoning jig to make the second cut that completes the rabbet.

11 **Cut the grooves for the drawer bottom.** To rip the ¼ × ¼-inch drawer bottom grooves in the fronts and sides, adjust the table saw blade to cut ¼ inch deep. Set the fence ⅜ inch from the blade and rip a kerf in the fronts and sides, forming the bottom edge of the grooves. Move the fence as necessary to cut the top edge of the grooves. With most blades, the fence movement will be about ⅛ inch. Rip the top edge of the grooves. If a sliver of wood remains in the center of the grooves, reset the fence a third time and rip out the sliver.

12 **Drill the drawer fronts for the pulls.** Lay out and drill the screw holes for the drawer pulls. Countersink the holes so the screw heads will sit flush with the inside of the drawers.

13 **Assemble the drawers.** Sand the inside surfaces of the drawer parts. Assemble the drawers on a flat surface. Glue and clamp the drawer sides to the rabbets in the ends of the drawer fronts. With the drawers in clamps, nail the sides to the fronts with 6d finishing nails. Glue and nail the backs in place between the sides. Align the bottom edge of the drawer back with the top edge of the drawer bottom groove.

Make certain the drawers are square by measuring diagonally across the corners. Sand the drawer bottoms and slide them into the bottom grooves. Nail the bottoms to the drawer backs with 2d common nails.

14 **Turn and attach the drawer pulls.** The drawer pulls can be turned on a lathe if you have one. If you don't, purchase commercially turned drawer pulls, which you can stain to match your wood. Glue and screw the pulls to the drawer fronts.

15 **Add the top.** The top is heavy enough to stay in place with no fasteners. If you like, you can keep it from being bumped out of place with cleats glued to the underside.

To attach the cleats, first place the top in position on the table. Reach up from below and draw the outline of the table frame on the bottom of the slate. Remove the top and turn it upside down on your bench. Bond four ½ × ½ × 8-inch strips of wood just inside the pencil lines. The type of construction adhesive that comes in tubes sticks well to the slate. Center one strip on each side of the table. The strips keep the top from moving if someone bumps it.

16 **Apply a finish.** If you made your table from a nice hardwood, you probably won't want to stain it. You can finish the wooden parts of the table with just about any finish you like. This table has two coats of boiled linseed oil on the slate to seal it.

SHAKER END TABLE

The simple grace of this Shaker-inspired end table will nestle comfortably into most any decor. Except for the drawer bottom, the table is built entirely of cherry, a wood the Shakers used often.

Building this little table doesn't require a lot of wood or shop space. For this reason, Rodale Press woodworking editors David Schiff and Rob Yoder decided to get together and build several of them at once, cutting down on machine set-up time. You'll probably want to build at least a pair. Then you can place one on each side of your bed or sofa.

If you've never built a table before, this project is an excellent place to start. Because it's small, mistakes won't cost you much wood. Meanwhile, you'll learn all the techniques necessary to build bigger tables. You'll need to hand-cut dovetails at the top of the front legs to receive the ends of the top rail. The joints won't be seen so they don't need to be beautiful. They're a good opportunity to practice. You'll get more practice dovetailing the back of the drawer to the sides. By then you'll be ready to move on to the real challenge: the half-blind

dovetails at the drawer front.

The bottom rail is locked into the front legs with a sliding dovetail joint. This joint takes a bit of fussing with the router set-up, but takes little skill to make. And it adds greatly to the strength and elegance of the table.

If you don't feel ready for all this dovetailing, you can make the project much simpler by eliminating the drawer. Replace the drawer and front rails with an apron identical to the back apron. Use the same mortise-and-tenon joinery used at the back apron.

The spare and simple lines of Shaker-style furniture emphasize the beauty of the wood. This means you'll want to pay particular attention to the stock you choose for each part of this table. As you choose the parts, you'll create a picture of the table in your mind. The fun and satisfaction in building the table comes from seeing that picture become reality.

1 **Surface the stock and prepare the leg blanks.** Most of the table is made of 4/4 (four-quarter) cherry. The

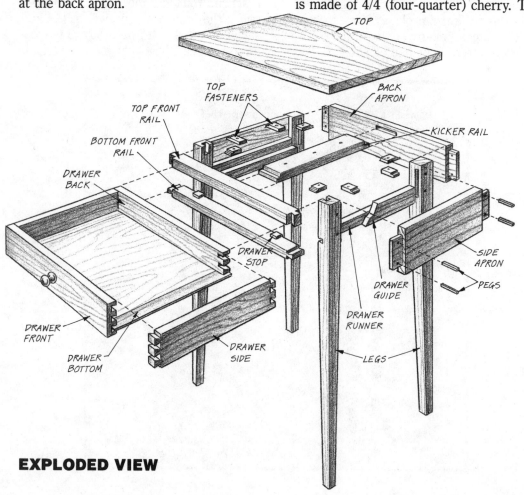

EXPLODED VIEW

exceptions are the legs, which are made of 6/4 (six-quarter) cherry and the drawer bottom, which is made from ½-inch-thick pine. Plane the 4/4 stock flat and ¾ inch thick.

Rip and plane the leg stock to 1⅜ inches square. Crosscut one end of each leg blank to square it up, but leave the blank 1 to 2 inches longer than the final 26-inch length.

2 **Glue up the top and drawer bottom.** Select your most attractive stock for the top. You'll need to glue up the top from at least two (and perhaps three) boards. Try to match the boards so that the grain flows together instead

of ending abruptly. Cut the boards so the glued-up blank will be at least 1 inch longer and wider than the finished top. Glue and clamp the top, then let the glue cure at least overnight. Follow the same procedure to glue up the drawer bottom.

3 **Mortise the legs.** Lay out the mortises in the legs, as shown in the *Mortise and Tenon Detail*. This is the time to decide how the legs will be oriented in the finished table. In general, you'll want to select the nicest-looking faces of the nicest legs for the front of the table. You'll also want the nicest faces of the rear legs to face the front of the table. Take a close look at grain di-

CUTTING LIST

Part	Quantity	Dimensions	Comments
Legs	4	1⅜″ × 1⅜″ × 26″	Cherry
Top	1	¾″ × 16″ × 21½″	Cherry
Side aprons	2	¾″ × 4″ × 13¼″	Cherry
Back apron	1	¾″ × 4″ × 17¾″	Cherry
Top/bottom front rails	2	¾″ × 1⅜″ × 16¾″	Cherry
Kicker rail	1	¾″ × 2″ × 12¼″	Cherry
Top fasteners	8	⁷⁄₁₆″ × 1 × 1½″	Cherry
Pegs	12	³⁄₁₆″ × ³⁄₁₆″ × 2″	Cherry
Drawer guides	2	½″ × 1½″ × 11¾″	Cherry
Drawer runners	2	½″ × ¹³⁄₁₆″ × 12¼″	Cherry
Drawer front	1	⅝″ × 2½″ × 15⅝″	Cherry
Drawer back	1	⁷⁄₁₆″ × 1⅞″ × 15⅝″	Cherry
Drawer sides	2	⁷⁄₁₆″ × 2½″ × 12¾″	Cherry
Drawer bottom	1	½″ × 12¾″ × 15⅛″	Pine
Drawer stops	2	¼″ × ¾″ × ¾″	

Hardware

13 flathead wood screws, #6 × 1″
1 Shaker-style knob, ⅞″ dia. Available from Smith Woodworks & Design, R.R. 5, Box 42, Califon, NJ 07830.

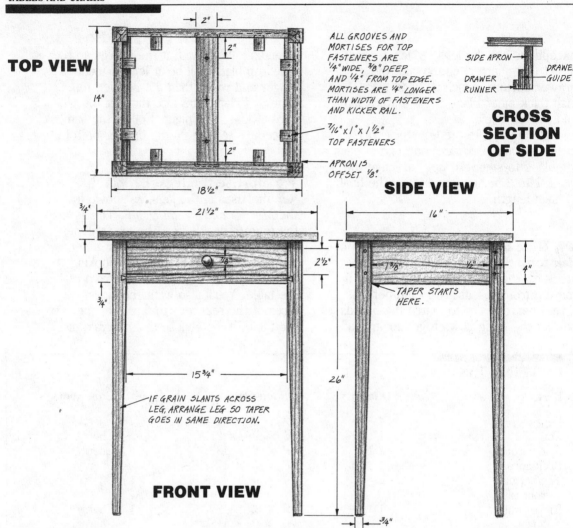

TOP VIEW

14"

2"

2"

2"

2"

ALL GROOVES AND
MORTISES FOR TOP
FASTENERS ARE
1/4" WIDE, 3/8" DEEP,
AND 1/4" FROM TOP EDGE.
MORTISES ARE 1/4" LONGER
THAN WIDTH OF FASTENERS
AND KICKER RAIL.

7/16" x 1" x 1 1/2"
TOP FASTENERS

APRON IS
OFFSET 1/8".

18 1/2"

SIDE APRON

DRAWER
RUNNER

DRAWER
GUIDE

**CROSS
SECTION
OF SIDE**

SIDE VIEW

3/4"

21 1/2"

16"

2 1/2"

1 3/8"

1/2"

4"

TAPER STARTS
HERE.

3/4"

26"

15 3/4"

IF GRAIN SLANTS ACROSS
LEG, ARRANGE LEG SO TAPER
GOES IN SAME DIRECTION.

3/4"

FRONT VIEW

rection when you make these decisions. If the grain slants across the width of the legs, they will look best if the legs taper in the same direction, as shown in the *Front View.* This will also help prevent tear-out when you finish plane and scrape the legs.

Once you have decided where the legs will go, mark where they'll go on their tops. Then mark the positions of the mortises that will receive the side and rear aprons. Lay them out, measur-

ing from 25½ inches from the bottoms of the legs. You'll cut the tops of the legs to length after cutting the mortises. The extra stock lessens the chances of splitting out a mortise while cutting it. Remember, the rear legs get two mortises each while the front legs get only one mortise each. Cut the mortises, as described in "Cutting Mortises and Tenons" on the opposite page. When laying out the

(continued on page 150)

CUTTING MORTISES AND TENONS

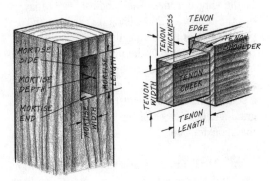

Mortise-and-tenon joints are one of the oldest methods of joining two pieces of wood together. They are also one of the most common joints in modern woodworking, whether industrial or hand crafted. With a history that spans many technological revolutions, it's not surprising that there are a variety of ways to cut the joint.

A good way to learn how to cut mortises is by drilling out most of the waste and then cleaning up the mortise with chisels. Mortises can also be cut with just chisels, a router, a square-bit mortising attachment for a drill press, or with specialized machines used mostly in industry. A good way to learn how to cut tenons is on the table saw. Tenons can also be cut with a handsaw; a dado cutter on the table saw or an industrial tenoner; or on a router table.

Reading about cutting mortises and tenons can be more confusing than actually cutting them. The confusion stems from the terms used. Various experts use different terms, and even terms like "length" and "width" are sometimes used in nonintuitive ways. This description will use the terms shown above. Notice that the length of the tenon corresponds to the depth of the mortise, the width of the tenon corresponds to the length of the mortise, and the thickness of the tenon corresponds to the width of the mortise.

1 **Lay out the mortises and tenons.** A mortise gauge is a specialized marking gauge with two scribing pins. The distance between the two pins is adjustable independent of the fence.

To lay out a mortise, first lay out the length, marking both ends with a sharp pencil. Adjust the distance between the pins of the mortise gauge to the width of the mortise. Adjust the fence of the mortise gauge to position the mortise as required by your plans. Scribe the width of the mortise between the end marks on the stock.

If you're cutting through mortises, square the end lines around to the opposite face and scribe the width on that face as well. Be as precise as you can when laying out the joint and squaring around to the opposite face. The strength of the joint depends on the fit of the parts, and the fit depends on the layout.

(continued)

CUTTING MORTISES AND TENONS—CONTINUE

STEP 1

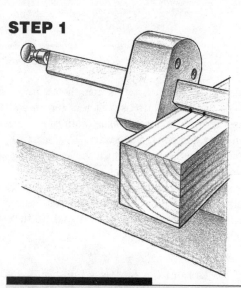

SHOP TIP: If you have a marking gauge but not a mortise gauge, prepare shims the exact thickness of your most common mortises. Set the marking gauge to mark the mortise edge farthest from the stock edge. Mark that edge, then insert the appropriate shim between the gauge fence and the stock edge to mark the nearer mortise edge.

To lay out a tenon, first lay out the *length*. Scribe a line all the way around the stock at this point. This scribe line marks the tenon shoulders. Now lay out the tenon *thickness* with the mortise gauge. Leave the distance between the pins adjusted exactly as you had it for the mortise. If necessary for your design, readjust the fence. Scribe the tenon thickness on the end of the stock and on both edges back as far

as the shoulder line. The handiest way to lay out the tenon *width* depends on the size and proportions of the tenon. In some cases it will be convenient to use the mortise gauge, in other cases it will be easier to use a marking gauge, and on occasion it will be easiest to use a square and awl. Lay out the width on the end grain and both faces of the stock back as far as the shoulder line.

2 **Drill out the mortise.** Begin the mortise by drilling out most of the waste. The best way to drill accurately is with a drill press with a fence clamped to the table. The fence should have a working face that is square to the drill press table. If you don't have a drill press, you can approximate the steps that follow with a doweling jig and a bit of imagination.

STEP 2

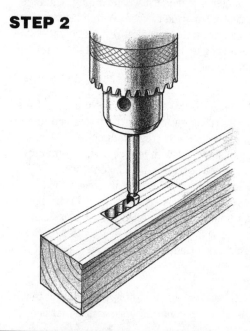

A second key to getting a good, accurate job is a bit with sharp spurs designed specifically for boring wood. Suitable bits include Forstner bits, brad-point bits, and Stanley Power Bore bits. The easiest to set up are the pilotless Forstner bits. Select a bit the exact diameter of the required mortise width. This will be easy if you designed your joints around the bits you have.

Place the stock on the drill press table with the mortise face up. Bring the bit down and align the spurs or rim of the bit exactly with the scribed mortise. Hold the stock in place by applying a little downward pressure with the bit. Bring the fence up alongside the stock and clamp it securely to the drill press table. Release the downward pressure, slide the stock over a little, and check that the bit still comes down exactly between the mortise layout lines.

If the mortises you are cutting are through mortises, put a piece of scrap alongside the fence and adjust the depth stop of the drill press so the bit will drill slightly into the scrap but no further. If you're cutting blind mortises, set the stop to drill the required mortise depth.

Begin drilling at the ends of the mortise. The fence will ensure that the bit aligns properly between the width layout lines, allowing you to concentrate on drilling right to the end layout lines. Drill both ends of the mortise, then drill overlapping holes between the end holes, removing as much waste as possible. The more you overlap the holes, the less you will have to pare out with chisels. Generally speaking, Forstner bits allow you to overlap the most without tending to jump over into the adjoining hole.

3 **Pare to the layout lines.** Some woodworkers prefer to clean up the mortise with the stock clamped to the workbench with the mortise face up. Others prefer to chisel horizontally with the mortise face toward them. Try both; neither has any inherent advantage.

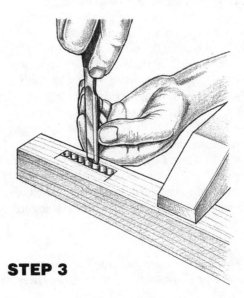

STEP 3

Clamp the stock to the workbench. Select a sharp chisel wide enough to span from the center of one overlapping hole to the center of the next one. Start the chisel right in the scribe line between two overlapping holes and push it in, paring off the ridge of wood between the holes. Guide the chisel so you don't undercut the mortise but still maintain the full width of the mortise. If the chisel strays, stop and realign it. There's a bit of a knack to this paring

(continued)

CUTTING MORTISES AND TENONS—CONTINUE

but it comes very quickly. If your mortise is a through mortise, pare about halfway through. If it's a blind mortise, pare all the way to the bottom. Repeat until you've removed all of the ridges between bored holes. If you're cutting through mortises, turn the stock around and clean up from the other side of the stock.

When the sides of the mortise are as flat and true as you can get them, lay the back of your chisel flat on the side of the mortise and begin slicing toward the corner. Slice as deeply as you can without resorting to a mallet. Now select a chisel the exact width of the mortise and push or drive it down the end of the mortise, squaring up the end. If it drives hard, take a preliminary cut removing less stock. Work from both sides of through mortises as you did when paring the sides. Square up both ends.

Give the completed mortise a thorough examination, paring off any areas that are not full width.

4 **Make a tenoning jig.** The drawing shows a simple, reliable, easy-to-use tenoning

jig that will keep your stock under control and perpendicular to the saw table. Make it out of ¾-inch particleboard with a pine or poplar fence. Accurate tenons begin with an accurate tenoning jig, so be fussy about keeping the sides of the base parallel, the corners of the brace square, and the fence square to the bottom surface of the jig. Glue and screw the particleboard together and glue the fence in place.

5 **Saw the cheeks and edges.** Install a sharp ripping blade on your table saw. You'll find that a ripping blade cuts more freely and much cooler than other tooth configurations when making end grain cuts.

Gather together all of the parts that require tenons of the same thickness in stock of the same thickness, and two or three scraps of the same thickness. Place one of the parts flat against the fence in the tenoning jig and clamp it to the upright. Position the jig so the stock is alongside the blade and adjust the blade height to ¹⁄₃₂ inch or so below the shoulder mark. Place the tenoning jig against the saw fence and

STEP 4

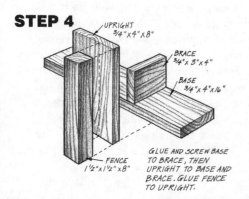

UPRIGHT
¾" x 4" x 8"

BRACE
¾" x 3" x 4"

BASE
¾" x 4" x 16"

FENCE
1½" x 1½" x 8"

GLUE AND SCREW BASE
TO BRACE, THEN
UPRIGHT TO BASE AND
BRACE. GLUE FENCE
TO UPRIGHT.

STEP 5

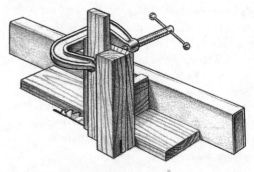

STEP 6

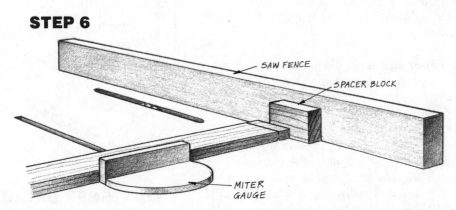

SAW FENCE

SPACER BLOCK

MITER GAUGE

adjust the fence to cut one of the cheeks. Set it to cut precisely down the line. Make sure the kerf will be on the waste side of the line. Saw the first cheek on all of the parts and scraps. Push the jig right on through, cutting a kerf in the fence as well as the stock. Make sure you don't have a hand near the rear of the fence where the blade will exit. If your tenons are of different lengths, readjust the blade height as necessary, but don't change the fence.

When you've made the first cheek cut on all of the parts and scraps, clamp one of the scraps in the jig in the same position as before. Readjust the fence to cut the second cheek. Cut the second cheek in the scrap, saw off the waste at the shoulder line with a handsaw, and test the fit in a mortise. Readjust the fence as necessary or place masking tape shims on the upright to get a good fit in your mortises. Then cut the remaining parts. Don't forget to readjust the height of the blade for different tenon lengths, if necessary.

Cut the tenon edges the same way you cut the cheeks. Depending on the shape of your parts, you may find it easier to clamp the stock

to the fence instead of the upright.

6 **Saw the shoulders.** Change to a smooth-cutting crosscut or combination blade. Clamp a spacer block to the saw fence well in front of the blade, as shown in the drawing. Adjust the blade height to cut the full depth of the shoulder and just barely score the tenon. This adjustment ensures that no tiny ridge of wood remains in the corner between the shoulder and the cheek. Put one of the parts against the miter gauge fence and line up the blade with the shoulder mark. Make sure the kerf will be on the waste side of the line. Hold the stock against the miter gauge fence, pull the stock and miter gauge back until the stock is in line with the spacer block on the saw fence, and move the saw fence over until the spacer block touches the end of the stock. Clamp it there. Saw the shoulders by butting the stock against the spacer block to position it, then holding it against the miter gauge fence while pushing it over the blade. Readjust the blade height and fence as necessary for different shoulder depths and tenon lengths.

mortises, note that the aprons should be recessed ⅛ inch from the outside faces of the legs, as shown in the *Top View.* When the mortises are complete, crosscut the tops of the legs to length.

4 **Taper the legs.** Each leg is tapered on its two inside faces. Make these tapers as described in "Tapering Legs" on page 124. After you have cut the tapers on the table saw, remove the saw marks with a few strokes of a sharp plane on each taper. Follow the plane with a hand scraper, if you have one, then sandpaper. Finally, use a block plane to chamfer the bottom edges of the legs slightly. This will prevent the legs from chipping when slid across a floor.

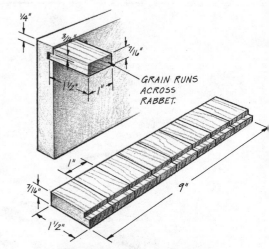

FASTENER DETAIL

5 **Make the aprons and rails.** Cut the aprons, the kicker rail, and the top and bottom front rails to the dimensions specified by the Cutting List. Make the tenons on the aprons, as described in "Cutting Mortises and Tenons" on page 145. Miter the tenons to meet in the corners, as shown in the *Top View.*

The top fasteners and the kicker rail fit in grooves in the aprons, as shown in the *Top View.* At the front of the table these same parts fit into mortises in the top rail. Cut the grooves in the aprons with a dado cutter on the table saw. Lay out the three mortises in the top rail, then drill out most of the waste with a ¼-inch bit. Finish up the mortises with a chisel. Scrape or sand the aprons smooth.

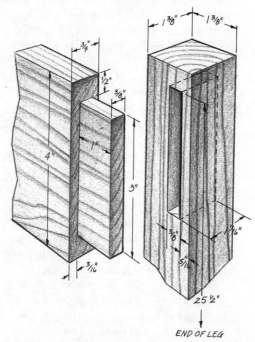

MORTISE AND TENON DETAIL

6 **Make the top fasteners and the kicker rail.** As shown in the *Fastener Detail,* the top fasteners are eight little blocks with a tongue on one end that fits into the grooves in the side rails and the mortises in the front top rail. The grain runs in the long direction so the tongue won't break off.

The easiest way to make the fasteners is to cut the tongues on all of them at once. Begin with a piece of stock that is $\frac{7}{16}$ inch thick, $1\frac{1}{2}$ inches in the direction of the grain, and about 9 inches across the grain, as shown in the drawing. (If you don't have a 9-inch-wide board to cut such a piece from, use two pieces about 5 inches across the grain.) After cutting a tongue along a 9-inch edge of this piece, you'll cut it up into eight 1-inch-wide top fasteners.

Set up a dado cutter in the table saw for a $\frac{1}{4}$-inch-wide cut. Set the cutter height to $\frac{3}{16}$ inch. Put a wooden auxiliary fence on the rip fence and position it to just graze the cutter. With this setup, with the stock flat on the saw table, cut a rabbet the length of one of the edges.

While you have the dado cutter on the table saw, cut the tongues on the ends of the kicker rail. Leave the fence right alongside the cutter but raise the cutter height to $\frac{1}{4}$ inch. With the miter gauge guiding the stock and the stock butted against the fence, rabbet both sides of both ends of the kicker rail. This will produce tenons $\frac{1}{4} \times \frac{1}{4} \times 2$ inches (the width of the kicker rail).

Now put the saw blade back on the saw and crosscut the eight 1-inch-wide top fasteners from the 9-inch piece.

7 **Drill holes in the fasteners and kicker rail.** Drill and countersink each top fastener for a #6 flathead wood screw. Also drill and countersink three holes for #6 screws in the kicker rail, as shown in the *Top View.* Drill the center hole straight through. As you drill the remaining two holes, rock the drill back and forth a bit to make the holes a little longer than they are wide. This will allow the screws to move as the tabletop expands and contracts along its width.

8 **Cut the top front rail joint.** Lay out a single dovetail centered on each end of the top rail, as shown in *Top Rail Dovetail Detail.* Saw out the dovetails with a fine-tooth gent's saw or on the band saw.

Trace the dovetails onto the tops of the front legs. Scribe the thickness of the rail on the inner face of the front legs and square down from the layout of the tail to the scribe line. Clamp the legs to your bench with the inner face up and chop out the dovetail mortises with a mallet and chisel. If you haven't chopped this kind of dovetail mortise before, see "Cutting Half-Blind Dovetails" on page 129.

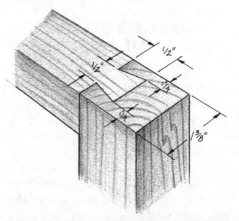

TOP RAIL DOVETAIL DETAIL

9 **Cut the bottom front rail joint.** The bottom rail joins the legs with a sliding dovetail. Begin this joint by clamping the legs to the bench with the front faces together, as shown in *Routing Sliding Dovetail Grooves*. Since the bottom of the bottom rail should line up with the bottom of the side aprons, lay an apron across the legs to mark the bottom rail position, as shown in the drawing. Mark the centerline of the bottom rail ⅜ inch up from there. Clamp a fence across the legs, one-half the width of your router base away from the centerline. Chuck a ½-inch, 14 degree dovetail bit in the router and set it for a ½-inch-deep cut. Rout the groove.

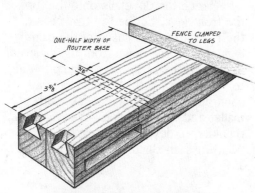

ROUTING SLIDING DOVETAIL GROOVES

Mount the router in the router table with the same dovetail bit in the collet. If necessary, reset the depth of cut to ½ inch. Adjust the fence to expose ¼ inch of the bit, as shown in *Routing Sliding Dovetails*. Now comes some trial and error. Find a scrap the exact thickness of the lower rail. Run first one side of the scrap over the bit, then the other side, forming a dovetail, as shown in the

drawing. Use a backer block, as shown, to provide support and prevent tear-out at the end of the cut.

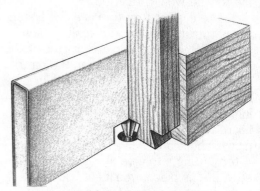

ROUTING SLIDING DOVETAILS

Test the fit of the dovetail in a groove. If it fits, go out immediately and buy a lottery ticket because you are unbelievably lucky. If the tail is too big for the groove, adjust the fence to expose more of the bit. If it is too loose, expose less of the bit. Keep in mind that to cut a tail you have to make one cut from each side; the width of the tail will change by twice the amount of the adjustment to the fence. Make test cuts until you get a good fit. Remember that this is the most visible joint in the table. When you get it right, cut a dovetail on each end of the bottom rail.

10 **Glue up the table.** It is possible to glue up the entire table at once, but David and Rob chose to do it in stages. Begin by joining the front legs and rails. Put glue in the dovetail mortises at the top of the front legs and in the dovetail grooves for the bottom rail. Assemble the rails to the legs and clamp them. Make sure that the assembly is square and flat.

Next, apply glue to the mortises in the back legs where the back apron joins. Fit the back apron into the mortises, clamp it, and check that it's square and flat. If you let these two assemblies dry before continuing with the table assembly, make sure there is no excess glue in the remaining mortises in the back legs.

To complete the assembly, apply glue to the remaining leg mortises. Put the kicker rail in place without glue and assemble the side aprons to the front and back leg assemblies. Make sure the assembly is square on the sides and on the top.

SHOP TIP: When making fine adjustments to a router table fence, take advantage of the fact that the fence doesn't need to be parallel to the table edge. By leaving one end of the fence clamped to the table and moving only the other end, fence adjustment at the bit will be only half as great as fence adjustment at the end. This makes fine adjustments easier to achieve.

11 Make and insert the pegs.
The practice of pegging mortise-and-tenon joints dates from before glue was used. Now that wood glue is stronger than the wood itself, the pegs are unnecessary. But pegs still lend a look of structural integrity to a joint.

You'll need 12 pegs, each $3/16$ inch

square and about 2 inches long. Make the pegs on the table saw from a scrap of cherry, as shown in *Cutting Pegs*. Set the table saw fence $3/16$ inch from the blade. Set blade height to slightly less than $3/16$ inch. Make one pass, then turn the piece end for end and make the second pass. Since the blade height is slightly less than $3/16$ inch, the peg will still be attached to the original stock with a thin sliver of wood. Break off the peg—don't try to cut it off on the table saw. It will come flying back at you. Cut the pegs to length.

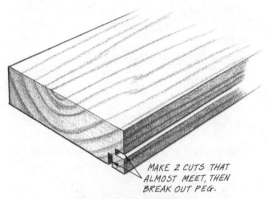

MAKE 2 CUTS THAT ALMOST MEET, THEN BREAK OUT PEG.

CUTTING PEGS

Lay out the peg positions on the sides of the legs and the back of the back legs, as shown in the *Side View*. Wrap a piece of tape around a $3/16$-inch bit about 1 inch from the end. Drill the holes to the depth of the tape. Square the tops of the holes with a small chisel. Shave a little taper on the ends of the pegs to make them easier to insert. Pound the pegs into the holes. Saw the pegs off about $1/8$-inch proud of the surface and shave them flush with a sharp chisel.

12 **Make and install the drawer guides and runners.** The distance from the inside of the side aprons to the drawer opening should be ½ inch. This is the thickness specified for the guides. Check this measurement and adjust the thickness of the guides if necessary. Then cut the guides and runners to size. Glue and clamp the guides in place, flush with the bottom of the aprons, as shown in the *Cross Section of Side.* When the glue sets, clamp the runners alongside the guides, flush with the bottom of the guides. You'll notice as you fit them that the top of each runner is ¹⁄₁₆ inch higher than the top of the bottom rail. This will allow you to create an even gap around the drawer front when you fit the drawer to the opening.

13 **Surface and install the top.** Scrape the dried, squeezed-out glue from the top. Check that the top is flat. If it isn't, hand plane it flat, then sand it smooth.

Lay the top upside down on the bench. Center the table on the top and mark the position lightly in pencil. Screw the kicker rail to the top with #6 × 1-inch flathead wood screws. Position the top fasteners and screw them to the top.

14 **Make the drawer front and sides.** Joint and plane stock for the drawer front, back, and sides to the thicknesses specified by the Cutting List. Measure the drawer opening. If your opening agrees with the dimensions in the *Front View,* cut the drawer parts to the dimensions specified by the Cutting List, which allow ⅛-inch total clearance (¹⁄₁₆ inch all the way around). If your drawer opening is off for any reason, adjust the sizes of the drawer parts to compensate.

With a dado cutter on the table saw, cut ¼-inch-deep grooves for the drawer bottom in the sides and front, as shown in the *Drawer Dimensions.* Cut through dovetails to join the sides to the back and half-blind dovetails to join the sides to the front, as shown in the drawing. For more on cutting dovetails, see "Cutting Through Dovetails" on page 67 and "Cutting Half-Blind Dovetails" on page 129.

15 **Make the drawer bottom.** Saw the drawer bottom to the dimen-

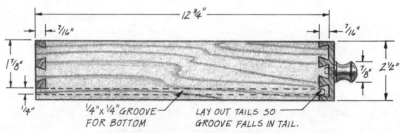

DRAWER DIMENSIONS

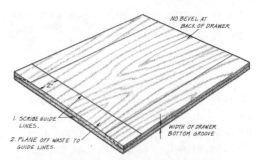

HAND PLANING BEVELS

sions specified by the Cutting List. The drawer bottom is beveled on three sides to fit in the grooves in the sides and front. David and Rob decided to make these bevels with a hand plane. The soft pine is easily planed and the bevel widths and angles don't need to be precise, so this job is surprisingly quick and fun. Use a marking gauge to scribe the ¼-inch depth around the perimeter of the bottom, as shown in *Hand Planing Bevels*. Then scribe a line 2 inches from the three edges indicating where the bevels will start. Plane away the waste with a smooth or jack plane. Bevel the sides first. If you get tear-out at the ends of these cross-grain cuts, the front bevel will remove the damage. You can sand the drawer bottom if you like, or just leave the plane marks.

16 **Assemble the drawer.** Dry assemble the drawer and bottom to make sure everything fits. Note that the drawer bottom should fit into the grooves with a gap of about ¹⁄₁₆ inch at the bottom of each groove. This allows for some wood movement.

Test fit the drawer in the table. If everything fits, glue and clamp the dovetails together and check that the drawer is square. Then slide in the bottom, but don't glue it. When the glue in the joints cures, remove the clamps. Drill pilot, shank, and counterbore holes for two #6 × 1-inch flathead wood screws to fasten the drawer bottom to the back. Insert the screws.

Drill a hole for the knob, centered on the drawer front, then glue the knob in place.

17 **Make and install the drawer stops.** The drawer stops are two pieces of cherry, ¼ inch thick × ¾ inch long, glued to the bottom rail, as shown in the *Exploded View*. When the inside of the drawer front hits them, the drawer can't go any farther. Cut the stops from the edge of a ¾-inch-thick scrap. Place the table upside down on the bench and put the drawer in place with the front flush with the rails. Push a stop in place between the drawer bottom and the bottom rail. Push it in until it touches the drawer front. Mark where the stop meets the back edge of the bottom rail. Cut both stops to this size. Then glue and clamp the stops to the rails.

18 **Apply a finish.** Give the table a final sanding, gently rounding all edges. David and Rob finished their table with three coats of Watco Danish oil. They let it cure for a few days, then added one coat of Waterlox to the top to prevent water marks. They waited a few more days, then rubbed the top with a very fine Scotch-Brite pad dipped in wax to break down brush marks and make the finish matte again. They used the wax only to lubricate the Scotch-Brite pad, and wiped it off before it dried.

THREE-PERSON BENCH

To David Page of Swarthmore, Pennsylvania, the word "bench" brings to mind a sturdy piece of furniture, seating built to be more robust than fancy. He designed this bench in that image. The joinery is simple, with most of the work being done on the table saw. It could also be built quite easily with hand tools.

Unlike many seating designs, the size of the bench is adaptable. If you need a longer bench, simply increase the length of the seat, stretchers, and back. You might want to add another leg if you make it more than 6 feet long. Shorten it in the same manner, eliminating the center leg if that would suit your needs. To soften the seat, make a cushion to lay on the seat. The 18-inch height given in the drawings is really a maximum and can be reduced by making the legs shorter. Red oak is a strong and attractive wood for this bench, but you can choose just about any wood, hard or soft.

1 **Select the stock and cut the parts.** Try to get boards wide enough for the seat boards and back so you will only have to glue up stock for the legs. Glue up as necessary to get the required widths. Joint the stock flat and plane it to the thicknesses specified by the Cutting List. Saw the parts to the required length and width. Joint the edges and sand the ends to clean up the saw marks on all of the parts except the legs.

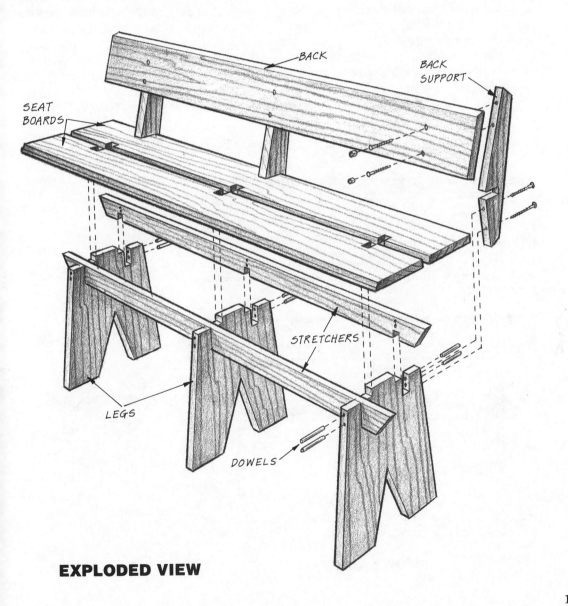

BACK

BACK SUPPORT

SEAT BOARDS

STRETCHERS

LEGS

DOWELS

EXPLODED VIEW

2 **Cut the stretcher slots in the legs.** Cut the slots for the stretchers while the blanks for the legs are still square. Lay out the slots and tenon on the top edge of the legs, as shown in the *Leg Joint Detail.* Screw a tall auxiliary fence to the miter gauge and stand each leg blank upright against the fence to cut the slots. Adjust the saw to cut 3 inches deep and make a cut on the waste side of the layout marks. Remove the stock between these cuts with a series of saw cuts, sliding the leg over 1/8 inch for each cut.

3 **Cut the tenons on top of the legs.** Readjust the saw to cut 7/8 inch deep and cut the ends of the tenons the same way you cut the slots.

To cut the tenon shoulders, raise the blade to achieve a 1½-inch depth of cut. Adjust the rip fence to 7/8 inch from the farther face of the saw blade. Cutting the shoulders is now a bit of a problem. The cut must stop before cutting into the tenon, but the leading edge of the cut will be on the bottom surface of the stock where you can't see it. To solve the problem, square over from the lead-

TOP VIEW

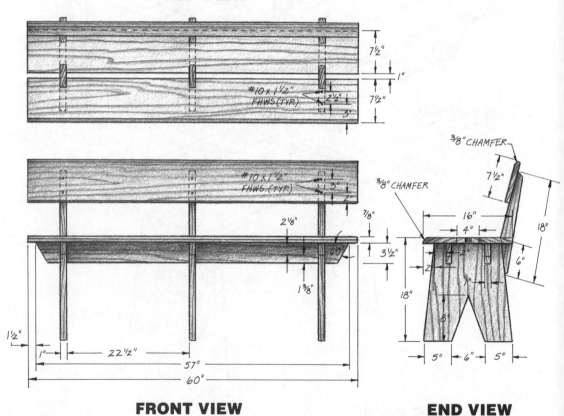

FRONT VIEW   **END VIEW**

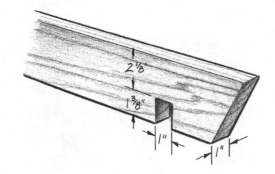

4 **Saw the tapered edges and notches in the legs.** Lay out the tapered edges and V-notches in the legs, as shown in the *End View*. To saw the tapers, first screw an extension fence to the miter gauge. Place one of the legs against the miter gauge extension fence and lay a straightedge along the laid-out taper. Adjust the miter gauge so the straightedge is parallel to the saw blade and lock it, then saw the tapered edges of the legs. Saw out the notch with a handsaw or band saw and clean up the saw marks with files and sandpaper.

5 **Make the stretchers.** Slots in the stretchers interlock with the leg board slots, as shown in the *Leg Joint Detail*. You can make certain the slots in the two stretchers are identical by clamping the stretchers together while cutting the slots. Cut the slots the same way you cut the slots in the legs, using the miter gauge to guide the stock while making multiple saw cuts.

Reset the miter gauge on the table saw to 60 degrees and cut the angled ends of the stretchers. Test assemble the legs and the stretchers without glue, adjusting the slot widths if necessary.

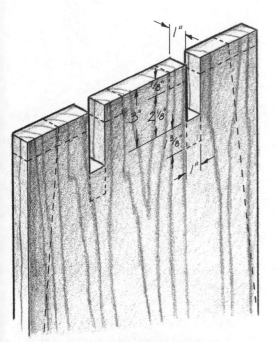

LEG JOINT DETAIL

ing edge of the blade to the fence and, from there, measure back along the fence 6 inches and clamp a stop block to the fence. Now feed the stock until it touches the stop block, then pull it back and cut the opposite shoulder. Complete the shoulder cut with a handsaw. Repeat for the other two legs.

6 **Cut the slots in the seat boards.** Lay out the leg tenon slots in the seat boards directly from the leg and stretcher assembly. Begin by clamping the seat boards to your workbench 1 inch apart. Invert the leg and stretcher assembly on top of the seat boards, positioning it as shown in the *Front View* and *End View,* and trace around the tenons. Cut the slots on the table saw as you did for the previous slots. You may find it helpful to provide extra support for the seat boards where they overhang the saw table.

The seat board that will become the rear seat board requires three additional 2-inch-deep slots for the back supports. Lay them out in line with the leg tenon slots. Test fit the seat boards on the leg and stretcher assembly.

7 **Drill for dowels and screws.** Drill the front and back edges of each leg for ⅜-inch dowels into the stretchers, as shown in the *Back Support Detail.* Make certain the legs are square to the stretchers and that the stretchers are fully seated before drilling.

Drill and counterbore screw holes in the seat boards, as shown in the *Top View.*

8 **Glue together the bench.** Sand the bench parts that are ready for assembly. On a flat surface, glue the stretchers into the slots in the legs. Square the legs to the stretchers, then glue the dowels into the predrilled holes. Check that the seat boards will fit the assembly, then let the glue dry. Trim the dowels flush with the edges of the leg boards.

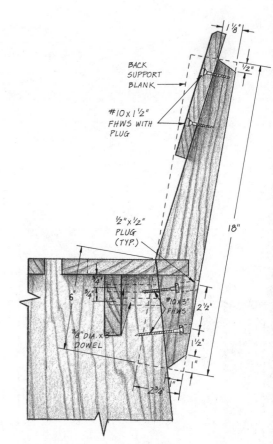

BACK SUPPORT DETAIL

Fit the seat boards onto the leg boards and stretchers. Drill pilot holes through the screw shank holes into the leg boards. Glue and screw the seat boards in place with #10 × 1½-inch flathead wood screws. Plug the screw holes in the seat with wood plugs cut from the same wood as the seat boards. (You can buy plugs if you don't have a plug cutter, but the color and grain match won't be as good as plugs that you cut from the same stock as the bench.) Sand the plugs flush with the seat boards.

9 **Cut out and attach the back support pieces.** Lay out the back supports, as shown in the *Back Support Detail*. Cut the shape of the back supports on the band saw, then joint or hand plane, file, and sand the sawed edges clean.

Drill and counterbore the back supports for #10 × 3-inch flathead wood screws. Hold the supports in position on the back edges of the legs and drill pilot holes for the screws. Glue and screw the back support pieces to the leg boards. Plug the screw holes in the back supports as you did in the seat boards. Sand the plugs flush.

10 **Attach the back to the back supports.** Chamfer the top front edge of the back with a ball-bearing chamfering bit. Lay out the position of the screws that fasten the back to the back supports, then drill and counterbore for #10 × 1½-inch screws. Sand the back, then clamp it in position on the back supports. Drill pilot holes through the shank holes, then glue and screw the back to the back supports.

11 **Chamfer the edge of the seat and back.** Rout a chamfer along the front edge of the front seat board. This helps keep the boards from cutting into your legs. Rout an identical chamfer along the top edge of the back. Sand the chamfers smooth.

12 **Apply a finish to the bench.** Finish the bench to suit your intended use. An oil finish won't show physical abuse as much as a finish that forms a surface film and it's easier to touch up. A lacquer or polyurethane, on the other hand, will resist spills better and will produce a better gloss if that's what you like. If you stain the bench, make sure the stain is compatible with the finish you choose; test them if the products are made by different companies. Be sure to let the finish cure completely before sitting on your bench.

CUTTING LIST

Part	Quantity	Dimensions	Comments
Legs	3	1″ × 16″ × 18″	Red oak
Stretchers	2	1″ × 3½″ × 57″	Red oak
Seat boards	2	⅞″ × 7½″ × 60″	Red oak
Back supports	3	1″ × 2¾″ × 18″	Red oak
Back	1	¾″ × 7½″ × 60″	Red oak

Hardware

12 dowels, ⅜″ dia. × 3″
18 flathead wood screws, #10 × 1½″
6 flathead wood screws, #10 × 3″
Wood plugs, ½″ dia. oak face grain (optional). Available from The Woodworkers' Store, 21801 Industrial Blvd., Rogers, MN 55374-9514. Part #23523 (pack of 50). Specify red oak.

PART FIVE

SHELVING AND STORAGE

FISHING ROD RACK

If your mind is on fishing even when your favorite fishing hole is frozen over, try making this tackle stand. It will help occupy your mind until the spring thaw. Fred Matlack of the Rodale Design Center designed it to be built with a minimum number of tools, so those of you with a tackle box bigger than your tool box can have a heyday. A handsaw or power saw, a coping saw, a square, a drill, a plane, a hammer, a nail set, and a tape measure are all you need. To make life even easier, Fred used materials that are readily available, already planed, from lumberyards and home centers. Go for it: When the season opens, your gear will be better organized than it's ever been before.

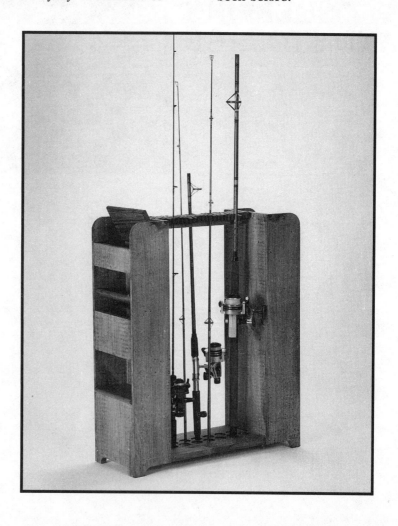

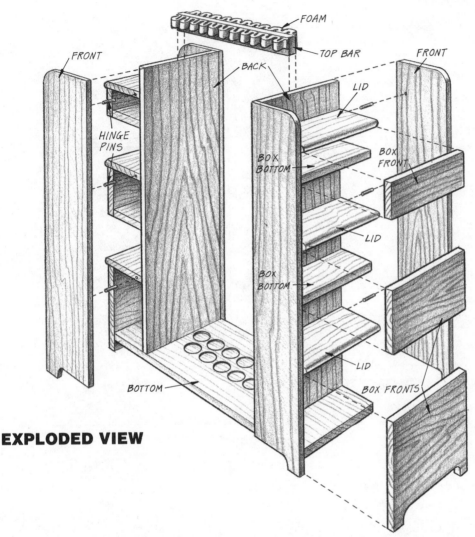

FOAM

TOP BAR

FRONT

BACK

FRONT

LID

HINGE PINS

BOX BOTTOM

BOX FRONT

LID

BOX BOTTOM

LID

BOTTOM

BOX FRONTS

EXPLODED VIEW

1 **Select the stock.** Phil made the stand out of pine, the grade commonly used for house trim. You'll need 12 feet of ¾-inch-thick × 9-inch-wide material. (A board that is nominally 10 inches wide is actually 9¼ inches wide, leaving you with ⅛ inch along each edge to plane away nicks and gouges.) You'll also need 5 feet of ⅝-inch-thick × 5-inch-wide pine for the lids, 10½ feet of ½-inch-thick × 5½-inch-wide (nominal

6-inch-wide) pine for the fronts, and a stick of wood, as specified by the Cutting List, for the top bar.

2 **Make the fronts.** Saw the stock for the fronts into four pieces, each 31 inches long. Make sure the ends are square. Lay out the hinge pin holes and the bottom edges of the box bottoms, as shown in the *Front View*. Notice that the

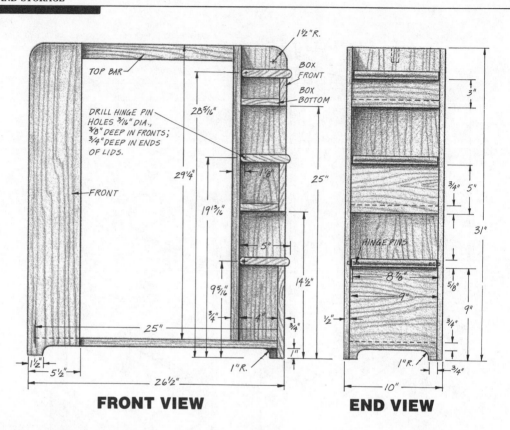

FRONT VIEW

END VIEW

CUTTING LIST

Part	Quantity	Dimensions	Comments
Fronts	4	$\frac{1}{2}'' \times 5\frac{1}{2}'' \times 31''$	Pine
Lids	6	$\frac{5}{8}'' \times 5'' \times 8\frac{7}{8}''$	Pine
Backs	2	$\frac{3}{4}'' \times 9'' \times 29\frac{1}{4}''$	Pine
Bottom	1	$\frac{3}{4}'' \times 9'' \times 25''$	Pine
Tall box fronts	2	$\frac{3}{4}'' \times 9'' \times 9''$	Pine
Medium box fronts	2	$\frac{3}{4}'' \times 9'' \times 5''$	Pine
Short box fronts	2	$\frac{3}{4}'' \times 9'' \times 3''$	Pine
Box bottoms	4	$\frac{3}{4}'' \times 9'' \times 4''$	Pine
Top bar	1	$\frac{3}{4}'' \times 1\frac{1}{2}'' \times 15\frac{1}{2}''$	Pine
Hinge pins	12	$\frac{3}{16}''$ dia. $\times 1\frac{1}{8}''$	Hardwood dowel

Hardware

10' high-density foam weather stripping, $\frac{3}{4}'' \times \frac{7}{16}''$
6d finishing nails

dimensions are all given from the bottom end of the piece. It's much more accurate to lay out a series of marks all from the same reference point than to measure from one mark to the next. If you look down from above at the four fronts, two of the fronts must have the hinge pin holes along the left edge, while the other two must have the holes along the right edge. Draw a line square across the fronts at the box bottom marks, then put an X just above the lines.

Wrap a piece of tape around a ³⁄₁₆-inch brad-point drill bit, exposing ³⁄₈ inch of the bit. Drill the hinge pin holes ³⁄₈ inch deep (up to the tape).

Finally, lay out the cutouts that form the feet and the rounded corners at the tops. Saw out both of these features with a coping saw, then smooth the sawed surfaces with sandpaper or a file.

3 **Make the lids.** You probably had to buy your ⅝-inch-thick stock for the lids 5½ inches wide. Don't cut the lids to length yet. Saw the stock to a trifle over 5 inches wide, then plane the edge smooth, reducing the width to 5 inches. Now draw a line down the center of each edge, dividing the thickness into two halves. These lines will help guide you as you round the edges. Plane both edges to a semicircular shape, as shown in the *Front View.* You don't have to be perfect but, if you want to, you can cut a template out of posterboard to check the shape as you go. The rounding should begin right at the line on the edge but the line should remain. The roundover is purely decorative along the opening edge of the lids but necessary for the lid to open along the hinged edge. When

you're done planing, sand out any remaining plane marks and sand off the lines on the edges. Now cut the stock into six pieces, each 8⅞ inches long.

Lay out the hinge pin holes in the lids. For the hinges to work properly, these holes must be concentric with the semicircular edges, centered between the two surfaces and ⁵⁄₁₆ inch from one edge. If you have one, a marking gauge is a convenient way to lay out these holes, but you can do as well with a tape measure if you're careful. Drill the holes ¾ inch deep, using tape to gauge the depth as you did before. Aim the holes as accurately as you can, parallel to the surfaces and the edge. While you have the ³⁄₁₆-inch bit in the drill, drill a hole through a scrap of wood and stick it in your pocket for the time being.

4 **Make all of the 9-inch-wide parts.** A glance at the cutting list will show six different parts totaling 13 pieces that are ¾ inch thick × 9 inches wide. Thanks, Fred; you're making this too easy. Dress the edges of your ¾-inch stock by planing it to 9 inches wide. Keep the edges straight and square. Now starting with the backs and continuing through the box fronts to the box bottoms, cut all of the parts to length. Label them as you go so you don't confuse them. If you have a power saw and want this to be a high-class job, use one of the special blades designed for fine crosscutting and mitering. They leave a very smooth edge.

Lay out the feet on the long (9-inch-high) box fronts. Saw them out with a coping saw and smooth the edges, just as you did with the fronts.

The only other part that needs any further work is the bottom. It gets shallow holes that keep the butt ends of the fishing rods from sliding around. You can drill them now or you can wait until after the stand is assembled. The layout that Fred used is shown in the *Bottom Detail*. Fred is planning a trip to bring back Moby Dick, so his holes are 1½ inches in diameter. You might want to check your tackle and make your holes ⅛ inch or so larger than the butts of your rods.

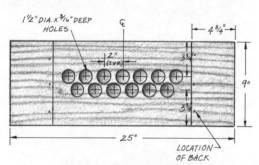

BOTTOM DETAIL

Saw the top bar to the dimensions specified by the Cutting List and smooth the edges.

Cut a piece of ³⁄₁₆-inch-diameter dowel to about 18 inches long. Sand it down so it slides easily through the hole in the piece of scrap you've been carrying around in your pocket. Cut the dowel into 12 hinge pins, each 1⅛ inches long. Chamfer the ends just a bit with sandpaper.

5 **Test assemble the stand.** If your craftsmanship so far is worth bragging about, keep it up; sand out all those almost imperceptible cross-grain ridges that the factory planer leaves behind.

They'll be ten times as visible after you've applied a finish. While you're at it, give all the edges a slight rounding-over with the sandpaper. If you have a machine sander and wind up erasing the layout lines that you drew on the bottom and fronts, replace them.

The stand is assembled with glue and 6d finishing nails but, before you get out the glue, assemble it with just a few nails to check that everything fits right and the lids open and close without sticking. Begin by nailing the bottom to one of the backs. Nail up through the bottom into the end of the back. Use two nails in the joint and leave at least ¼ inch of the nails exposed. Next, nail on one of the fronts. A couple of nails into the back and one into the bottom should suffice. Make sure the back is perpendicular to the bottom before nailing the front to the bottom. Again, leave enough of each nail exposed that you'll be able to pull it.

Lay the stand flat with the assembled front down. Fit hinge pins into one end of three of the lids. Stand them on end on the assembled front with the pins engaging the pin holes in the front. Now insert hinge pins into the ends of the lids sticking up at you and fit the opposing front onto the pins. Nail it in place as you did the first one. Remember that you have nails sticking out of the other side, so slip some blocks of scrap under the assembly to protect your work surface.

Fit two box bottoms in place just above and aligned with your layout lines. Nail them there. Finish up this end of the stand with the three box fronts. Nails through the two fronts should be sufficient; don't nail them to the box bottoms at this point.

Now stand it up and check it out. Check that all the parts fit without gaps and that the lids function smoothly, opening all the way without jamming. If anything is amiss, mark the parts that need trimming and take notes of what needs to be done before you introduce irreversible glue. Before tearing it down, repeat all of these trial assembly steps on the other end of the stand. Keep in mind that at this point you have both time and materials invested in the project; protect your investment by taking your time and getting it right before it's too late.

Disassemble the stand, stacking and arranging the disassembled parts so you can reassemble them in the same locations using the same nail holes. If your work area is cramped and you're afraid the parts will get mixed up, label them on an edge that won't show after final assembly. Protect the soft pine from the hammer pulling the nails by holding a scrap of ¼-inch plywood under the hammer. When the stand is all apart, go through your notes and do all of the required fixes. Repeat the trial assembly, if necessary, to make sure everything will work right when you're done.

6 **Glue it all together.** Final assembly is a repeat of the trial assembly but with glue and more nails. Many of the joints involve gluing end grain, a joint that is prone to failure if it isn't done right. The secret is to prime the end grain with glue, let it soak in, scrape off what didn't soak in, then apply fresh glue and assemble the joint.

Another frequent cause of failure is the false assumption that enough glue on one surface will transfer to the other surface so you don't need to apply glue to both surfaces. It doesn't work that way; all you get is more glue squeezing out and running down the sides without improving the bond. Brush glue thinly on both surfaces, and don't use those ten brushes on the ends of your hands; they don't have enough bristles to work the glue into the wood pores. Use a real brush—a plumber's disposable flux brush is ideal.

Now do it the same way you did it before. Apply the glue to each joint as you come to it so it's fresh when the joint comes together. When you come to the lids, don't glue the hinge pins in either the lid or the fronts; they won't run away. When you bring the second front down over the lids, tap the nails in just a bit and then pry it back up until the hinge pins almost slip out, but don't. Now you can insert the box bottoms and box fronts without scraping all the glue off as they slide into place. Using the old nail holes will make it a lot easier to keep everything properly aligned as you assemble all of these parts. When all of the box bottoms and box fronts are in place, drive the nails almost home. Leave them just a little proud so your hammer never strikes the pine. Use about one nail every 4 inches on longer joints, never fewer than two to a joint on shorter ones. When one end of the stand is fully assembled, use a nail set to drive the nails below the surface. Then assemble the other end. Don't attach the top bar yet.

7 **Apply a finish.** Allow a day for the glue to fully cure, then clean up the joints. If there are places where the fronts are not flush with the adjoining parts, a stroke or two with your plane should fix it. Fill the nail holes with a blond wood filler. Scrape off the little beads of glue that squeezed out of the joints, then sand the joint lines. Any piece of metal with a reasonably sharp, square edge will do as a scraper. If you wiped off glue while it was still wet, sand those areas. Traces of glue will interfere with your finish. When you're done touching up, clean off all of the wood dust. A vacuum cleaner will do a good job provided you use a brush attachment on the end of the hose. You can also do a good job with a cloth dampened with paint thinner.

SHOP TIP: You can
make a very effective tack cloth by dampening cheesecloth with very diluted clear finish like varnish or polyurethane. Rather than mixing up fresh thinner with fresh finish, save the thinner that you use to clean your brushes. Keep it in a tightly closed jar until your next need for a tack cloth.

The quickest route to an attractive finish is one of the penetrating oil finishes known as Danish oil. It's more than just an oil, it's really a thinned-down varnish that soaks into the wood. It protects the wood and accentuates the grain but doesn't create a film on the surface the way a varnish or polyurethane does. Apply the oil with a brush, rag, or small sponge. As it soaks into the wood and the wood begins to look dry, apply more. Keep this up for a half-hour. You'll find

that the end grain of pine is very thirsty. After a half-hour, wipe the stand dry with clean rags. You don't want to leave any on the surface.

The rags are now a problem. They qualify perfectly as the notorious "oil-soaked rags" that fire marshalls and safety experts warn us about. If you dump them in a pile you're not asking for a fire, you're begging for one. Hang them up like diapers on a clothesline where they can get plenty of ventilation. After a day or so they'll be stiff—and safe.

Allow this first coat of finish to cure for a day or two, then give it a second application. Much less will soak in this time. Apply the oil the same way you did the first application, then rub down the entire stand with a Scotch-Brite pad while the oil is wet on the surface. It will take you a half-hour to rub it down, so by the time you're done it will be time to wipe it dry. Again, hang out the laundry to avoid a fire.

Danish oil is not your only choice, of course. You can finish the stand with varnish, polyurethane, or even paint. If you do, be careful that you don't let your finish run down onto the hinge pins. These finishes that build a film will also glue your hinge pins in place if you let them.

8 **Attach the rod grips.** Your fishing rods will be held in place against the top bar by pleats of foam weather stripping. Strips of carpet also work well.

To lay out the top bar for the foam, begin ¼ inch from the end of the top bar and put a mark every ⅝ inch down its length. You should come out ¼ inch from the other end. Mark the other side of the bar in the same way. Unroll the weather stripping and mark it every 2½ inches with a felt-tip marker.

Form the pleats by stapling the marks on the weather stripping to the marks on the top bar, as shown in the *Rod Holder Detail*. Peel a few inches of backing paper from the foam and staple the end of it to the first mark on the top bar. Move the next mark on the foam into position over the next mark on the bar and staple again. Peel back the backing paper as you go and don't let the foam stick to itself until you have it in position. Continue pleating and stapling until you've stapled the foam to the last mark on the bar. Install the foam on the other side of the bar in the same way. The whole job will use exactly 10 feet of foam.

The last step in assembly is attaching the top bar. Fit it in position between the two backs and nail it with two nails on each end.

You're done. Fill it up with your gear and go back to daydreaming about your next fishing trip.

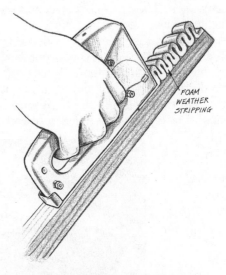

FOAM WEATHER STRIPPING

ROD HOLDER DETAIL

COOPERED-FRONT CABINET

Small cabinets like this one have many uses. They can hold spices in the kitchen, guard keys in the office, or house small collectibles and notions. Or they can just showcase your woodworking talents, holding nothing. Whatever you do with it, you will enjoy making it. Hand-cut dovetails join the bottom to the sides. The top is dadoed and screwed to the sides for simplicity. The screws are out of sight, well above eye level. A simple coopered door encloses the cabinet.

Coopering is the process of making curved wooden panels, usually barrels and buckets. The same techniques are useful in cabinetry. The process is a simple matter of cutting bevels on the edges of boards and gluing the boards together.

EXPLODED VIEW

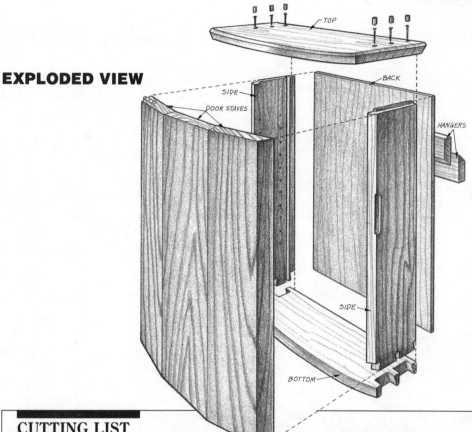

TOP

SIDE

DOOR STAVES

BACK

HANGERS

SIDE

BOTTOM

CUTTING LIST

Part	Quantity	Dimensions	Comments
Top	1	$7/8'' \times 5\frac{3}{4}'' \times 14''$	Walnut
Sides	2	$5/8'' \times 3\frac{3}{4}'' \times 16\frac{1}{4}''$	Walnut
Bottom	1	$5/8'' \times 5\frac{1}{8}'' \times 12\frac{1}{2}''$	Walnut
Back	1	$\frac{1}{4}'' \times 11\frac{3}{4}'' \times 16''$	Walnut plywood
Door staves	3	$7/8'' \times 4\frac{1}{2}'' \times 15\frac{1}{2}''$	Walnut
Hangers	2	$\frac{1}{2}'' \times 2'' \times 11\frac{1}{4}''$	Hardwood

Hardware

6 drywall screws, #6 × 1¼"

2 knife hinges. Available from The Woodworkers' Store, 21801 Industrial Blvd., Rogers, MN 55374–9514. Part #26245.

6 hardwood plugs, ⅜"

1 magnetic catch. Available from The Woodworkers' Store. Part #26559.

4 shelf brackets, ¼". Available from The Woodworkers' Store. Part #30437.

1 glass shelf, ¼" × 2¾" × 11⅛"

1 **Select the stock and cut the parts.** Spread out your stock and examine it. Choose the pieces with the straightest grain for the top, bottom, and sides. Make the doors from the more figured pieces. Joint and plane the wood to the thicknesses specified by the Cutting List. Saw the parts to length and width, but make the door staves about 1 inch longer and ½ inch wider than called for. You'll cut them to fit later. Don't cut the curves on the front edges of the top and bottom yet.

2 **Dado the top.** With a ⅜-inch bit in your table-mounted router, cut ⅛-inch-deep dadoes in the top, as shown in the *Cross Sections of Top*. When you are through routing, leave the bit adjusted to a ⅛-inch depth of cut for the next step.

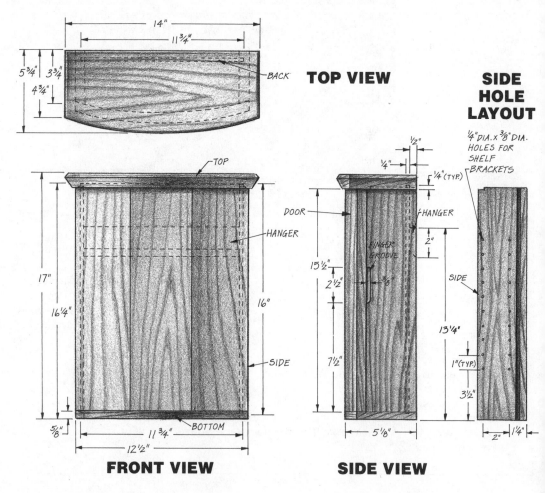

TOP VIEW

SIDE HOLE LAYOUT

FRONT VIEW

SIDE VIEW

CROSS SECTIONS OF TOP

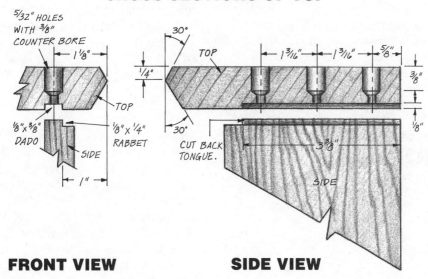

FRONT VIEW   **SIDE VIEW**

3 **Rabbet the sides.** The top ends of the cabinet sides are rabbetted to create a tongue. Reset the router table fence so that only ¼ inch of the bit is exposed. Rout a rabbet in the end of a piece of scrap that is the same thickness as the sides. Stand it on end and hold it firmly against the fence as you pass it by the bit. Test the resulting tongue in the dado that you cut in the cabinet top. Adjust the fence, if necessary, until you get a good fit, then rabbet the actual sides. Trim the front of each tongue with a dovetail saw, as shown in the *Cross Sections of Top.*

4 **Drill the top.** Drill three ⁵⁄₃₂-inch holes through the bottom of each dado, as shown in the *Cross Sections of Top.* Counterbore these holes from the top with a ⅜-inch bit.

5 **Dovetail the bottom into the sides.** Lay out and cut the dovetail joint on the bottom and sides, as shown in the *Dovetail Layout.* For more detailed instructions, see "Cutting Through Dovetails" on page 67.

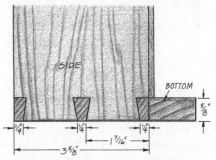

DOVETAIL LAYOUT

6 **Cut the grooves for the back.** Adjust a ¼-inch straight bit in your table-mounted router to cut ¼ inch deep. Clamp a fence ½ inch away from the bit. Rout the grooves for the back in the top, bottom, and sides. Note that the groove in the bottom runs full length. The groove in the top runs ¼ inch into the side dadoes. The grooves in the sides stop ¼ inch from the bottom but run out the top.

SHOP TIP: Use an adjustable drafting triangle to set up angled cuts. Many adjustable triangles have a small magnifying lens over the scale to help in making adjustments as fine as a fraction of a degree.

7 **Bevel the sides.** Tilt the blade on the table saw to 77 degrees, as shown in the *Side Bevel Detail.* Rip the bevel on the sides, allowing ¹⁄₃₂ inch for cleanup. Plane the sawed edges smooth.

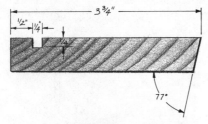

SIDE BEVEL DETAIL

8 **Drill the holes in the sides for the adjustable shelf brackets.** Drill the holes for the shelf brackets, as shown in the *Side Hole Layout.*

9 **Rout the finger groove.** Rout the finger groove in the outer surface of the right side of the cabinet, as shown in

the *Side View.* This groove allows you to reach behind an edge of the door to open it. Make the cut with a ½-inch-diameter core box bit in your table-mounted router. Set up the fence so the bit is about two-thirds exposed. Experiment to get a profile you like.

10 **Test assemble the cabinet.** Assemble the parts of the cabinet without glue. Fit the dovetails together first. Then slide the back in place and seat the top on the sides. Using the holes in the top as guides, drill ³⁄₃₂-inch pilot holes in the sides. Screw the top in place temporarily with 1¼-inch drywall screws. Leave the cabinet assembled temporarily.

11 **Bevel the door staves.** On the table saw, bevel the door staves to the width and angle shown in the *Door Cross Section.* Adjust the jointer fence to the same angle and joint the sawed edges to remove the saw marks.

12 **Glue up the door.** Before attempting to glue up the coopered door, test your clamp setup. Begin the practice run by placing two identical bar clamps on a flat surface. Place cauls and shims on the clamp bars, as shown in *Gluing Coopered Panels.* Put the staves in place and slowly tighten the clamps. Experiment with the clamps and shims until the joints come together tightly on both sides. The joints should be tight when the outer edges of the outside staves are about 1 inch above the center stave.

Once you have the clamping system

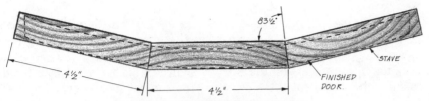

DOOR CROSS SECTION

worked out, loosen the clamps. Apply glue to the joints and reclamp the door. Let the glue dry overnight.

13 Plane the door. Shape the outside of the door to a gentle curve with a hand plane. Plane the inside to match with a hollowing plane or curved-blade spokeshave. If you don't have either of these tools, you can use a disk sander or simply leave the flat surfaces showing.

14 Fit the door. Crosscut the door on the table saw to fit between the cabinet top and bottom. Allow about 3/32-inch total clearance. Once you've cut the door to length, center it from side to side in the cabinet. Mark the width by tracing along the cabinet sides.

Trim the door to width on the table saw by placing it with the convex side up over an 8-inch-wide supporting board. Run the door and support together through the saw. Saw it slightly oversize and hand plane to the mark. Hold it by hand on the benchtop because you're liable to split it if you clamp it or put it in a vise.

15 Hang the door. The door swings on knife hinges. Cut the mortises in the top and bottom edges of the door first. Position the hinges so the pivots are halfway into the door, as shown in the *Hinge Detail*. The hinges should be flush with the surface when

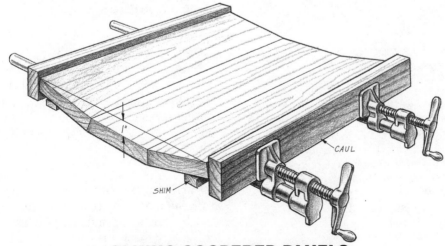

GLUING COOPERED PANELS

you are finished. By backing out the screws that hold the cabinet top, you can fit the door and hinges in place. Then trace the location of the hinges on the cabinet top and bottom and cut the matching mortises.

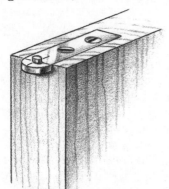

HINGE DETAIL

16 **Lay out the top and bottom curves.** Once the door is hung, trace its curve onto the cabinet top and bottom. Disassemble the cabinet. Saw the bottom curve, then scrape and sand it smooth. On the top, draw a new curved line parallel to the door tracing but ¾ inch outside it. Don't cut this curve yet.

SHOP TIP: Draw parallel curves with the help of a compass. Set the compass for the distance between the two curves. Start at one end of the original curve and swing an arc to the side where you want the new curve. Move the compass down the original curve about ¼ inch and repeat. Keep repeating this for the length of the curve. Draw a line tangent to all the arcs to lay out the new curve.

17 **Cut the bevels on the top.** The top has a 30 degree beveled profile around the sides and front, as shown in the *Front View* and *Side View*. You can cut these bevels with a 30 degree bevel pattern router bit (available from Paso Robles Carbide Inc., Paso Robles, CA 93446, part #TA-263).

Chuck the 30 degree bevel bit in the router table and rout the bevels on the ends of the top. The dimensions are given in the *Cross Sections of Top*. Push the stock past the bit with a 6-inch-square backup block to minimize splintering when the bit exits the stock. Now shape the curved front edge, as explained in "Routing Curved Edges" on the opposite page.

18 **Make the hanger.** The finished cabinet hangs from a beveled hanger glued to the cabinet back. A matching hanger is screwed to the wall. Cut the hangers to the shape and dimensions shown in the *Hanger Detail*. Glue one hanger to the back of the cabinet. Use a clamp pad on the inside of the cabinet back to avoid marring it.

19 **Glue up the cabinet.** Finish sand all of the cabinet parts. Apply glue to the pins, tails, and dadoes. Assemble the cabinet as before. Don't forget to slide the back in before attaching the top. Tighten the screws and plug the counterbores.

20 **Finish the cabinet.** Touch up any areas that need sanding and apply your favorite finish. When the finish is dry, hang the door by first install-

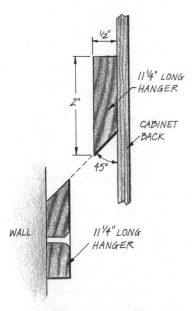

HANGER DETAIL

ing the hinges in the cabinet and then sliding the door onto the hinges. Attach the magnetic catch. Have a glass cutter cut the shelf and smooth the edges.

21 **Hang the cabinet.** Drill and countersink $5/32$-inch holes every inch along the length of the second mounting cleat. Line up one of these holes with a stud when you hang the cabinet. Drive a 2-inch drywall screw through the hole and into the stud. If the best location for the cabinet requires that this mounting screw be close to one end of the cleat, drive a second screw into the wall even if it only goes into plaster. This second screw will prevent the cleat from tilting. Hang the cabinet on the wall and install the shelf.

ROUTING CURVED EDGES

The easiest way to rout a decorative shape on a curved edge is to use a bit with a ball-bearing pilot. But some bits aren't available with a pilot, and sometimes the shape that you need doesn't have a suitable surface for a pilot to follow. What do you do then? If the curved edge is circular—that is, if it's a segment of a circle—you can use a curved fence, as shown in *Curved Router Table Fence*. Here's how to go about it.

1 **Check the curve.** Before going any further, check that the curve you want to shape is, indeed, circular. If you laid it out with tram-

mels or a beam compass, then you know that it's circular. If the curve was traced from another part of the project or from a pattern, experiment with trammels or a beam compass to see if you can reproduce the curve. If you can, it's circular.

If you can produce a circular curve that comes very close but isn't an exact match, you may want to adjust the design to match the circular curve. A circular curve may have been intended and you may improve the appearance of your project by adopting the circular curve.

(continued)

ROUTING CURVED EDGES—CONTINUED

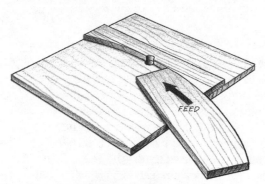

CURVED ROUTER TABLE FENCE

If the curve isn't circular and you can't adjust the layout, then you can't shape the edge using a curved fence.

2 **Saw the curve.** When you have a circular curve to work with, saw the curve in the workpiece. Saw just outside the line in one continuous cut. Save the cutoff. You'll use it as a fence when routing.

3 **Back up the cutoff.** If the cutoff is less than 3 inches wide, glue it edge to edge with a piece of scrap of the same thickness. If you'd rather not wait for the glue to dry, stick the scrap and the cutoff to each other with double-faced tape.

4 **Smooth the curves.** Sand the saw marks from both the workpiece and the cutoff, preserving the fit of the two pieces to each other as much as possible. Coarse sandpaper is fine for this smoothing. A handy trick is to stick sandpaper to the edge of one piece to sand the

other, then switch the sandpaper to the other piece and sand the first.

5 **Cut out the bit recess.** Before you can use the cutoff as a fence, you need to cut a recess in the curved edge. The location of the recess, which houses the bit, is shown in the *Bit Recess Layout.* To lay out the recess, first find the *minimum* cutting diameter of the bit. (You can get this dimension from the manufacturer's catalog or by direct measurement.) Divide the diameter by 2. The center of the recess is this distance from the curved edge of the fence. To find the diameter of the hole, add ¼ inch to the bit's *maximum* cutting diameter. If you have a hole saw this size or slightly larger, use it to cut the recess. If you don't have the correct size hole saw, lay out the recess with a compass and saw it out with a coping saw.

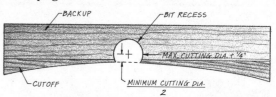

BIT RECESS LAYOUT

6 **Shape the curved edge.** Chuck your edge-forming bit in the router. Position the fence so that it's cutting the desired profile. You can gauge the location largely by eye, but it's a good idea to clamp the fence in place and then test your setup by routing a sample. Guide the curved piece along the fence, and you'll find you can rout the curved edge with full control. Make any necessary adjustments, and then rout the actual workpiece.

LISA'S CHEST

If this project looks complicated or demanding, look again. At first glance it looks much more complicated than it really is. The chest is a ¼-inch plywood box with solid wood along the edges to reinforce it and make it easier to join together. Stock molding from a lumberyard gives the plywood the look of raised panels. A solid wood top completes the chest. The lock on the chest is optional, and the handles are mostly for show.

The chest is a wonderful keeper of pillows and blankets, stuffed toys, sweaters, or just about anything in a bedroom or playroom that needs its own place. It's just the right height to sit on for putting on shoes and socks.

1 Cut the parts to size. The solid wood parts for your chest can be any species you like. Look for straight stock without any major defects. If surfaced stock ⅞ inch thick is difficult for you to find, or if you would prefer a less heavy appearance, substitute ¾-inch stock. Choose a plywood that goes well with the solid wood. A 5-ply birch plywood will make a stronger chest than 3-ply lauan but isn't necessary for most situations. The molding can be any stock molding from your lumberyard. It doesn't need to match the molding shown in the *Molding Detail* as long as it's wide enough to cover the edges of the chest top. Cut the solid wood parts to the sizes specified by the Cutting List. (You'll cut the plywood to size after you assemble the frames.)

2 Drill dowel holes in the frame members. The frame rails and stiles are joined with dowels. Lay out the holes, as shown in the *Joinery Detail*. Use a doweling jig when you drill the holes.

EXPLODED VIEW

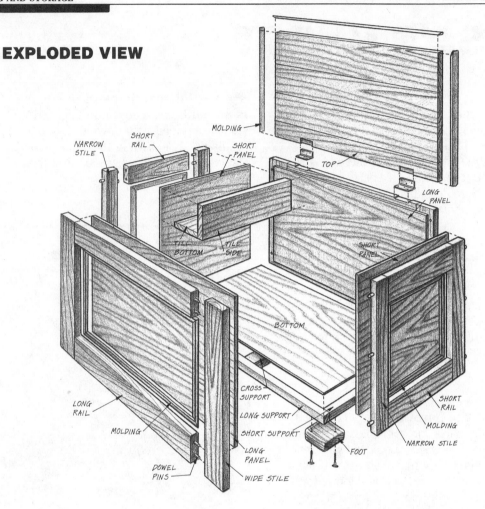

MOLDING

NARROW
STILE

SHORT
RAIL

SHORT
PANEL

TOP

LONG
PANEL

TILL
BOTTOM

TILL
SIDE

SHORT
PANEL

BOTTOM

LONG
RAIL

MOLDING

CROSS
SUPPORT

LONG SUPPORT

SHORT SUPPORT

SHORT
RAIL

MOLDING

NARROW STILE

FOOT

DOWEL
PINS

LONG
PANEL

WIDE STILE

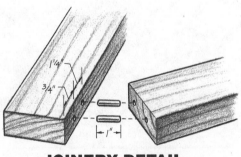

1¼"

¾"

1"

JOINERY DETAIL

3 **Glue together the frames.** Glue and clamp the frames together on a flat surface. Make sure the frames are square.

4 **Drill dowel holes to align the frames.** The four frames are doweled and glued together to form the chest. These dowels help hold the chest together during trial fitting of the plywood and help align the frames during glue-up. Drill the ¼-inch dowel holes at each corner of the chest, as shown in the *Front View* and *Side View.*

5 **Glue bottom supports to the frames.** Glue and clamp the supports flush with the bottom edges of the frames. Run the long supports the full length of the front and back frames. Center the short supports from side to side on the side frames.

6 **Cut the plywood to fit.** Test assemble the four frames without glue. Make certain the chest is square. Then cut the plywood panels to fit inside. The front and back (long) panels butt against the side frames. The side

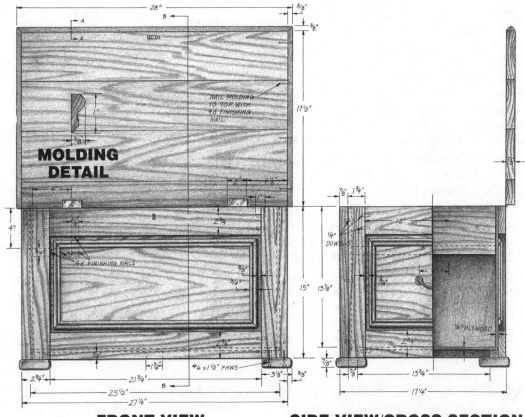

MOLDING DETAIL

FRONT VIEW

SIDE VIEW/CROSS SECTION

(short) panels fit between the front and back panels. Slide the plywood panels into place within the assembled frames. Cut the plywood bottom to fit within the panels. Make sure the panels fit without pushing the frame joints apart.

7 Cut the molding pieces and glue them to the panels. Lightly scribe a line on the panels along the inner edges of the frames. Remove the panels. Lay out the molding positions ⅜ inch inside the scribed lines. With the table saw miter gauge set at 45 degrees, miter the ends of the molding pieces to fit inside this layout.

To glue the molding to the plywood panels, first clamp four pieces of molding to their panel without glue. Remove one piece at a time, apply glue, and clamp it in place on the panel. Then remove, glue, and clamp another piece of the molding. Continue until you've glued the moldings to all four panels. If you don't have clamps with deep enough throats to clamp the molding in position, tack it in place with fine wire nails, leaving the nail heads protruding. After the glue dries, pull the nails and fill the nail holes.

8 Glue the wooden frames to the plywood panels. Disassemble the chest frames and sand them. Glue and clamp the frames to the plywood panels. Use the scribe lines on the panels to align the frames. The bottom of the plywood rests on the bottom supports. Clean up any glue that has squeezed out, then let the glue dry.

9 Glue the chest together. Glue 1-inch dowels in the dowel holes in the end frames. On a flat surface, glue and clamp the chest together. Make sure there is no squeezed-out glue on the bottom supports, then put the bottom in place. Letting the glue dry while the bottom is in place ensures that the bottom will fit after the glue dries. Measure diagonally across the corners at the top to be sure the top opening is square. If the opening is sqaure, the diagonal measurements will be equal.

10 Glue the bottom cross support and plywood bottom. Glue the cross support across the center of the chest between the long supports. Toenail it to the bottom supports with 4d finishing nails.

Glue the plywood bottom into the chest. Since you can't clamp it in place, tack it to the bottom supports with small brads.

11 Install the chest till. The till is the small open compartment in the chest. Sand the till bottom and side. Glue the till bottom and clamp it to the inside of the chest with hand screws. Make certain it is level from side to side and front to back. Reinforce the glue by nailing through the front and back panels into the ends of the till bottom with 4d finishing nails.

Glue the till side to the till bottom. Nail it in place through the front and back panels with 4d finishing nails. Set the nails and fill all the holes.

12 Make and install the feet. Chuck a ¼-inch-radius roundover bit in a table-mounted router. Round-over the top and bottom edges of each foot. Turn the chest upside down and position the feet so they overhang the sides and ends by ⅜ inch, as shown in the *Front View* and *Side View*. Lay out two screw holes in each foot, one into a long rail and one into a short rail. Drill and countersink shank holes for #6 × 1½-inch flathead wood screws. Reposition the feet on the chest and mark and drill pilot holes in the rails. Sand the feet, then glue and screw them in place.

SHOP TIP: When cutting or routing small parts, keep your fingers away from the cutters. A rubber-sole mason's float, sold in most hardware stores, makes a great push stick.

13 **Make the top.** To minimize cupping, glue up the top from several boards, alternating heart-side up and heart-side down, as shown in the *Side View*. Leave the boards 1 or 2 inches

CUTTING LIST

Part	Quantity	Dimensions	Comments
Long rails	4	⅞″ × 2¾″ × 21¾″	
Short rails	4	⅞″ × 2¾″ × 12″	
Wide stiles	4	⅞″ × 2¾″ × 15″	
Narrow stiles	4	⅞″ × 1¾″ × 15″	
Long supports	2	⅞″ × ⅞″ × 25½″	
Short supports	2	⅞″ × ⅞″ × 13¾″	
Long panels	2	¼″ × 14⅛″ × 25½″	Plywood
Short panels	2	¼″ × 14⅛″ × 15″	Plywood
Bottom	1	¼″ × 15″ × 25″	Plywood
Cross support	1	⅞″ × 1¾″ × 13¾″	
Till bottom	1	¾″ × 4″ × 15″	
Till side	1	¾″ × 4¾″ × 15″	
Feet	4	⅞″ × 3⅛″ × 3⅛″	
Top	1	⅞″ × 17½″ × 27¼″	

Hardware

44 grooved dowel pins, ¼″ × 1″
4d finishing nails
¾″ brads
⅜″ × 1″ × 24′ stock molding
1 pair butt hinges with brass screws, 2″ × 1½″
1 chest lock with strike. Available from The Woodworkers' Store, 21801 Industrial Blvd., Rogers MN 55374–9514. Part #28241.
2 handles. Available from The Woodworkers' Store. Part #32060.

longer than specified by the Cutting List and crosscut them to length on the table saw after the top is glued together. Sand the top.

14 **Hinge the top to the chest.** Lay out and cut hinge mortises in the top edge of the chest back. See "Mortising Hinges" on page 33 for detailed instructions. Mark and drill the screw holes. Temporarily screw the hinges to the chest with one screw. Hold the chest top in place and mark the position of the hinges. Rout the hinge mortises in the top. Drill the screw holes and attach the top to the chest.

15 **Add the chest lock.** The lock is optional. If you decide to install one, lay out the mortise for it in the front frame and plywood panel. Position it so the keyhole is centered. Follow the dimensions and directions for the lock you buy. Rout out the mortise and mark the position of the keyhole. Make the keyhole by drilling two holes, one above the other, through the frame. Drill the bottom hole slightly smaller than the top hole. Shape the keyhole with files. Screw the lock in place.

Close the lid to position the lock strike. Mortise the strike into the top of the chest if necessary. Screw the strike to the top of the chest.

16 **Attach the molding to the edge of the top.** The molding is slightly wider than the top is thick. Trim it *after* you've installed it. First, miter the ends of the front molding piece. Miter the front ends of the side moldings and crosscut them to length. Glue and nail the front molding piece in place so that the top of the molding is flush with the top of the lid. Glue and nail the front 3 inches of the end molding pieces, but only nail the rest. This allows for seasonal movement of the top. Set the nails and fill the holes.

With a block plane, trim the molding flush with the bottom of the lid.

17 **Attach the handles.** The chest handles are optional and mostly decorative. If you want them to be functional, glue a small rectangle of ¼-inch plywood to the inside of the chest opposite the handle locations. Lay out and drill holes through the sides of the chest for the handle screws. Place washers under the heads of the screws and screw the handles to the chest.

18 **Finish the chest.** Our chest was personalized with a name and a date. Carve or paint these features on your chest before you finish it. A durable finish such as polyurethane or lacquer will work well.

LOW BOOKCASE

It's difficult to have too many bookcases; they're useful for too many things besides books. This one is short enough to fit under most windows and narrow enough to serve as a bedside table. The shelves are deep enough to hold larger books and photo albums.

The construction is quite simple but also quite solid. The shelves are dadoed in place. The top supports are dovetailed to the sides. It's a good chance to practice cutting dovetails because when the top goes on it covers the dovetails. The bookcase shown is made of pine and finished with a mahogany stain and tung oil varnish. The back is ¼-inch plywood.

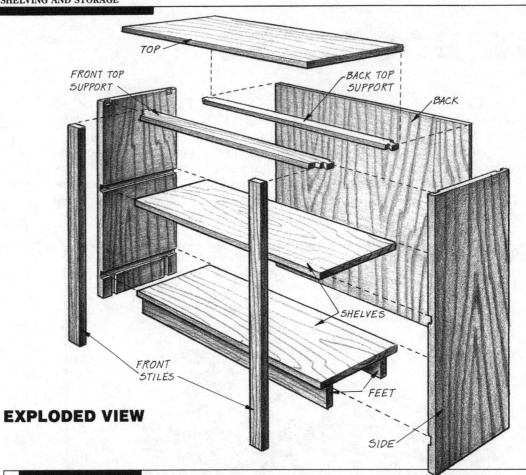

TOP

FRONT TOP
SUPPORT

BACK TOP
SUPPORT

BACK

SHELVES

FRONT
STILES

FEET

SIDE

EXPLODED VIEW

CUTTING LIST

Part	Quantity	Dimensions	Comments
Sides	2	¾" × 12½" × 29¾"	Pine
Front top support	1	¾" × 2½" × 33¾"	Pine
Back top support	1	¾" × 1½" × 33¾"	Pine
Shelves	2	¾" × 12¼" × 33¾"	Pine
Feet	2	¾" × 2½" × 33¾"	Pine
Front stiles	2	¾" × 1½" × 29¾"	Pine
Top	1	¾" × 14" × 38"	Pine
Back	1	¼" × 27¼" × 33¾"	Plywood

Hardware

6 drywall screws, #6 × 1¼"
2d finishing nails

1 Cut the stock to size. Cut the parts to the sizes specified by the Cutting List. Edge-glue narrow boards to make the wide pieces, if necessary. All of the parts are solid wood except the back, which is plywood.

2 Dado the sides. Mount a dado head on the table saw. Adjust its width to match the thickness of the shelves. Set the depth of cut to ⅜ inch. Cut the dadoes, as shown in the *Front View* and *Side View.*

With the same dado setting, groove the sides for the feet, as shown in the *Side View.* Set the fence 1¼ inches from the blade and cut one groove on each piece. Then set the fence 10½ inches from the blade and cut the other groove on each piece.

To avoid cutting too far, clamp a stop block to the fence, as shown in the

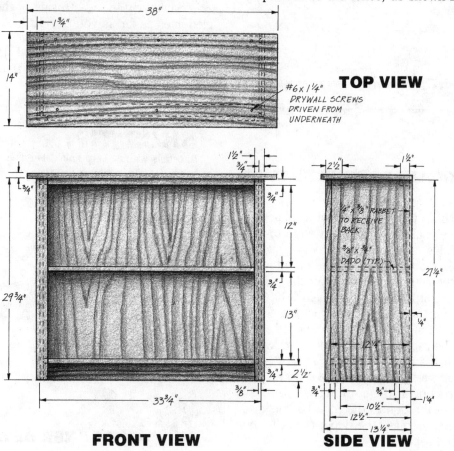

TOP VIEW

#6 x 1¼"
DRYWALL SCREWS
DRIVEN FROM
UNDERNEATH

FRONT VIEW

SIDE VIEW

¼" X ⅜" RABBET
TO RECEIVE
BACK

⅜" X ¾"
DADO (TYP.)

Stopped Groove Detail. Feed the boards until they hit the stop. Then carefully back out of the cut. The dado cutter will leave stopped grooves that curve up at the stopped end. Finish the grooves with a chisel.

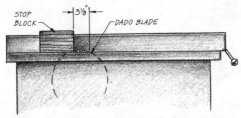

SHOP TIP: To make sure dadoes are the right width, cut a sample in a piece of scrap. Test fit the adjoining piece. If necessary, you can adjust the cutting width of stack dadoes by slipping paper shims over the arbor, between the chippers.

STOPPED GROOVE DETAIL

3 **Rabbet the sides.** Cut a rabbet for the back along the back edge of both sides, as shown in the *Side View.* Cut the rabbet in two passes on a table-mounted router. Adjust a ¾-inch-diameter straight bit to a ³⁄₁₆-inch depth of cut for the first pass. Adjust the fence so that ¼ inch of the bit is exposed. Rout the rabbets. On one side you will start at the top and rout until you get to the bottom shelf dado. On the other, start routing at the bottom shelf dado and rout through to the top. To finish the cuts, increase the depth of cut to ⅜ inch and repeat.

4 **Dovetail the top supports and sides.** The top supports are dovetailed into the top of the sides. Begin by laying out the tails on the top supports, as shown in the *Corner Details.* Note that the front top support has a notch for the stile next to the dovetail. Cut the notches and tails with a dovetail saw.

Hold the supports in position on the sides and trace around the dovetails. Set a marking gauge to the thickness of the supports. Scribe a line across the inside face of the sides to indicate how deep to cut the sockets. Square down from the tracings to the scribe lines.

Saw along the waste side of the angled lines as far as you can without cutting beyond any of the other layout lines. Chop out the waste with a chisel. For more information, see "Cutting Half-Blind Dovetails" on page 129.

SHOP TIP: Lay out dovetails with a sharp knife. The line is narrower and more precise than a pencil line.

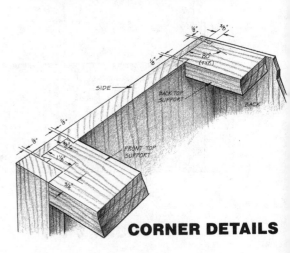

CORNER DETAILS

5 **Assemble the case.** Finish sand the sides, shelves, top supports, and feet. Put them together without glue to be sure everything fits. Clamp the joints tightly. Measure the diagonals—the case is square when the diagonals are equal. When everything fits well, take the case apart and reassemble it with glue. Again, measure the diagonals to make sure the case is square. Let the glue dry overnight.

6 **Attach the stiles.** Sand the stiles and glue them to the front of the case. Make sure they are flush along the sides.

7 **Apply the finish.** You'll find it easier to reach all the corners and crevices if you apply your finish before you attach the top and back. Sand the remaining parts and apply your favorite finish. The bookshelf in the photo was stained with an oil-base mahogany stain followed by three coats of a tung oil varnish. Be sure to finish both sides of the top to help prevent warping.

8 **Attach the top and back.** Drill and countersink three $5/32$-inch-diameter holes in each top support. The placement of the holes isn't critical. Drill one hole near each end and one roughly in the middle. Place the top on the case. Position it flush with the back edge and center it from side to side. Drive $1\frac{1}{4}$-inch drywall screws through the holes you just drilled and into the top.

To attach the back, tip the case over on its face. Be sure to put a pad underneath to avoid marring the finish. Place the back in its rabbets and nail it in place with 2d finishing nails. Drive a nail every 5 inches along the rabbets, shelves, and top support.

DOVETAILED BLANKET CHEST

For all their simplicity, blanket chests can be quite elegant. This example, made from poplar by Brent and Linda Kahl of Richland, Pennsylvania, has feet that give it a more airy, less heavy appearance than some. Blanket chests are popular for over-the-summer storage of winter blankets or comforters. Fit a piece of aromatic cedar flakeboard in the bottom if you like. The chests are handy year-round as a seat at the foot of a bed.

The Kahls painted this chest, but poplar can also be given a clear finish. The green tinge sometimes found in the heartwood quickly turns to a mellow brown with exposure to light.

1 **Select the stock and cut the parts.** If you really want to make this chest with historic authenticity, you'll have to find 18-inch-wide boards for the main parts. If you have trouble

finding them, try some of the advertisers in the classified sections of woodworking magazines. Feel free to substitute some other species of wood if you can get it wide enough. If you decide to glue up narrower boards to get the needed width, try to match the grain so the joint line isn't too conspicuous.

Plane the stock flat and to the thicknesses specified by the Cutting List. Saw the parts to width and length. Leave the till side and till bottom $\frac{1}{16}$ inch thicker than the dimension given. Leave the till lid $\frac{3}{4}$ inch thick for the time being. You'll plane it thinner after cutting a cove in one edge.

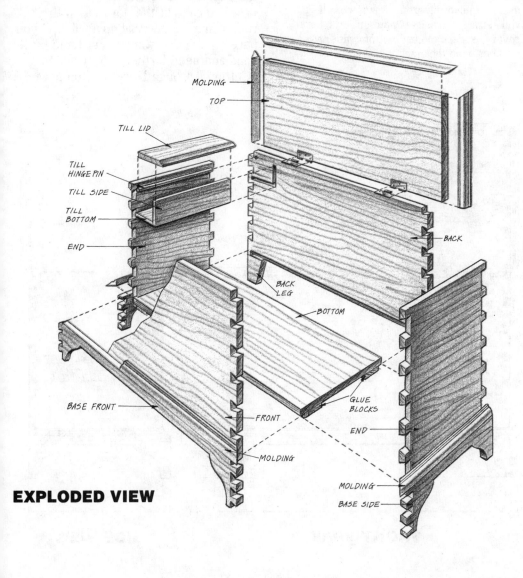

MOLDING
TOP
TILL LID
TILL HINGE PIN
TILL SIDE
TILL BOTTOM
END
BACK
BACK LEG
BOTTOM
BASE FRONT
FRONT
GLUE BLOCKS
END
MOLDING
MOLDING
BASE SIDE

EXPLODED VIEW

SHOP TIP: Keep wide panels flat while you work by controlling the air flow to the panel surfaces. Stack the panels with uniform thickness stickers between them. (Stickers are pieces of wood ¾ to 1 inch square, and as long as the panels are wide.) The stickers allow the panels to take up or give off moisture uniformly from all surfaces. If you stack the panels without stickers, cover the stack top and bottom with plywood or wrap the stack in plastic.

2 **Dovetail the corners of the chest.** The *Front View* gives the layout of the dovetails. Notice that the layout ends at the bottom with an extra-wide tail instead of a pin. This layout allows you to cut a through rabbet for the bottom without leaving a gap visible from the rear of the chest. The base covers the gaps at the ends.

You can cut the dovetails with a router in a commercial dovetail jig if you have one. If you want to cut them by hand and need further help, refer to "Cutting Through Dovetails" on page 67.

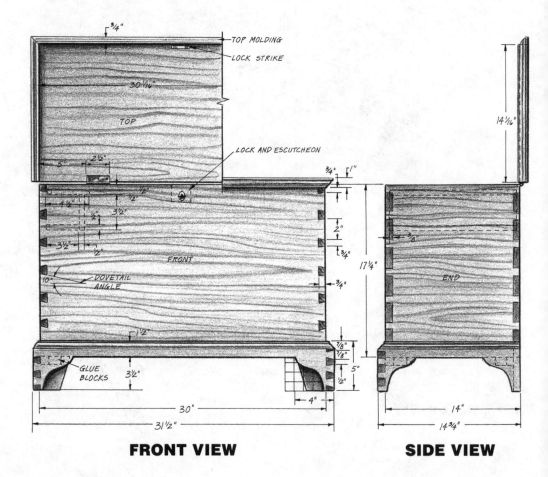

FRONT VIEW   **SIDE VIEW**

3 **Dado the front and back for the till boards.** The till side and bottom fit in stopped dadoes routed in the front and back of the chest. Lay out the dadoes and clamp a fence to the front and back to guide the router. Use a ½-inch straight bit in a plunge router. Square the ends of the dadoes with a chisel. Plane the till side and bottom until they just slip snugly into their dadoes.

4 **Rout the rabbets in the front, back, and ends for the bottom.** Make the rabbets with a ¾-inch straight bit in a router or with a dado blade on your table saw. To cut them on the table saw in a single pass, adjust the dado head to cut ⅜ inch deep × ¾ inch wide. If you use a router, adjust the depth of cut to ⅜ inch but take at least two passes to cut the ¾-inch width.

CUTTING LIST

Part	Quantity	Dimensions	Comments
Front/back	2	¾" × 17¼" × 30"	Poplar
Ends	2	¾" × 17¼" × 14	Poplar
Till side/bottom	2	½" × 3½" × 13³⁄₁₆"	Poplar or other hardwood
Till lid	1	½" × 4¼" × 12⅜"	Poplar or other hardwood
Till lid hinge pin	1	½" dia. × 13¼"	Hardwood dowel
Bottom	1	¾" × 13¼" × 29¼"	Hardwood plywood
Base front	1	¾" × 5" × 31½"	Poplar
Base sides	2	¾" × 5" × 14¾"	Poplar
Back legs	2	¾" × 3" × 3½"	Poplar
Top	1	¾" × 14¹⁄₁₆" × 30¹⁄₁₆"	Poplar
Molding stock	1	¾" × 1" × 64"	Poplar; cut to fit.
Glue block stock	8	¾" × ¾" × 18"	Poplar; cut into 2" pieces.

Hardware

6d finish nails
1" wire nails
1 pair brass butt hinges, 1½" × 2½"
1 half-mortise chest lock with escutcheon and key. Available from Paxton Hardware, Ltd., 7818 Bradshaw Road, Upper Falls, MD 21156.

5 **Drill holes for the till hinge pin.** The till lid hinge pin extends ⅜ inch into holes in the front and back, as shown in the *Till Lid Details*. Drill the ½-inch-diameter × ½-inch-deep holes.

6 **Make the till lid.** The hinge pin is a dowel that fits into a cove routed along the entire back of the lid. Rout the cove with a ½-inch-diameter core box bit in a table-mounted router. Center the cove in the edge of the ¾-inch stock, then plane off ⅛ inch from each surface, reducing the lid to ½ inch thick. Glue and clamp the hinge pin into the cove, centering it from end to end. Shape the lid with a hand plane, as shown in the *Till Lid Details*. Scrape and sand the lid smooth, rounding the edges so they don't catch on blankets going into the chest.

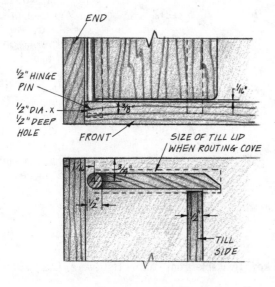

TILL LID DETAILS

7 **Glue together the chest.** Sand the till parts and the inside surfaces of the chest. Cover your bench with a piece of plastic to protect it from glue, then lay the back on it with the inside facing up. Apply glue to the dovetails that join the ends to the back and assemble them. If light tapping with a mallet won't bring the joint together, apply clamp pressure. By clamping down onto the bench, the bench top acts like a caul, distributing the clamp pressure evenly along the back.

When the ends and back are assembled, glue the till side and bottom into the dadoes in the back and insert the till lid hinge pin into its hole. Now apply glue to the dovetails that join the ends to the front and to the till dadoes in the front. Position the front. Start the dovetails on the side with the till first. Tap them together evenly, inserting the till parts in the dadoes and hole in the front as the parts approach. A 2 × 4 caul will help distribute mallet blows. When the till parts are started in the dadoes, start the dovetails at the other end of the front. Bring the joints together fully, using clamp pressure as necessary. Use cauls under the clamps to distribute the clamp pressure.

Measure diagonally across the top opening to check that the assembly is square. If the two diagonals are not equal, the chest isn't square. Apply clamp pressure across the longer diagonal until the assembly is square.

When the glue is dry, clean up the dovetails with a sharp hand plane or a sander. Finish sand the outside of the chest.

8 **Nail the chest bottom into the bottom rabbet.** Sand the inside of the chest bottom and set it in the rabbet. Nail through the sides into the edges of the bottom with 6d finishing nails. The base will cover the nails.

9 **Dovetail the base pieces.** The three base pieces dovetail together at the front corners. Lay out the dovetails, as shown in the *Front View.* Adjust the layout as necessary so the base will fit snugly around the chest. Cut them the same way you cut the dovetails in the chest.

10 **Saw the feet on the base pieces.** Make a pattern of the feet out of stiff paper, as shown in the *Front View.* Lay out the feet on the base pieces and saw them to shape with a coping saw or band saw. Clean up the sawed edges with a fine rasp and sandpaper. A sanding drum on a drill press is a handy way to clean up the curved edge of the feet.

SHOP TIP: If nails tend to split the stock you're nailing, drill pilot holes for them. Cut the head off of one of the nails and chuck it in a drill. Drill the pilot hole with this nail as though it were a bit. The pilot hole will be exactly the right diameter and slightly shorter than the nail, which is good.

11 **Assemble the base and rout the molded edge.** Glue and clamp together the base dovetails. To make sure the assembled base will fit the chest perfectly, tape waxed paper around the front bottom corners of the chest and glue the base together in position on the chest. When the glue is dry, remove the base from the chest to rout the molding along its top edge.

The *Molding Detail* shows the shape that the Kahls use. You can rout it in a single pass with a Roman ogee bit. Chuck the bit in a table-mounted router and adjust the height to produce the shape that you want. You can guide the stock with either a fence or a ball-bearing pilot on the bit. Shape the long front edge first. For the last inch or so of the cut, push the base with a block of scrap to support the wood as the bit exits, minimizing tear-out. Then shape the two sides. The side shaping will remove any unavoidable tear-out at the ends of the front molding.

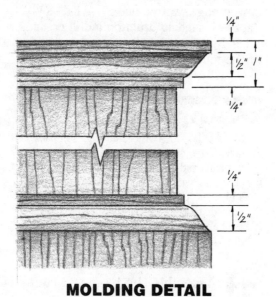

MOLDING DETAIL

12 **Attach the base to the chest.** Glue and clamp the base to the chest. Position the bottom of the chest flush with the bottom of the straight sections between the feet. Nail the base to the chest with 6d finishing nails and fill the nail holes.

13 **Attach the back legs and glue blocks.** Glue the plain back legs to the chest and side base pieces, as shown in the *Back Leg Detail*. Support all of the legs by gluing and clamping ¾ × ¾ × 2-inch blocks behind them, as shown in the *Front View* and *Side View*.

14 **Make and attach the top edge molding.** Rout the edge of the top molding with the same router table setup that you used for the base pieces.

Cut and miter a side molding from the molding stock. Cut the piece about ⅛ inch longer than necessary so that it sticks out past the back when held in place. Tape or clamp it in place. Cut a matching miter on the end of the molding stock and hold it in place on the front of the chest top, against the first side piece. Make sure that you're holding it tight against the top *and* the side molding. Mark the length of the top on the back of the molding stock. Note the direction of the second miter and which side of the mark the blade must be on, then cut the miter. Tape or clamp this front molding to the top. Miter the remaining molding stock to match the front molding. Hold it in place on the remaining side and mark it for length at the back. Mark the first piece for length in the same manner and cut both side pieces to length.

Glue the front molding in place, applying glue along the entire length. Because the top will expand and contract in width with changes in humidity, you shouldn't glue the full length of the side moldings. Glue the front 3 inches in place and nail the remainder with 1-inch wire nails. Sand the chest top.

15 **Cut the hinge mortises and attach the top.** Lay out the hinge mortises in the chest top and the top edge of the chest back. Cut the mortises as explained in "Mortising Hinges" on page 33. Drill for screws and install the hinges.

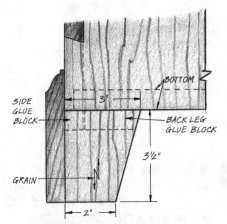

BACK LEG DETAIL

16 **Add the chest lock and escutcheon.** The Kahls' chests have a half-mortise chest lock and brass escutcheon. Your lock and escutcheon may differ. Lay out and rout the mortise for the lock, centering the keyhole on the front of the chest. Set the lock in place and mark for the keyhole. To make the keyhole, drill two holes in the front of the chest, one just over the other. Then shape the keyhole with small files. Screw the lock in place and attach the escutcheon with small brads.

Lower the lid and mark where the strike must be attached. Mortise the strike into the lid, if required by your lock set, and attach the strike.

17 **Finish the blanket chest.** If you managed to find wide boards for the chest, you will probably want to apply a clear finish. Apply linseed or tung oil, let it soak in, and wipe off the excess. (The linseed oil to use is called "boiled" linseed oil, not "raw" linseed oil. Boiled linseed oil is not actually boiled; it's linseed oil with dryers that help it harden faster. While some woodworkers heat linseed oil to help it penetrate, heating it is extremely dangerous because it is so flammable. Just buy boiled linseed oil and rub it in. Or use tung oil.)

Let the oil dry for a day or two. Repeat the application procedure two or three times. When the oil is thoroughly dry, rub it down with #0000 steel wool or an ultrafine Scotch-Brite pad. Apply a paste wax and buff it well.

If you prefer to paint the chest, try a milk paint. Rub it down with steel wool until the paint is nearly rubbed through in places. Then brush on a glaze and wipe it off. The glaze adds depth and color to the finish. Glazes are readily available from paint stores. If you are unable to find milk paint at a local store, write to The Old Fashioned Milk Paint Company, 436 Main Street, Groton, MA 01450-0222.

PAINTED CUPBOARD

This tall, two-door cabinet has rather plain lines, but builder Rick Wright of Schnecksville, Pennsylvania, has added a bit of spice by selectively painting various parts. There is nothing wrong with plain lines and a natural finish, of course—this cabinet will hold your kitchen, dining room, or pantry items regardless of the finish. If you do decide to paint parts of the cupboard, mask off the unpainted areas for a clean, professional result.

Two of the shelves in the cabinet are adjustable. You can easily add additional shelves.

1 Select the stock and cut the parts. Choose a wood for the appearance that you want; both hard and soft woods are suitable.

Edge-glue narrower boards as necessary for the wider parts, then plane your stock flat and to the required thickness. Saw the parts to the lengths and widths specified by the Cutting List, with the following exceptions: Prepare one long piece for the side trim and cut it to length after routing the shape, and prepare the six door rails as one piece 13 inches wide. You'll rip it to width after coping the ends.

2 Rout dadoes in the cupboard sides. The sides require stopped dadoes for the drawer shelves and the fixed shelf. The drawer shelf dadoes stop ⅜ inch from the front edges. The shelf dadoes stop ¾ inch from the front edges. Lay out the dadoes. Clamp a straightedge to the sides to guide the router and rout the dadoes in several passes of increasing depth. Square the front ends of the shelf dadoes with a chisel.

3 Cut out the feet in the sides. Lay out the foot cutout, as shown in the *Foot Pattern*. Saw out the shape and clean up the sawed edges with files and sandpaper.

EXPLODED VIEW

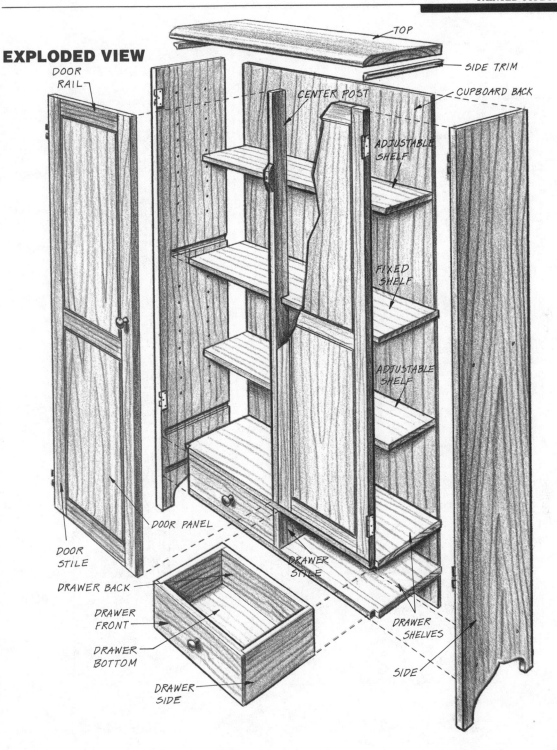

DOOR
RAIL

TOP

SIDE TRIM

CUPBOARD BACK

CENTER POST

ADJUSTABLE
SHELF

FIXED
SHELF

ADJUSTABLE
SHELF

DOOR PANEL

DOOR
STILE

DRAWER BACK

DRAWER
FRONT

DRAWER
BOTTOM

DRAWER
SIDE

DRAWER
STILE

DRAWER
SHELVES

SIDE

201

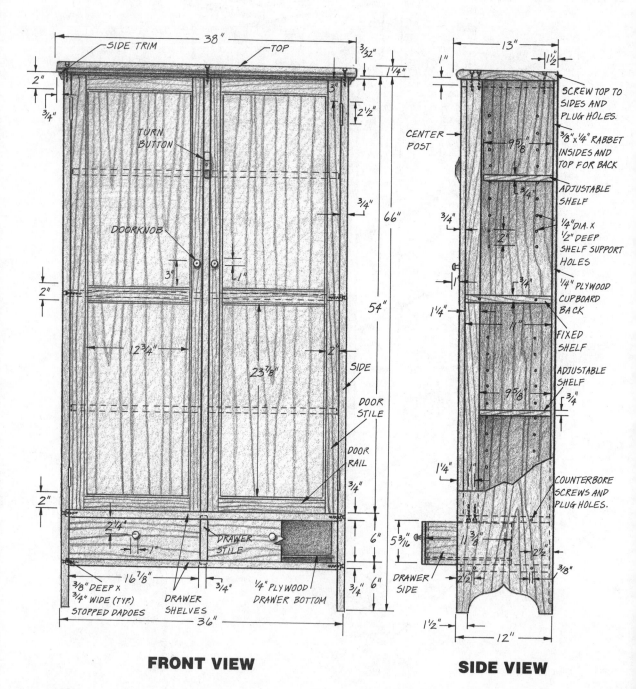

FRONT VIEW

SIDE VIEW

CUTTING LIST

Part	Quantity	Dimensions	Comments
Sides	2	¾" × 12" × 66"	
Drawer shelves	2	¾" × 11¾" × 35¼"	
Drawer stile	1	¾" × 6" × 11¾"	
Top	1	1¼" × 13" × 38"	
Fixed shelf	1	¾" × 11" × 35¼"	
Adjustable shelves	2	¾" × 9⅝" × 34¼"	
Center post	1	¾" × 1¼" × 54"	
Cupboard back	1	¼" × 35¼" × 64⅜"	Plywood
Trim	2	¾" × 1" × 12"	
Drawer fronts	2	¾" × 5³⁄₁₆" × 16¹³⁄₁₆"	
Drawer sides	4	¾" × 5³⁄₁₆" × 11⅜"	
Drawer backs	2	¾" × 4⁹⁄₁₆" × 15⁵⁄₁₆"	
Drawer bottoms	2	¼" × 11¼" 15¹³⁄₁₆"	Plywood
Door stiles	4	¾" × 2" × 53¹³⁄₁₆"	
Door rails	6	¾" × 2" × 13⁹⁄₁₆"	Length may vary; see step 18.
Door panels	4	¼" × 13⁷⁄₁₆" × 24½"	Plywood
Turn button	1	¾" × ¾" × 3"	Hardwood

Hardware

#8 × 1½" flathead wood screws
⅜" wood plugs
⅝" wire nails
4d finishing nails
4 wooden knobs, 1" dia., with screws
½" O.D. flat washer
8 pin-style shelf supports. Available from Woodworker's Supply, 5604 Alameda Place NE, Albuquerque, NM 87113.
2 pairs brass butt hinges, 1½" × 2½"

4 Rabbet the sides for the back. The back fits in rabbets in the sides. You can rout the rabbet with a ball-bearing piloted bit if you have one, or with an unpiloted bit, guiding the router with its fence. The back does not continue all the way to the floor; stop the rabbet 2 inches from the bottom.

5 Drill holes for the adjustable shelves. Drill holes for the adjustable shelf supports, as shown in the *Side View*. Most pin-style supports require ¼-inch-diameter holes. Make the holes ½ inch deep. If you don't have a stop collar or depth gauge, wrap tape around the bit to mark the correct depth.

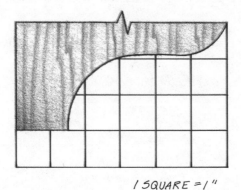

1 SQUARE = 1"

FOOT PATTERN

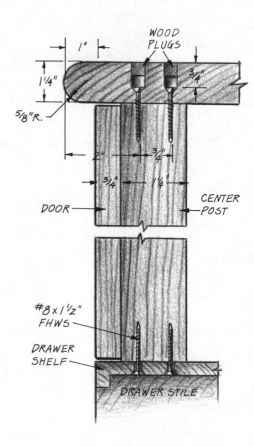

SHOP TIP: When a project involves dado joints that you intend to rout, make a thickness gauge before surfacing your stock. Make the gauge by routing a dado in a piece of scrap using the same bit that you will use later to cut the dadoes. Joint the stock, then plane it to a thickness that snugly fits the dado in the scrap.

6 **Counterbore and drill the cupboard sides for screws.** Glue and screws hold the drawer shelves and fixed shelf in the dadoes in the sides. Lay out the positions of the screws on the cabinet sides. Make sure they are centered in the dadoes. Drill the ³⁄₈-inch counterbores first, then drill the ⁵⁄₃₂-inch screw shank holes, as shown in the *Screw Details*. If you have a combination bit that bores the counterbore, countersink, shank, and pilot holes all at once, you can drill these holes after the cupboard is glued together.

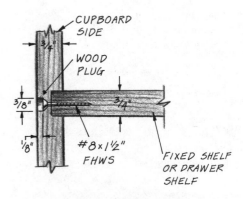

SCREW DETAILS

7 **Rout the drawer stile dado in
the drawer shelves.** Lay out and
rout a ¾-inch × ⅜-inch dado for the
drawer stile across the center of the
drawer shelves. Rout these dadoes as
you did the dadoes in the cabinet sides.
Stop each dado ⅜ inch from the front
edge of the drawer shelf.

8 **Notch the drawer shelves and
drawer stile for the blind da-
does.** Dado joinery is concealed by stop-
ping a dado short of an edge where it
would otherwise show, then cutting a
matching notch in the piece housed in
the dado. The *Blind Dado Detail* shows
this treatment. The depth of the notch
(*C*) should be exactly the depth of the
dado (*D*). The width of the notch (*B*)
must be great enough to reach beyond
where the dado begins to narrow because of the rounded end (*A*).

Notch the drawer stile and drawer
shelves to match their respective dadoes. Cut the notches with a dovetail

saw, or stand the pieces on edge against
an auxiliary fence screwed to your miter
gauge and saw them on the table saw.

9 **Drill for the center post screw
holes.** The center post fits between the cupboard top and the upper
drawer shelf. Drill screw holes down
through the top and up through the upper drawer shelf, as shown in the *Screw
Details.* Center the drawer shelf screw
holes in the drawer stile dado. Countersink the holes so the screw heads won't
interfere with the drawer stile. Counterbore deeply through the top, as shown in
the drawing.

10 **Drill screw holes in the top.**
Screws secure the top to the cupboard sides, as shown in the *Front View*
and *Side View.* Counterbore deeply for
these screws as you did for the center
post screws. Drill the shank holes.

BLIND DADO DETAIL

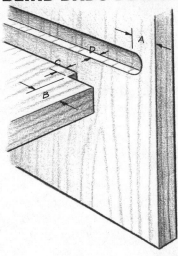

11 **Notch the fixed shelf around the center post.** Cut a ¾-inch-wide notch in the fixed shelf to fit around the center post. Center the notch in the front edge of the shelf. Raise the table saw blade to cut 1¼ inches deep. Stand the shelf on edge against a tall auxiliary fence screwed to your miter gauge to cut the sides of the notch. Chisel out the waste between the saw kerfs.

12 **Shape and rabbet the top.** Plane the front edge and ends of the top to the shape shown in the *Screw Details*. File and sand the profile smooth.

Rout a ⅜ × ¼-inch rabbet in the top for the back. Note that the rabbet doesn't run the full length of the top—it stops 1⅜ inches from each end so that it's just long enough for the back. Square the ends of the rabbet. Finish sand the rest of the top.

13 **Glue and clamp the cupboard together.** Sand the drawer shelves, cupboard shelves, and the inside of the cupboard sides. Test assemble the cupboard with clamps but without glue, and make sure the cabinet is square. Drill screw pilot holes through the screw shank holes you made earlier. Drill through the top into the sides and center post, and through the sides into the drawer shelves and fixed shelf. Remove the drawer stile and mark the bottom of the center post for screws. Disassemble the cupboard and drill the bottom of the center post for screws.

Assemble the cabinet on its back on a flat surface. Begin by gluing and screwing the upper drawer shelf to the center post. Support the center post with the fixed shelf as you glue and clamp the drawer stile between the two drawer shelves. Glue and screw the drawer shelves and fixed shelf into the side dadoes. Glue and screw the top in position on the sides. Make sure the assembly is square, then let the glue dry.

14 **Plug the screw holes.** Cut wood plugs from scrap with a plug cutter in the drill press. Make the plugs from the same wood as the cupboard. Glue the plugs in the holes with the grain running the same direction as in the cupboard. Saw the plugs off nearly flush with the surrounding wood, then sand them flush. If you don't have a plug cutter, precut wood plugs are available from most mail-order tool suppliers.

15 **Glue the back on the cupboard.** Glue and clamp the ¼-inch plywood back into the rabbbets in the back edges of the cupboard. Nail it to the drawer shelves and fixed shelf with ⅝-inch nails.

16 **Attach the trim to the cupboard top.** Shape the trim with ⁵⁄₁₆-inch-radius roundover and cove bits in a table-mounted router. Dimensions are given in the *Trim Detail*. Sand the molding, then cut it to length and nail it in place with 4d finishing nails. If you're using a hardwood, predrill the nail holes with a small bit. Glue the molding to the cabinet only at the center so the top can swell and shrink without splitting.

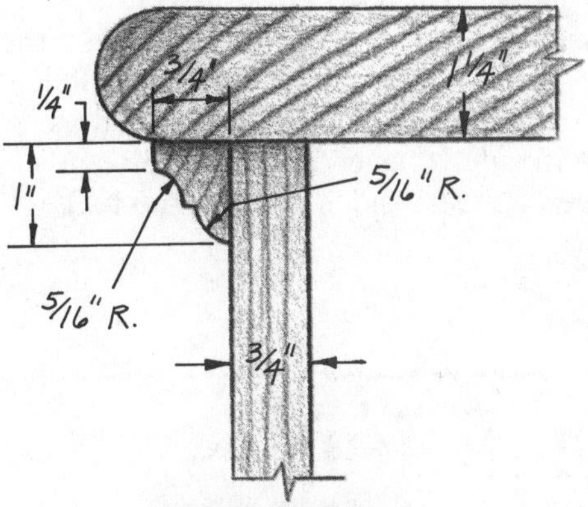

TRIM DETAIL

17 Make the cupboard drawers. The drawer sides are rabbeted, glued, and nailed into the drawer fronts. The backs are simply butted, glued, and nailed in place. Since there are always small variations in construction, cut the drawer parts to fit the actual openings. Adjust the dimensions, if necessary, to get 1/16-inch side-to-side and top-to-bottom clearance. The *Drawer Detail* shows the relationship of the drawer parts.

Cut the rabbets in the drawer fronts on the table saw. Rip the drawer bottom groove 5/16 inch deep. Bore a screw shank hole in the fronts for the knob screw.

Sand the drawer pieces, including the bottoms. Glue and nail the sides into the front rabbets, then glue and nail the backs between the sides. Nail the parts together with 4d finishing nails. Predrill nail holes if your wood is hard. Slide the bottom into the bottom groove from the back and nail it to the drawer back with 5/8-inch wire nails. Don't glue the bottom. Screw on the wooden knobs.

18 Cut the door joints. Rick uses a matched pair of special router bits for his door joinery. These bits are variously called cope-and-pattern, cope-and-stick, or rail-and-stile bits. The sidebar on page 208 explains their use. If this is the first time that you will use cope-and-stick cutters, make a complete small door out of scrap to familiarize yourself with the operation. Then cut the door joints.

The depth of the grooves cut by different router bit sets is not standardized so the overall length of the rails may vary. Rick uses the #184-0405 set by Eagle America (P.O. Box 1099, Chardon, OH 44024), which cuts a 3/8-inch-deep groove. If your bit set cuts a groove of a different depth, you will need to adjust the 13 9/16-inch length of the rails to make doors that are 16 13/16 inches wide.

19 Glue the doors together. Sand the door stiles, rails, and panels. Assemble the door frames around the

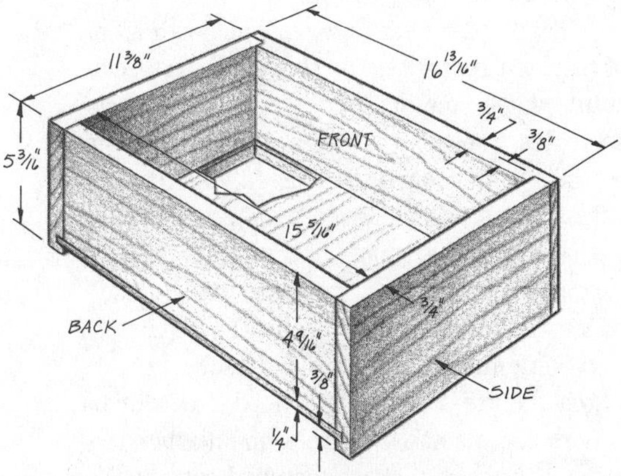

DRAWER DETAIL

panels on a flat surface, gluing the rail tongues into the stile grooves as you go. Don't glue the panels into the grooves. Clamp the frames together. Check to make certain the doors are square and flat and let the glue dry.

20 **Hang the cupboard doors.** Trim the cupboard doors so they fit in the openings with ³/₁₆-inch total clearance from top to bottom and ⅛ inch from side to side. Lay out the hinges on the cupboard sides and cut the hinge

ROUTING COPE-AND-STICK JOINTS

Shaping the inner edge of a frame for a raised panel adds a nice decorative touch but complicates the joinery at the corners of the frame. Mitering the rail and the stile so the shape on the edge of the rail matches the shape on the edge of the stile is fine for picture frames but not strong enough for doors. The traditional solution to the problem is to miter only the shaped edge and to mortise and tenon the rest of the width of the parts. That solution is still a good one for a skilled and experienced woodworker who can achieve both a tight-fitting miter and a well-fitted mortise and tenon in the same joint. There's an easier way for those who prefer to work with machines.

The cope-and-stick joint is cut with a pair of matched router bits or shaper cutters. One cutter shapes the decorative edge of the rails and stiles, the other cutter shapes the ends of the rails to fit around the shaped edge of the stiles. The two cutters must match, one being a perfect negative image of the other. A close examination of any factory-made raised-panel door will show how the joint works.

Some manufacturers make each of the matched cutters as a single, solid cutter or bit. Others use a stack of cutters on an arbor to make up each of the two matched cutters. You can buy sets that cut a groove for a raised

panel or a rabbet for panes of glass, and you can choose among a variety of decorative shapes. Sets that use stacked cutters often allow you to interchange individual cutters to switch between panels and panes or change decorative shapes without having to buy an entire new set. The steps in making a door are the same for all of the cutter arrangements.

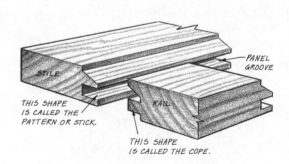

PANEL GROOVE

STILE

THIS SHAPE IS CALLED THE PATTERN OR STICK.

RAIL

THIS SHAPE IS CALLED THE COPE.

1 **Prepare the rails and stiles.** Plane and saw the stiles to final thickness and overall width, but leave them ¼ inch longer than final length. Select wide boards for the rails. For a single door, select a board wide enough for both rails plus a saw kerf and an allowance for mortises. Make the depth of the mortises ⅟₃₂ inch less than half the thickness of the hinge barrel. Fit the hinges to the mortises and drill for screws.

Set the doors in the opening and mark the position of the hinges on the door stiles. Lay out and cut the hinge mortises in the stiles. See "Mortising Hinges" on page 33 for more detailed instructions. Fit the hinges and drill for screws. Install the knobs. Hang the doors and make whatever adjustments

planing off saw marks. If you're making more than one door of the same width, try to get as many rails as you can from a single board. Saw the rail boards to final length, but don't rip them from the wide boards. When sawing them to length, keep in mind that the overall length of a rail is greater than the distance between the stiles because of the way the coped end of the rail wraps around the shaped edge of the stile.

If you intend to reinforce the joints with dowels, lay out exactly where each rail will be cut from the wide boards, then lay out and drill the dowel holes in the rails. Lay out the final length of the stiles ⅛ inch from the ends of the stile blanks, then lay out and drill the dowel holes in the stiles. When drilling the dowel holes, keep in mind that the combined depth of the dowel holes in the rails and stiles must be greater than the length of the dowels because of the way the two parts intermesh.

2 Begin with the coping cut. Chuck the coping cutter in a table-mounted router and adjust the height. The correct height may vary depending on your set of bits. The rabbet on the back side of the rail should be at least ³⁄₁₆ inch deep. Adjust the fence so that the cutter just grazes the end grain of the tenon. When the fence and height are properly set up, cope the end grain on both ends of the wide rail pieces.

3 Rip the rail pieces into individual rails. Rip the rails to width, allowing for a stroke of the plane to clean up the saw marks. If you're reinforcing your joints with dowels, be sure to follow your layout exactly. Plane off the saw marks.

4 Shape the edges. Chuck the sticking cutter in the router. (Or rearrange the cutters, depending on your bit set.) Place a rail flat on the router table. Adjust the height of the cutter so that the grooving cutter is exactly the height of the tenon on the ends of the rails. Test the setup on some scrap and make any necessary adjustments. When a coped rail is fitted to a shaped stile, the surfaces of the two should be flush. When the adjustment is right, cut the pattern on the edge of both the stiles and the rails. If your door is two panels high, you have three rails; be sure to cut the pattern on both edges of the middle rail.

After assembly, trim the top and bottom of the doors, cutting the stiles to final length.

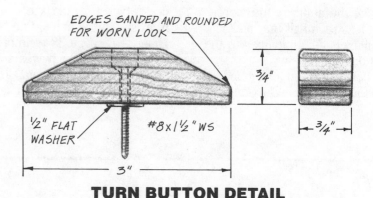

EDGES SANDED AND ROUNDED FOR WORN LOOK

3/4"

3/4"

1/2" FLAT WASHER

#8 x 1 1/2" WS

3"

TURN BUTTON DETAIL

are needed to acheive uniform clearances all the way around. When the doors fit the opening properly, shape the turn button, as shown in the *Turn Button Detail,* and install it on the center post.

21 **Apply a finish.** You have many finishing options with this cupboard. If you choose to paint it, you may paint certain details as Rick did, leaving other parts natural. Mask off unpainted areas, and pick colors that complement your home. Rick painted the door panels inside and out, as well as the side trim, shelves, and knobs. You can even paint the entire cupboard if you like. Seal the unpainted wood with a penetrating oil, such as tung oil, or brush on an easy polyurethane finish.

WALL-HUNG CORNER CUPBOARD

The corners of a room are not easy to decorate or furnish. That explains the popularity of this cabinet, made by Rick Wright of Schnecksville, Pennsylvania. Another reason for its popularity is its strong presence in a room and its functional design. This cabinet decorates without looking like pure decoration. Rick made his out of pine, but there's no reason you couldn't make it out of a hardwood like walnut or cherry.

1 Select the stock and cut the parts. Few woodworkers can obtain good, clear cabinet wood 12 or more inches wide, so you'll probably have to glue up the backs and the shelves. See the *Shelf Layout* for an economical way to glue up and lay out the shelves. If you have to glue up the door panel, try to match the grain so the glue line is inconspicuous.

Joint all the stock flat, then thickness plane it and saw it to the dimensions specified by the Cutting List. Don't cut out the shelves yet, and leave the door rails as one piece about 4½ inches wide × 8 inches long. It will make the joinery easier later.

2 Rabbet and dado the cupboard backs. Rout a ⅜ × ¾-inch rabbet in the back edge of the left (12-inch-wide) back. Rout the rabbet on your router table with a ¾-inch-diameter straight bit, guiding the cut against a fence.

Rout ⅜-inch-deep × ¾-inch-wide dadoes in the left and right backs for the cupboard shelves. The *Back Pattern* shows the layout of the dadoes. To rout the dadoes, first clamp the backs, edge to edge, on your bench. Clamp a straight-

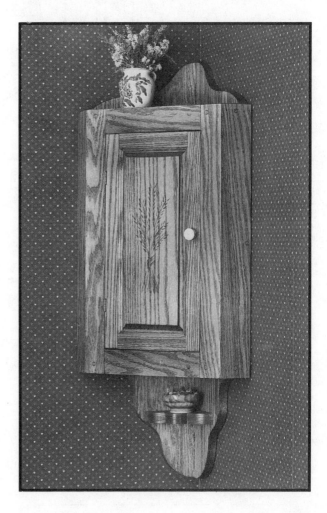

EXPLODED VIEW

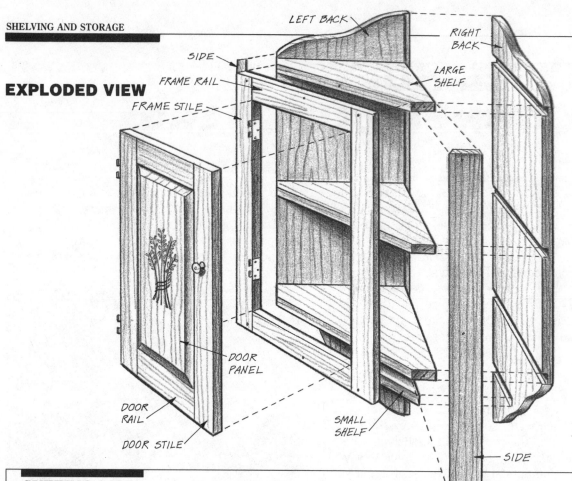

LEFT BACK

RIGHT BACK

SIDE

FRAME RAIL

FRAME STILE

LARGE SHELF

DOOR PANEL

DOOR RAIL

DOOR STILE

SMALL SHELF

SIDE

CUTTING LIST

Part	Quantity	Dimensions	Comments
Left back	1	$\frac{3}{4}'' \times 12'' \times 36''$	Pine
Right back	1	$\frac{3}{4}'' \times 11\frac{5}{8}'' \times 36''$	Pine
Large shelves	3	$\frac{3}{4}'' \times 11\frac{5}{8}'' \times 11\frac{5}{8}''$	Pine
Small shelf	1	$\frac{3}{4}'' \times 5\frac{1}{2}'' \times 5\frac{1}{2}''$	Pine
Frame rails	2	$\frac{3}{4}'' \times 2'' \times 11\frac{3}{16}''$	Pine
Frame stiles	2	$\frac{3}{4}'' \times 2'' \times 22''$	Pine
Sides	2	$\frac{3}{4}'' \times 2'' \times 22''$	Pine
Door rails	2	$\frac{3}{4}'' \times 2'' \times 8\frac{3}{16}''$	Pine
Door stiles	2	$\frac{3}{4}'' \times 2'' \times 18''$	Pine
Door panel	1	$\frac{3}{4}'' \times 7\frac{3}{4}'' \times 14\frac{3}{4}''$	Pine

Hardware

Fluted or grooved dowels, $\frac{1}{4}'' \times 2''$
14 wood plugs, $\frac{3}{8}''$ dia.
Flathead wood screws, #8 $\times$ $1\frac{1}{2}''$

1 pair cabinet butt hinges, $1\frac{1}{2}''$
1 porcelain knob with screw, $\frac{3}{4}''$ dia.
1 magnetic catch for door

edge in place to guide the router and rout the dadoes across both pieces. Routing both dadoes at the same time ensures that they will line up.

Make stopped dadoes for the small bottom shelf. Notice on the *Back Pattern* that the two stopped dadoes are of unequal length. Square the stopped ends of the dadoes with a chisel.

3 Cut the back patterns. Make cardboard patterns for the curves on the top and bottom of the cupboard backs. Trace the patterns onto the backs. Saw out the shapes with a band saw or coping saw. Smooth the sawed edges with files and sandpaper.

4 Drill the backs for wood screws. The shelves are glued and screwed into the dadoes. Lay out the screw holes, as shown in the *Top View,* centered in the dadoes. Drill 5/32-inch screw shank holes; countersink them.

5 Cut the shelves to size. Lay out the shelves, as shown in the *Shelf Layout.* Saw the back edges of the shelves on the table saw. Clamp the left and right backs together and fit the large shelves in their dadoes. Mark the shelves where the 45 degree corners extend beyond the cabinet backs. Saw off the corners at the marks so the shelves will fit as shown in the *Top View.*

The small shelf cannot be marked directly. Take an accurate measurement of the exposed length of the stopped dadoes. Lay out the corner cutoffs to these measurements and cut them square to the back edge.

6 Assemble the cupboard backs and shelves. Sand the inside of the backs and both sides of the shelves. Assemble the backs and shelves without glue and drill screw pilot holes in the shelves in line with the shank holes in the backs. Glue and screw the four shelves into the dadoes in the narrow (right) back. Make sure the edges of the shelves are flush with the edges of the back. Glue and screw the wide (left) back to this assembly. Make sure the cupboard is not twisted by checking that the backs lie flat against a flat surface such as your table saw table. If necessary, clamp the assembly to the flat surface while the glue dries.

7 Dowel the face frame together. Lay out dowel holes in the ends of the frame rails, as shown in the *Face Frame Detail.* Drill the 1/4-inch holes 1 inch deep. Drill the holes on the drill press or with a commercially available doweling jig.

Lay out the holes in the stiles with the help of commercially available dowel

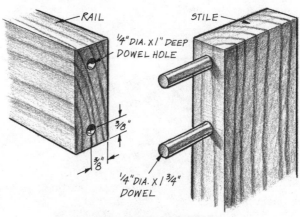

FACE FRAME DETAIL

TOP VIEW

2½"

12"

5½"

11⅝"

SMALL SHELF

2½"

⅜"

LARGE SHELF

¾"

¾"

15³⁄₁₆"

112½°

2"

SHELF LAYOUT

4⁵⁄₃₂"

45°

9⅛"

37"

FRONT VIEW

DOOR RAIL

FRAME RAIL

11³⁄₁₆"

7³⁄₁₆"

2"

2"

2"

8³⁄₁₆"

36"

22"

18"

14"

SIDE

FRAME STILE

DOOR STILE

DOOR PANEL

2"

2"

BACK

BACK PATTERN

ONE SQUARE = 1"

4"

¾"

10½"

¾"

36"

9¼"

⅜" DEEP DADO (TYP.)

¾"

5¼"

5½"

¾"

10"

⅜"

11⅝"

12"

centers. First, insert the centers into the rail holes. Lay a rail and stile on a flat surface and bring the two parts together. Check that they're flush at the end of the stile. Press them together firmly to mark the stile. Drill the holes 1 inch deep in the stiles. Assemble the frame with glue and ¼ × 2-inch fluted or grooved dowels and clamp it. Ensure that the frame is square by checking that both diagonals measure the same. If necessary, square the frame with a third clamp running in the direction of the longer diagonal.

8 **Bevel the edges of the sides.** The joint between the sides and the stiles is beveled. If you have a jointer, adjust the fence to 112½ degrees from the tables and joint an edge of each side. Adjust the depth of cut to make a very shallow cut and take successive passes until the bevel just reaches the outside corner.

If you don't have a jointer, tilt the table saw blade 22½ degrees from vertical. Set the fence so the outside face of the side will be just over 2 inches wide, rip the bevel, then plane off the saw marks, bringing the outside width to 2 inches.

9 **Install the sides.** Lay the cabinet on one of the backs on the bench and lay the opposing side in position. Adjust it so the inside of the beveled edge of the side is aligned with the corners of the shelves, then clamp it. Lay out the three screw holes shown in the *Front View*, then drill counterbore, shank, and pilot holes as before. Remove the side, apply glue, and put it back in place.

Clamp it to the cabinet back, then drive the three screws. Repeat for the other side.

10 **Bevel the edges of the face frame to fit between the sides.** With the jointer or table saw adjusted to the same angle you used to bevel the sides, bevel the edges of the stiles. The stiles must contact both the sides and the front of the shelves, so proceed cautiously. If you remove too much wood, there's no good way to remedy the error. A hand plane set to take a very fine shaving is the best way to make final adjustments to the fit.

11 **Glue and screw the face frame in place.** When you've trimmed the face frame to fit snugly between the sides, lay out the screw holes shown in the *Front View*, then drill counterbore, shank, and pilot holes. Glue and screw the frame in place. Plug the counterbores in the face frame and sides with plugs cut from the same stock as the cupboard. Cut them with a plug cutter on your drill press. Glue them in the counterbores with the grain running the same direction as the surrounding wood. Plane and sand the plugs flush with the frame pieces.

12 **Cut the door joints.** The frame of the frame-and-panel door is easily shaped and joined with the help of a matched set of cope-and-stick bits in a table-mounted router. Rout a cope on the ends of the wide board you made for the rails, then rip the rails to width. Rout a stick pattern on the stiles. See "Routing Cope-and-Stick Joints" on page 208 for more information.

13 **Make and carve the door panel.** Bevel the edges of the door panel to fit the grooves cut in the stiles and rails. Cut the bevel on the table saw, as shown in the *Panel Raising Detail*. Stand the panel on edge against the auxiliary fence and rip the bevel around the panel edges. Scrape and sand the bevel to clean up the saw cut.

Lay out the wheat stalk design on the door, as shown in the *Front View*. Carve the pattern, as explained in "Carving a Wheat Shock" on the opposite page.

14 **Assemble the door.** Sand the door parts. Assemble the frame around the panel, gluing the rail tongues into the stile grooves. Clamp the door together on a flat surface, making sure that all four corners are square.

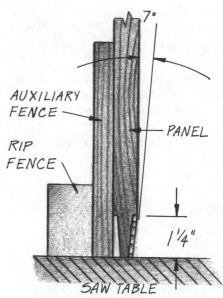

PANEL RAISING DETAIL

SHOP TIP: A door panel must be free to expand and contract across its width with changes in humidity. To prevent squeezed-out glue from the frame joints from gluing the panel in place, apply finish to the panel before assembling the frame. Give the panel the complete finish, including wax and a buffing. Incidentally, prefinishing has the added advantage of preventing an unfinished edge of the panel from showing when the panel shrinks in dry weather.

15 **Hang the door.** Plane the edges of the door so it fits the opening in the face frame with ¹⁄₁₆ inch of clearance in both height and width. Lay out the hinges on the door, as shown in the *Front View*. Cut the hinge mortises, as explained in "Mortising Hinges" on page 33. You will probably need to hand plane a slight bevel on the unhinged stile of the door to allow it to close without leaving an unsightly gap.

16 **Apply a finish.** Remove the hinges and give the entire cabinet a final sanding. An oil finish is both easy and appropriate for this cabinet. The choices include Danish oil, tung oil, and boiled linseed oil. Apply three coats for luster and protection. If you prefer, you can apply a urethane or varnish. When the finish is dry, rehang the door and install the pull and a door catch. If you like, substitute a wooden turn button for the magnetic catch listed in the Cutting List.

Hang the cabinet by screwing or bolting it through the back into both walls of the corner.

CARVING A WHEAT SHOCK

Carving a wheat shock is quite easy and requires a minimum of carving tools. You'll find that one of the most important steps in carving is laying out the design. Lay it out clearly so you can see where to cut.

1 **Draw the carving design on the door panel.** Sand the panel. Draw the wheat stalk design on paper. Tape the design in place on the panel with a sheet of carbon paper underneath. Trace over the design with a sharp pencil.

2 **Carve the stalks.** The stalks are thin, curved lines made with a V-cut, as shown in the *Carving Detail.* You can make the cuts with either a veiner or a bench chisel. The veiner cuts a V-bottom groove. If you use a veiner, begin at one end of the stalk and push the chisel along the line marking the bottom of the

groove. If you use a straight chisel, cut the stalks with a series of downward chopping cuts. First tilt the chisel in one direction about 15 degrees to cut one wall. Then tilt the chisel 15 degrees in the other direction to remove the waste and complete the groove. Carve the stalks that bind the shock in the same manner.

3 **Carve the wheat kernels.** Make each individual kernel with two cuts from a 7 mm #8 sweep gouge. Each of the cuts is made with the gouge about 15 degrees from vertical, one from each side of the kernel. The curved sweep of the gouge makes the curved edges of the kernels. A small gouge from a set of palm chisels gives a very similar result. Carve the double line of kernels for each of the wheat stalks.

CARVING DETAIL

CUT KERNELS WITH #8 SWEEP 7 MM GOUGE.

CUT V-GROOVE STALK WITH VEINER OR STRAIGHT CHISEL.

BATHROOM CABINET

The typical metal mirrored bathroom cabinet is often more convenient for the house builder than for the house occupant. You can do a lot better. Make this cabinet to replace or supplement your current one and your family will thank you for it.

You can build the cabinet as shown in the drawings or you can rearrange the shelves or even the overall dimensions to meet your own requirements. Before you start rearranging, however, study the drawings. You'll notice that this cabinet is cleverly designed to use the same size parts for both shelves and dividers. The identical parts make building it a piece of cake.

If you'd rather hide the contents, use mirrors instead of clear glass, or glue in a plywood panel. The joinery is simple—doweled butt joints—but provides good practice in basic, accurate layout.

1 **Select the stock and cut the parts.** Make the cabinet from whatever wood suits your taste and pocketbook. Just make sure the wood is

EXPLODED VIEW

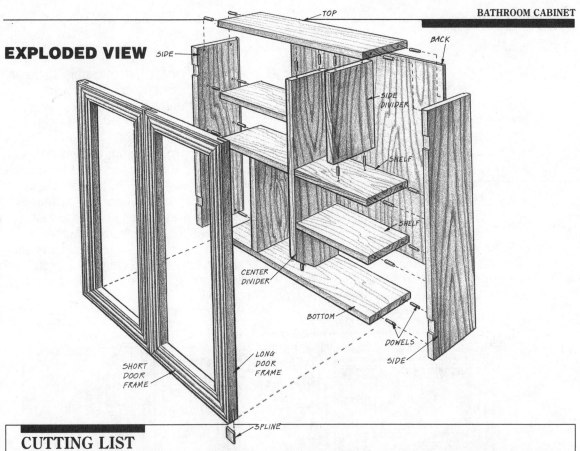

TOP

BACK

SIDE

SIDE
DIVIDER

SHELF

SHELF

CENTER
DIVIDER

BOTTOM

DOWELS

SIDE

SHORT
DOOR
FRAME

LONG
DOOR
FRAME

SPLINE

CUTTING LIST

Part	Quantity	Dimensions	Comments
Long parts	3	⅝″ × 4½″ × 18½″	Top, bottom, and center divider
Short parts	6	⅝″ × 4½″ × 8¹⁵⁄₁₆″	Shelves and side dividers
Sides	2	⅝″ × 4¾″ × 19¾″	
Back	1	¼″ × 19⅛″ × 19⅛″	Plywood
Short door frames	4	¾″ × 1¼″ × 9⅞″	
Long door frames	4	¾″ × 1¼″ × 19¾″	
Spline stock	1	⅛″ × ¾″ × 10″	Joins door corner miters.
Filler strip stock	1	¼″ × ⅜″ × 12′	Glass retainers

Hardware

Grooved dowels, ¼″ × ¾″   2 pieces clear glass, ¹⁄₁₆″ × 8″ × 17⅞″
4d finishing nails   2 magnetic catches
2 pairs butt hinges, 1″ × 1½″

straight, flat, and dry. The cabinet shown is made of pine.

Cut the parts to the dimensions specified by the Cutting List. It's important to cut the parts to the exact lengths and thicknesses specified so the joints will close. Use a stop block clamped to a miter gauge fence extension to get accurate, uniform lengths.

2 Lay out the dowel joints. The cabinet parts join together with dowel-reinforced butt joints. You need to lay out the dowel holes accurately to get well-fitted joints. Use a flexible stainless steel ruler (sold by art supply stores), an awl, a marking knife, a marking gauge, and dowel centers to lay out the dowel holes.

Begin by laying out end grain dowel holes on all the long and short parts. Adjust a marking gauge to half the thickness of the stock. Check the setting by scribing the end grain of a piece first from one face, then from the other. When the gauge is set properly, the second scribe mark will coincide exactly with the first. Scribe all the long and short parts.

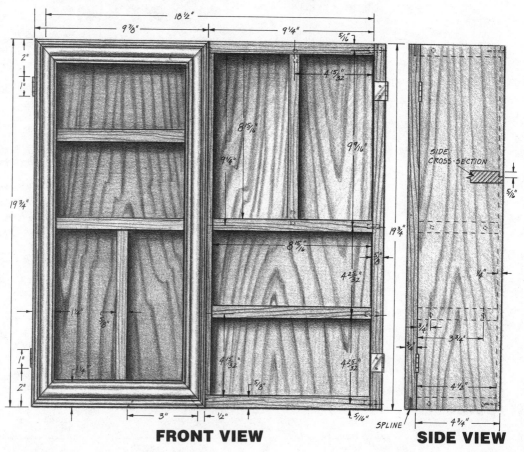

FRONT VIEW   **SIDE VIEW**

Set the marking gauge to ¾ inch and mark the centerlines 1 inch from each edge. Drill ¼-inch-diameter × ⅜-inch-deep holes at each mark.

Lay out the centerlines of the dowel holes in the faces of the long parts, short parts, and sides. The centerlines are shown in the *Front View.*

Arrange the parts, as shown in the *Front View,* with the front edges of the boards down so the front edges will be flush.

3 **Drill the remaining holes.** Lay out these holes with dowel centers. Taking each joint in succession, put the dowel centers in the end grain holes. Line up the dowel center points with the centerline on the adjoining part. Press the two together. Repeat for each joint. Drill ¼-inch-diameter × ⅜-inch-deep holes at each mark.

4 **Cut the rabbet for the back.** Rout a ¼-inch × ⁵⁄₁₆-inch rabbet in the back inside edges of the sides for the cabinet back. Chuck a ½-inch straight bit in a table-mounted router. Adjust the fence to expose ¼ inch of the bit. Guide the sides along the fence from right to left to cut the rabbet.

5 **Assemble the cabinet.** Sand the dividers and shelves, and the inside of the top, bottom, and sides.

Assemble the cabinet on its back without glue to make sure everything fits, then disassemble it. Glue the center shelves to the center divider. Glue the side dividers to the center shelves. Then glue the cabinet top and bottom to the

dividers. Glue the other two small shelves to the center divider and complete the cabinet by gluing on and clamping the sides. Clamp the top to the bottom across the center divider. Make sure the cabinet is square by measuring across diagonal corners. When the diagonals are equal, the cabinet is square.

SHOP TIP: To improve the strength of an end grain glue joint, apply glue to the end grain and let it soak in. Scrape off the excess after a few minutes and apply fresh glue to both joining surfaces just before bringing them together.

6 **Add the cabinet back.** When the glue is dry, apply glue to the cabinet back and nail it to all of the other parts with 4d finishing nails.

7 **Make the door frame pieces.** Make the door frame molding in two long pieces. Later, you will cut the individual parts to length. Rout the molding with a table-mounted router, guiding the pieces against a fence from right to left. Cut the profile in multiple passes with a straight bit and a beading bit, as shown in the *Molding Detail.*

8 **Miter and assemble the door frame.** Sand the door frame pieces. With the miter gauge on the table saw set at 45 degrees, miter the door frame members to length. Test assemble each door on the bench to ensure that the

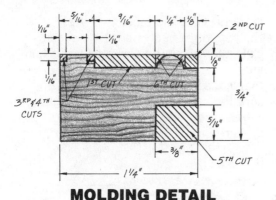

MOLDING DETAIL

joints are exact. Glue and clamp the door frames together. If you don't have a set of corner clamps for assembling miter joints, use a band clamp or even a tourniquet made from several wrappings of strong cord. Measure the doors across opposite corners to make sure they are square. Lay them, weighted if necessary, on a flat surface while the glue dries.

9 **Reinforce the door frame miters with splines.** The miter joints in the doors must be reinforced with splines. Both the splines and the spline slots are cut on the table saw. Cut the slots first.

Make a jig to cut the splines, as shown in *Spline Slotting Jig*. Adjust the saw blade to cut ¾ inch deep and adjust the fence to center the slot in the door frames. Feed the jig along the fence to cut the slots. Slot all four corners of both doors.

Rip the spline material from the edge of ¾-inch-thick scrap. The splines should slip snugly into the slots. Cut the spline material into roughly oversize splines. Glue them into the spline slots.

When the glue dries, trim them flush with the frame edges with a chisel or hand plane.

10 **Rout the door pulls.** Mount a ball-bearing piloted chamfer bit in a table-mounted router. Set it to cut a ½-inch chamfer. Cut a 3-inch-long chamfer in the bottom of each door, as shown in the *Front View*.

11 **Cut the hinge mortises and hang the doors.** Mortise the hinges into the cabinet sides only. Locate the hinges, as shown in the *Front View*. For detailed instructions, see "Mortising Hinges" on page 33. Lay out the hinge mortises directly from the hinges with a sharp knife. Mark the depth of the mortises with a marking gauge set to the thickness of the closed hinge. Chisel out the waste to the layout lines. Fit the hinges in place and mark and drill for screws. Screw the hinges to the cabinet.

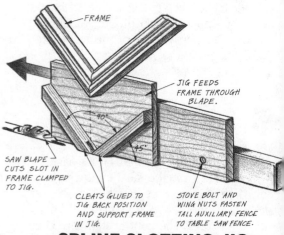

SPLINE SLOTTING JIG

Set the doors in place on the cabinet and mark the position of the hinges with a knife. Remove the hinges from the cabinet and position them on the doors. Mark and drill for screws, then screw the hinges in place. When all the hinges have been fitted, remove them. Reattach the doors after applying a finish and installing the glass.

12 **Finish the cabinet and doors.** After final sanding, apply a finish to the doors and cabinet. If you intend to use the cabinet in a bathroom, use a highly water-resistant finish such as polyurethane or high-gloss exterior enamel.

13 **Install the glass and door catches.** Set the glass in place and fit the filler strips to the frame rabbet. Attach the strips with hot-melt glue or small screws drilled and countersunk at a slight angle into the frame.

Attach a magnetic door catch to each bottom shelf near the door pull cutout.

Mount the cabinet by screwing through the cabinet back into the wall with #10 × 2-inch roundhead wood screws. Locate the studs in the wall and fasten at least two screws into a stud.

PART SIX

TOYS

ROCKING HORSE

There are many breeds of horse, even among rocking horses. You'll like this one for its simple construction methods and the interesting way the horse rocks (or swings, in this case). All of the parts are made from surfaced 4/4 (four-quarter) stock. While the horse requires no carving or creative painting, it offers an opportunity to be as creative and decorative as you like. Build it now; your bronco buster will want the car keys before you know it.

1 **Select the stock and cut the parts.** Any clear stock, hardwood or softwood, is appropriate. If you buy surfaced hardwood, it will probably be 13⁄16 inch thick, the thickness specified by the Cutting List and on the drawings. Surfaced softwoods will probably be ¾ inch thick, which is ample. Edge-glue to obtain the required widths if you need to. Plane the footrests to ⅝ inch thick. Cut all of the parts to the dimensions specified by the Cutting List.

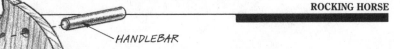

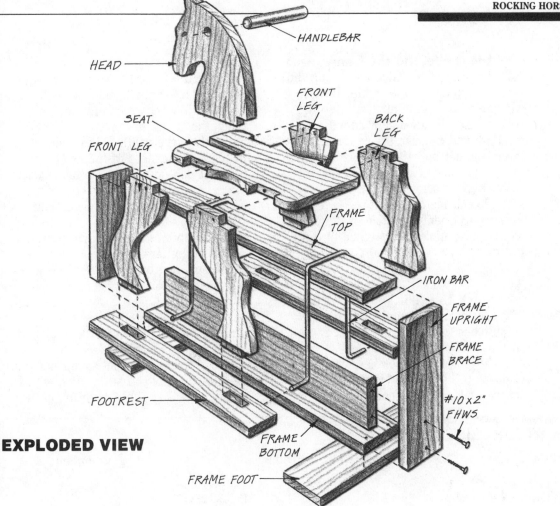

HANDLEBAR

HEAD

FRONT LEG

SEAT

BACK LEG

FRONT LEG

FRAME TOP

IRON BAR

FRAME UPRIGHT

FRAME BRACE

FOOTREST

#10 x 2" FHWS

FRAME BOTTOM

FRAME FOOT

EXPLODED VIEW

2 **Build the frame.** The frame is glued and screwed together. Lay out, counterbore, and drill ³/₁₆-inch shank holes in the uprights, as shown in the *Side View*. Hold the uprights in position against the ends of the frame brace and mark the brace for pilot holes. Drill pilot holes slightly smaller than the shank holes. Sand the parts, then glue and screw the uprights to the brace with #10 × 2-inch flathead wood screws.

Lay out the positions of the screws that fasten the frame top and bottom to the uprights. Drill counterbore and shank holes for the screws. Position the top and bottom on the uprights and mark for the pilot holes. Drill the pilot holes, then sand the top and bottom. Glue and screw them to the uprights. When gluing the frame bottom, glue it to the brace as well as the uprights and clamp it while the glue dries.

3 Add the feet to the frame. Sand the frame feet. Glue and clamp the feet to each end of the frame. If there is any slight bow in a foot, turn it so the concave side is down. For added strength you can also screw the feet to the frame bottom. If you do, screw them from below and countersink the screws so they won't scratch the floor.

Plug all the counterbored screws. Be sure to orient the grain of the plugs so that it's parallel to the grain of the boards.

4 Notch the seat board. Cut the seat board to length. Lay out the leg notches, neck cutout, and seat outline, as shown in the *Patterns*.

Cut out the leg notches with a dado blade on the table saw. For stability, screw a tall auxiliary fence to your miter gauge and hold the seat on edge against it. Make a $^{13}/_{16}$-inch-deep dado cut in the center of a leg notch, then widen the notch with successive cuts until you reach the layout marks.

Adjust the width of the dado cut to match the thickness of the head. Stand the seat on end against the tall auxiliary fence on the miter gauge and cut the notch for the head as deeply as you can.

5 Shape the seat board. Saw the seat corners, the scoops for the rider's legs, and the rest of the neck notch with a band saw or coping saw. Be sure to stay within the layout line on the neck notch. Clean up the sawed corners with files and sandpaper. Clean up and soften the edges of the side scoops with a rasp, spokeshave, and sandpaper. Finish the edges of the neck notch with a wide chisel. Try the neck blank in the

CUTTING LIST

Part	Quantity	Dimensions	Comments
Frame uprights	2	$^{13}/_{16}$″ × 3¾″ × 10¼″	
Frame brace	1	$^{13}/_{16}$″ × 3¾″ × 25⅞″	
Frame top/bottom	2	$^{13}/_{16}$″ × 3¾″ × 27½″	
Frame feet	2	$^{13}/_{16}$″ × 3¾″ × 13¾″	
Seat stock	1	$^{13}/_{16}$″ × 7⅞″ × 19″	
Footrests	2	⅝″ × 2¾″ × 23″	
Head stock	1	$^{13}/_{16}$″ × 7⅞″ × 11⅞″	
Front leg stock	2	$^{13}/_{16}$″ × 4″ × 11¾″	
Back leg stock	2	$^{13}/_{16}$″ × 4½″ × 12″	
Handlebar	1	¾″ dia. × 6″	Hardwood dowel

Hardware

21 wood plugs, ½″ dia.
2 solid steel curtain rods, ¼″ × 30″ or equivalent
12 large fencing staples to fit around ¼″ rod
21 flathead wood screws, #10 × 2″

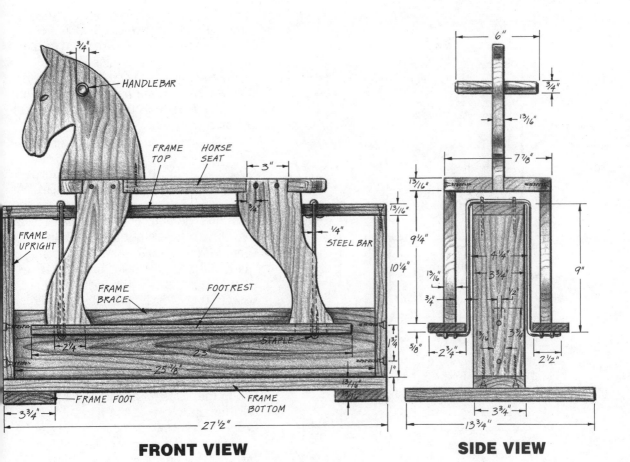

FRONT VIEW

SIDE VIEW

notch frequently to get a good fit between the two.

6 Mortise the footrests. Lay out the mortises in the footrests from the *Patterns*. Drill out the waste between the layout lines with a ¾-inch drill bit in the drill press. Use a fence clamped to the drill press table to make sure the holes are all in a straight line. Put a scrap under the board to protect the bit and prevent tear-out as the bit exits. Square up the mortises with a chisel.

7 Cut out the head and legs. Make a full-scale pattern of the horse's head and legs from the *Patterns*. Trace the patterns onto the wooden blanks. Cut the ends of the legs and the bottom edge of the head on the table saw.

Cut out the shape of the head and legs on the band saw. Saw the curves first. Check the layout of the notches by holding the head and legs up to the seat and footrest before sawing the notches. File and sand the curved edges to even them out and remove the saw marks.

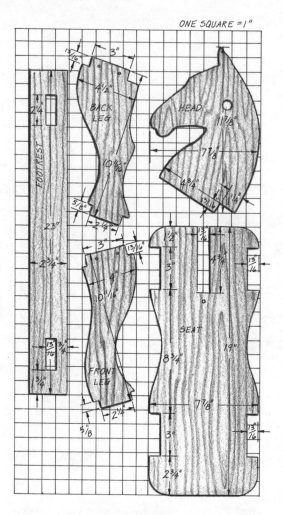

ONE SQUARE =1"

PATTERNS

8 **Drill and counterbore the legs and head.** Drill and counterbore screw shank holes through the top leg tenons and through the seat behind the head notch, as shown in the *Side View* and *Patterns.*

9 **Bore the handlebar hole.** Lay out and drill the ¾-inch hole for the

handlebar. Make sure this hole is perpendicular to the head. Round-over the ends of the dowel with files and sandpaper, then glue it in the hole. If you like, you can pin the handlebar by drilling a ³⁄₁₆-inch hole from the back of the head and driving in a dowel.

10 **Assemble the rocking horse.** Sand the legs, head, and seat. Fit the legs into the mortises in the footrests and the notches in the seat. Check that the shoulders of the tenons are seated firmly against the seat bottom. Mark and drill pilot holes in the seat, then glue and screw the legs to the seat with #10 × 2-inch flathead wood screws. Make sure the legs are square to the seat. Leave the legs in the footrests while the glue dries to make sure the legs are properly aligned.

Glue the horse's head into the head slot in the seat. Mark and drill a pilot hole for the screw at the back of the head, then screw the head to the seat. Apply a bar clamp across the width of the seat, clamping the head in place. The clamp will help give a good glue bond between the seat and the head, but won't make up for a poor fit.

11 **Attach the footrests.** Glue the legs into the mortises in the footrests. Make sure the footrests are square to the legs.

12 **Make and position the metal hangers.** The horse hangs from the frame on metal hangers. Bend the hangers from solid steel curtain rods or other ¼-inch mild steel rod. Starting at one end, clamp the rod in a vise so that the edge of the vise is exactly at the inside of the first required bend. Bend the rod 90 degrees. Mark the inside of the next bend, clamp it in the vise, and bend it 90 degrees in the opposite direction. Continue with the third and fourth bends, then cut off the extra with a hacksaw. Slipping a piece of ½-inch pipe over the rod will make the last bend easier. Bend and cut an identical second hanger. Check each bend with a framing square.

Put the hangers in place on the frame and the horse in place on the hangers, then mark the hanger positions. Remove the horse. Drill holes for the staples that hold the hangers to the frame top.

13 **Apply the finish.** Apply the finish before final assembly. You can paint the horse, stain it, or use a clear, natural finish. Be as decorative or simple as you want. Let the finish dry.

SHOP TIP: Use a straightedge to adjust a miter gauge to an angle that you have already laid out. Hold the straightedge along the layout line so that its end extends well beyond the edge of the board. Position the two on the saw table so the extended part of the straightedge is against the side of the blade but doesn't touch any teeth. Now hold the board in this position and bring the miter gauge up to it. Clamp the miter gauge fence at the angle of the board.

14 **Attach the horse to the frame.** Begin by stapling the hangers to the frame. The staples will protrude from the underside of the frame top. Turn the frame upside down and bend the tips of the staples over 90 degrees with pliers. Then bend over the rest of the protruding staple, driving the tip into the wood, as shown in the *Staple Detail*.

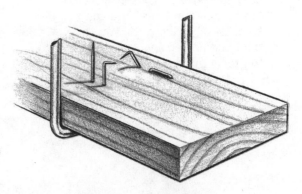

STAPLE DETAIL

Next, set the horse upside down on padding on your bench. Put the upside-down frame in place between the horse's legs with the hangers in place on the bottom of the footrests. The staples that hold the hangers to the horse go into the tenons, not the footrests. Drill pilot holes for the staples and drive the staples in. With the horse's head hanging over the end of the bench, drive in the rear leg staples. Reposition the upside-down horse so the front shoulder is over the bench while you drive each front leg staple.

Set the horse upright and call in the local bronco buster for a test.

CHILD'S TOOL BOX

Kids learn by imitation. If you're a woodworker with kids, you've got a decision to make. You can let the kids use *your* tools to imitate you (not recommended for the well-being of the kids *or* the tools) or you can make them a set of tools of their own.

This box of tools by Darryl Yeager of Bellwood, Pennsylvania, includes seven common tools. You can make some or all of them, or you can just take the general idea and make imitations of the tools that you use.

If a wooden toy breaks, it can leave sharp splinters, so make the tools from good hardwoods. The woods listed in the Cutting List are the woods shown in the photo. They're appropriate but certainly not required. Go through your collection of hardwood scraps and pick out suitable pieces. Feel free to alter the dimensions given in the Cutting List and drawings to suit the scraps that you have.

You can turn the round parts on a lathe if you have one, or you can buy them in the form of dowel rods or from the catalog supplier listed in the Cutting List.

CUTTING LIST

Part	Quantity	Dimensions	Comments
Tool box			
Ends	2	¾″ × 5″ × 6″	Oak
Bottom	1	¾″ × 5″ × 10½″	Oak
Sides	2	⅜″ × 3″ × 12″	Oak
Handle	1	⅝″ dia. × 11¼″	Birch dowel*
Wrench blank	1	¾″ × 2½″ × 8″	Elm
Hammer			
Head	1	1¼″ × 1½″ × 3″	Ash
Handle	1	1″ × 1″ × 3½″	Walnut
Shaft	1	½″ dia. × 4″	Birch dowel*
Square			
Handle	1	¾″ × 1½″ × 4″	Cherry
Blade	1	¼″ × 1¼″ × 7″	Oak
Pliers blanks	2	¾″ × 1¼″ × 7¼″	Birch plywood
Saw			
Blade	1	¼″ × 1½″ × 7″	Oak
Handle	1	¾″ × 3½″ × 4″	Cherry
Screwdriver			
Handle	1	1″ × 1″ × 3½″	Walnut
Blade	1	½″ dia. × 4″	Birch dowel*
Drill			
Chuck	1	1½″ dia. × 1¾″	Ash dowel*
Handle	1	1″ × 1″ × 3½″	Walnut
Shaft	1	⅝″ dia. × 4″	Birch dowel*
Bit	1	½″ dia. × 2″	Birch dowel*

Hardware

Tool box
    4 wood screws, #6 × 1¼″
    4 wood plugs, ⅜″ dia.
    14 finishing nails, 4d
Square
    2 brass nails, ½″
Pliers
    1 axle peg, ¼″ dia. Available from Cherry Tree Toys, Inc., P.O. Box 369, Belmont, OH 43718
        (1-800-848-4363). Part #4.
Saw
    2 brass nails, ½″
Drill
    1 wheel, ⅝″ × 2″ dia. Available from Cherry Tree Toys. Part #40.
    2 axle pegs, ⁵⁄₁₆″. Available from Cherry Tree Toys. Part #10.

*Available from Cherry Tree Toys.

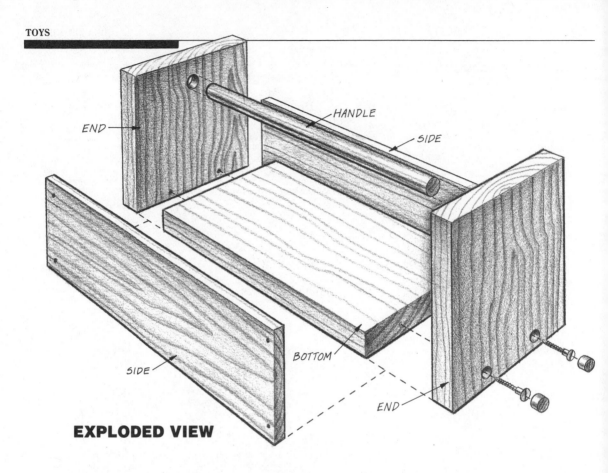

END

HANDLE

SIDE

SIDE

BOTTOM

END

EXPLODED VIEW

1 Make the tool box. Joint the tool box parts flat and smooth, plane them to the thicknesses specified by the Cutting List, and saw them to length and width.

The parts are joined together with simple butt joints, then glued and nailed or screwed, as shown in the *Side View* and *End View.* Lay out the screw holes in the ends. Drill counterbores ³⁄₁₆ inch deep at the layout marks. Drill ⁹⁄₆₄-inch screw shank holes for #6 screws centered in the counterbores.

Lay out and drill the stopped handle holes in the box ends. Make sure you drill them in the sides opposite the screw counterbores.

Finish sand the inside surfaces of the box parts. Hold the box bottom in a vise with an end sticking up. Hold a box end in place on the bottom and drill a pilot hole in the bottom through one of the shank holes in the end. Glue and screw the end in place, then drill the second pilot hole and install the second screw. Assemble the second box end in the same way, this time inserting the handle into the handle holes when you screw the end in place.

Lay the assembled parts on the bench and put one of the sides in position. Lay out the nail locations, as shown in the *Side View.* Select a twist drill slightly smaller in diameter than a 4d nail

234

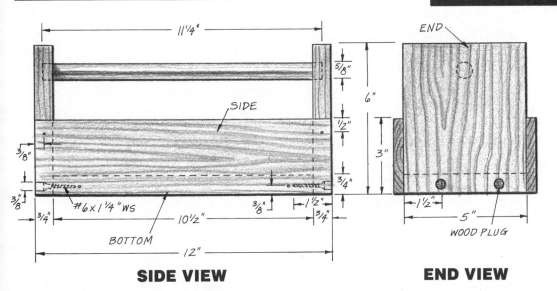

SIDE VIEW   **END VIEW**

and chuck it in your drill. Hold the side flush with the bottom and one end and drill a pilot hole at one of the nail locations. Apply glue to the mating surfaces and nail the side in place with a 4d finishing nail in the pilot hole. Check that the edges are still flush, then drill the remaining pilot holes and drive in the remaining nails. Turn the assembly over and install the second side in the same way.

Cut screw hole plugs out of matching scrap with a plug cutter on the drill press and plug the screw holes. If you don't have a plug cutter, buy plugs at a hardware store or from Cherry Tree Toys (address in Cutting List).

2 **Make the wrench.** If you happen to have a piece of elm, use it for the wrench. Elm is more resistant to

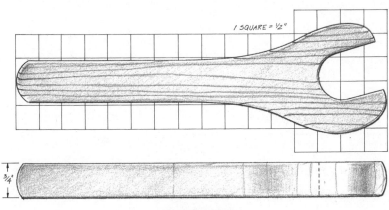

WRENCH

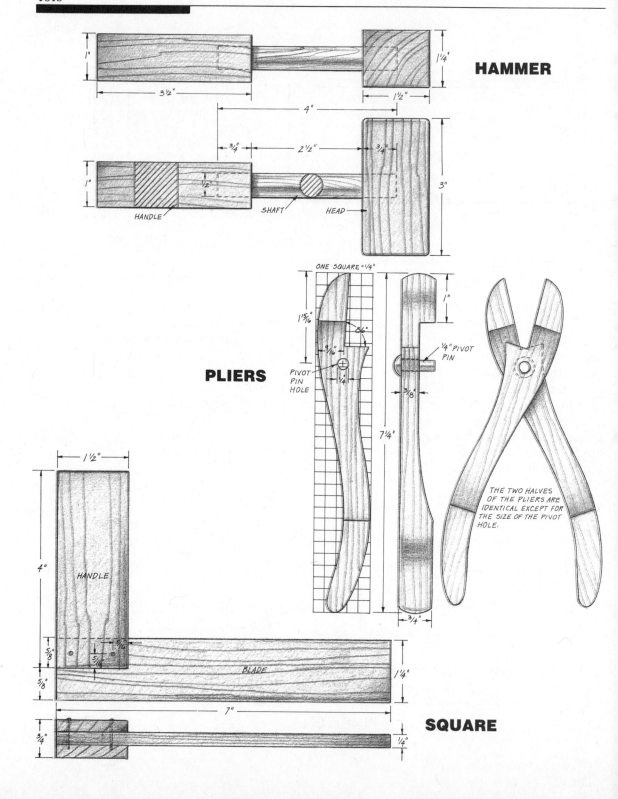

HAMMER

HANDLE

SHAFT

HEAD

PLIERS

ONE SQUARE = 1/4"

1 5/16"

8°

9/16"

1/4

PIVOT
PIN
HOLE

1/4" PIVOT
PIN

3/8"

7 1/4"

3/4"

1"

THE TWO HALVES
OF THE PLIERS ARE
IDENTICAL EXCEPT FOR
THE SIZE OF THE PIVOT
HOLE.

1 1/2"

HANDLE

4"

5/8"

5/16"

3/16"

5/8"

BLADE

1 1/4"

7"

3/4"

1/4"

SQUARE

splitting than most woods. Plane the blank smooth on both sides, then lay out the wrench pattern on the blank. Drill a 1-inch-diameter hole to create the back of the wrench jaws or throat. This makes a nice clean curve requiring little sanding. Saw out the wrench with a coping saw or scroll saw. Clean up the sawed edges with a file and sandpaper. Round the edges somewhat for the feel of a real wrench.

3 **Make the hammer.** Saw out the hammer head and handle and plane all of the surfaces smooth. Drill the shaft holes in the hammer head and handle as shown in the *Hammer* drawing. Check the fit of the shaft in the holes. It must not be too tight or you risk splitting the wood when you glue the hammer together. If the fit is very tight, sand the shaft down slightly. Glue the hammer together. When the glue is dry, sand the hammer, rounding the edges of the head and handle.

4 **Make the square.** Carefully made out of stable wood, this square can be a working tool, not just a toy. Plane the parts to uniform thickness and saw them to the dimensions shown in the *Square* drawing. Cut the slot in the handle of the square in two or three passes with a tenoning jig on the table saw. Back up the handle with a scrap piece of wood in the tenoning jig to prevent tear-out as the blade exits.

Sand the two parts of the square. Apply glue to the slot in the handle and insert the blade. Drill a small hole in the handle for one of the brass nails that

hold the blade and drive in the nail. Check that the blade is square to the handle with a second square or drafting triangle, then drill and drive the second nail.

5 **Make the pliers.** The pliers are the only tool in this set made from plywood. Hardwoods tend to split if any pressure is applied to the plier handles. Use a thin-veneer birch plywood with no voids, such as Finnish birch, Baltic birch, Apple-ply, or die board. Make a pattern for a pliers half, including the pivot pin hole, and trace two halves on your blanks.

Drill the pivot pin holes in the blanks. For the pliers to work properly, the pivot pin must fit loosely through one hole and tightly in the other. Drill both holes at 1/4-inch diameter, then ream one of them with sandpaper wrapped around a 3/16-inch dowel until the pivot pin turns easily in it.

Lay out the half-lap shown in the *Pliers* drawing edge view on both blanks. Be sure to lay it out so the lap cutout doesn't cut away the outline on the side. The two sides must be identical, not symmetrical. Saw out the lap with a coping saw or scroll saw and clean up the cut with files and sandpaper. Saw out the outline and clean up the sawed edges. Round the edges of the pliers slightly with sandpaper.

To assemble the pliers, insert the pivot peg through the reamed hole in one plier half and glue it in the snug-fitting hole in the other half. Use a minimal amount of glue so squeeze-out doesn't glue the pivoting half.

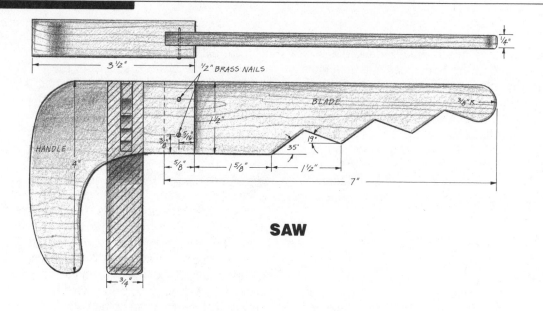

SAW

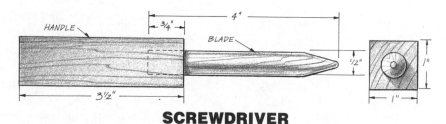

SCREWDRIVER

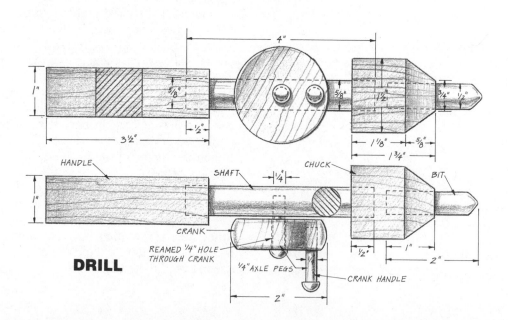

DRILL

6 **Make the saw.** Plane the two saw parts to the thicknesses specified by the Cutting List and saw them to the given dimensions. The blade fits in a slot in the saw handle. Saw this slot in two or three passes on the table saw. Adjust the blade to cut ⅝ inch deep and clamp the fence ¼ inch from the blade for the first cut. Readjust the fence to make additional cuts as needed to widen the groove to fit the blade.

Cut the handle and blade to shape with a coping saw or scroll saw. Clean up the sawed edges with files and sandpaper, rounding-over the handle edges slightly.

To assemble the saw, glue the blade into the slot in the handle. Drill a small hole in the handle for one of the brass nails that hold the blade and drive in the nail. Check that the top of the blade is in line with the top of the handle, then drill and drive the second nail.

7 **Make the screwdriver.** Plane the sides of the handle smooth, then drill the hole for the blade. Test the fit of the screwdriver blade in the hole. If the fit is very snug, sand the end of the

dowel slightly so the blade slides easily into the hole.

Glue the blade into the handle of the screwdriver. Sand or carve a blunt point on the end of the screwdriver blade so it looks a bit like the end of a crayon. Or, sand a flat tip like a screwdriver for slotted screws if you prefer. Sand the rest of the screwdriver to ease sharp edges.

8 **Make the drill.** If you have a lathe, you can turn the handle, shaft, chuck, and bit all in one piece, making the handle round instead of square. Just follow the dimensions shown in the *Drill* drawing.

To make the drill without a lathe, begin with the chuck. Square the end of a piece of 1½-inch-diameter dowel by sawing it off on the table saw. Scribe a line around the dowel ⅝ inch from the squared end with a marking gauge. Mark the center of the squared end. Scribe a ¾-inch-diameter circle in the squared end. This is easy to do with a ¾-inch-diameter brad-point drill bit. Place the pilot of the bit at the penciled center mark and scribe the circle with the spur of the bit. Clamp the dowel in a vise. With a block plane, chamfer the end from the mark scribed with the marking gauge to the mark scribed with the drill bit. When you've removed most of the waste with the plane, finish up with a file and sandpaper. When you're happy with the chamfer, saw the chuck from the end of the dowel.

Drill holes for the shaft, as shown in the *Drill* drawing. Drill the hole for the bit in the chamfered end of the chuck. Make sure the shaft and bit fit easily into these holes. Round the nose of the drill

SHOP TIP: When gluing dowels into drilled holes, make sure the excess glue can escape from the hole as the dowel is seated. If the fit is loose, the glue can escape up the sides of the dowel. If the fit is tight, carve one or two small vent grooves along the dowel for the depth of the hole. The vent grooves will relieve the pneumatic pressure created by the pistonlike dowel.

bit with a rasp or sandpaper.

Drill a ¼-inch hole in the center of the crank, then ream it with sandpaper wrapped around a ³⁄₁₆-inch dowel so it turns easily around a ¼-inch axle peg. Drill a ¼-inch hole for the crank handle in the outside edge of the crank. Set the shaft in a small V-block on the drill press and drill the ¼-inch hole for the axle.

Sand the drill parts, then glue the drill shaft into the handle and chuck. Glue the drill bit into the chuck. Glue the crank handle into its hole on the crank. Finally, insert the axle through the crank and glue it into the hole in the shaft. Make sure the crank wheel turns easily.

9 Apply a finish. To complete the child's tool box and tools, apply a nontoxic finish. Darryl uses vegetable oil. Mineral oil also works well. Rub the oil in with your hands. Let it soak into the wood and, after several minutes, wipe away any remaining oil. Repeat the process the next day. You can touch up the tools any time with another coat of oil if they begin to appear dry or worn.

HELICOPTER

Helicopters are every bit as much fun as airplanes. They have a distinctive sound and kids often see them up closer because they fly slower and lower.

This little model, designed by Darryl Yeager of Bellwood, Pennsylvania, can be held nicely in the hand. The propellers turn, giving the toy a greater realism. You can choose the wood you like to make the helicopter, but the cherry, walnut, and birch that Darryl uses are attractive, strong hardwoods that result in a colorful toy.

1 Select the stock and cut the parts. Ripping and planing parts as small as the helicopter parts is not safe with most machines. So, rip and plane larger pieces of wood and then work with hand tools after cutting the parts to size.

To cut out the ¼ × ¼-inch landing gear and cross supports, begin with a piece of ¾-inch-thick stock about 1 foot long. Adjust the blade height to ⅜ inch and clamp the fence ⁹⁄₃₂ inch from the blade. Saw a kerf into the edge of the stock with the face of the stock against the fence. Turn the stock end for end, hold the edge with the kerf against the fence, and saw out the corner of the stock. When the corner is freed at the end of the cut, it will be between the blade and the fence and could shoot back at you. For your protection, push the

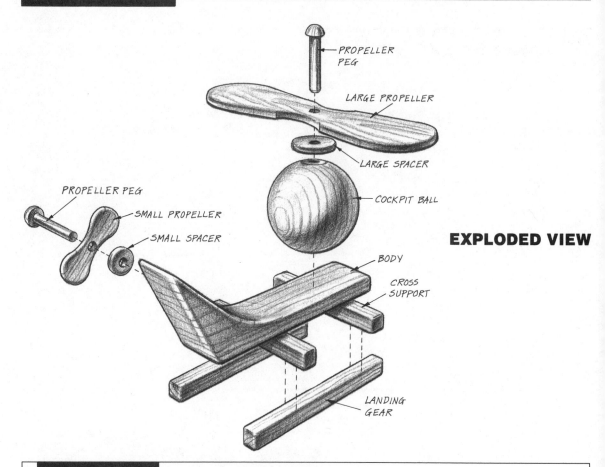

PROPELLER PEG

LARGE PROPELLER

LARGE SPACER

COCKPIT BALL

PROPELLER PEG

SMALL PROPELLER

SMALL SPACER

BODY

CROSS SUPPORT

EXPLODED VIEW

LANDING GEAR

CUTTING LIST

Part	Quantity	Dimensions	Comments
Large propeller	1	$1/8'' \times 7/8'' \times 4''$	Walnut
Small propeller	1	$1/8'' \times 1/2'' \times 1\,3/8''$	Walnut
Large spacer	1	$1/8'' \times 3/4''$ dia.	Birch
Small spacer	1	$1/8'' \times 1/2''$ dia.	Birch
Body	1	$3/4'' \times 1\,1/2'' \times 4''$	Cherry
Cross supports	2	$1/4'' \times 1/4'' \times 2''$	Cherry
Landing gear	2	$1/4'' \times 1/4'' \times 2\,3/4''$	Walnut

Hardware

1 cherry ball, $1\,1/2''$ dia. Available from Cherry Tree Toys, Inc., P.O. Box 369, Belmont, OH 43718. Part #46.

2 birch pegs, $7/32'' \times 1\,1/16'' \times 3/8''$. Available from Cherry Tree Toys. Part #2.

stock with a piece of scrap held against the fence, pushing the stock and the freed corner all the way past the blade. Plane the saw marks from the small corner piece, reducing it to $\frac{1}{4} \times \frac{1}{4}$ inch. Crosscut the landing gear and cross supports from the planed 1-foot-long piece.

Rip the propeller and spacer stock from the edge of a piece of wood as thick as the width of the helicopter parts. Be generous with the length; it's a lot easier to handle a piece 1 foot long

than it is to handle a piece only a few inches long. Rip them a bit oversize, then hand plane them to $\frac{1}{8}$ inch thick, removing the saw marks. Don't cut the parts to length yet.

If you turn the cockpit ball yourself, prepare a $2 \times 2 \times 2$-inch blank to make the turning easier.

2 **Make the props and spacers.**
Make a paper pattern for the two

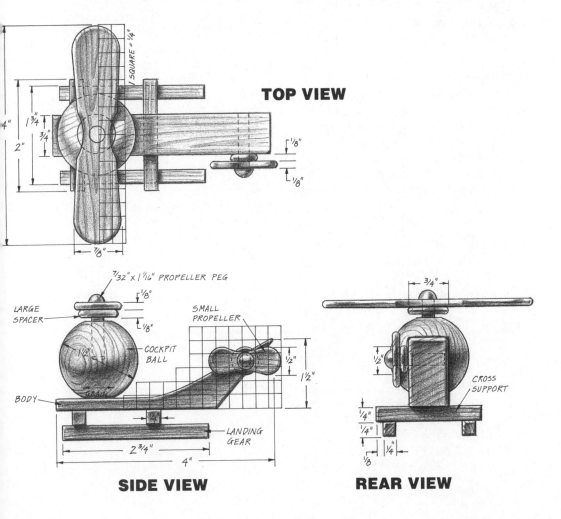

TOP VIEW

SIDE VIEW

REAR VIEW

propellers, as shown in the *Top View* and *Side View*. Trace them onto the stock with carbon paper. Be sure to mark the hole centers. Draw the spacers directly on the stock with a compass. Drill the holes before cutting out the outlines. Drill the spacer holes the same diameter (⁷⁄₃₂ inch) as the propeller pegs. Drill the propeller holes ¼ inch in diameter so the propellers will spin freely.

Saw out the propellers and spacers with a coping saw or scroll saw. Smooth the sawed edges with a file and sandpaper. Round the edges slightly.

3 Turn the cockpit ball. If you have a lathe and want to turn the ball instead of buying one, chuck the 2 × 2 × 2 blank in the lathe with the lathe centers in the side grain. Turn a 1½-inch-diameter round ball and sand it smooth. Saw off the spigots where the lathe centers held the ball.

4 Flatten and drill the cockpit ball. The cockpit ball needs a small flat on the top and bottom where it joins the propeller and body. If you turned your own ball, put the flats where you sawed off the spigots. If you bought a ball, be sure to locate the flats on the side grain so the ball will glue well to the body.

Sand the flats to a diameter of about ⁵⁄₈ inch. A disk or belt sander works well for this, but sandpaper over a hardwood block will also do just fine.

Mark the center of one of the flats for a hole for the propeller peg. Drill the hole ⁷⁄₃₂ inch diameter × ⅞ inch deep.

5 Cut out and drill the helicopter body. Make a paper pattern of the helicopter body profile and center of the rear propeller peg from the *Side View*. Trace it onto the stock with carbon paper. Drill the ⁷⁄₃₂-inch hole for the peg first, then saw out the body with a coping saw or band saw. Sand out the saw marks. Round the nose and the tail fin of the body with sandpaper if you like.

6 Assemble the helicopter. Finish sand all the parts of the helicopter. Start the assembly by gluing and clamping the cross supports to the helicopter body. Then glue and clamp the landing gear to the supports. When they are dry, glue and clamp the cockpit ball to the helicopter body. The exact position is not critical, just keep it centered on the body.

Brush some glue into the propeller peg hole in the ball. Slip the propeller peg through the large prop, then push the peg through the large spacer. Position the spacer on the peg so the propeller spins freely but doesn't wobble excessively, then push the peg into the hole in the ball. Tap it down until the spacer just contacts the ball. Glue the small propeller peg into its hole as you did the large one.

7 Apply a nontoxic finish. The finish you choose must be nontoxic. Darryl uses vegetable oil. It works well and is safe. Mineral oil also works well. Rub the oil into the wood several days in a row and again whenever the toy begins to look dry.

DOLL BED WITH STORAGE CHEST

DOLL BED WITH STORAGE CHEST

When Jean Nick of Kintnersville, Pennsylvania, heard through the grapevine that Santa was bringing a doll to her daughter, she decided that it needed its own home. It didn't need a doll *house*. It needed a *chest* that would store the doll together with its clothes and other accessories. But since a storage chest by itself might not capture the enduring interest of her daughter, Jean made a bed for the doll that just fit inside the chest. Now it made perfectly good sense for the doll to retire for the night in its bed, in its chest, together with all its accoutrements. *Voilà,* the seed of good housekeeping is planted.

Jean built a strong chest to withstand plenty of wear and tear. She used ¼-inch birch plywood almost exclusively. Since she doesn't have a shop, Jean designed it so she could build it with a few hand tools. The joinery consists mainly of butt joints glued and nailed with ¾-inch brads. To furnish the bed, Jean made a mattress and pillow from foam and covered them with cotton ticking.

This project was designed for an 18-inch doll. Alter the dimensions to suit the occupant, if necessary. If you decide you want a natural finish on your chest, you may want to choose a different hardwood plywood.

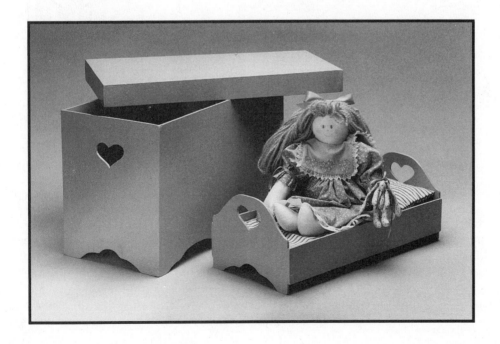

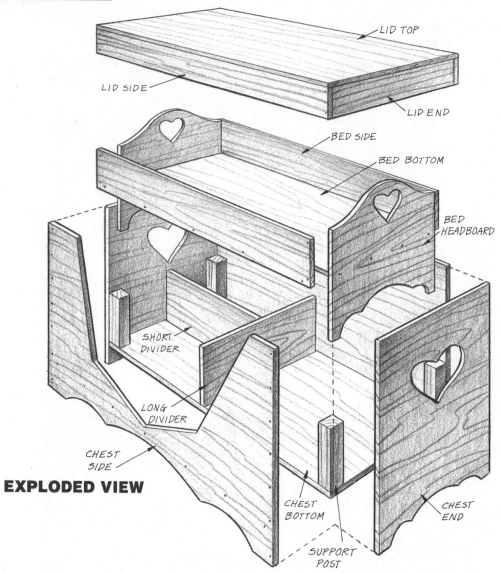

LID TOP

LID SIDE

LID END

BED SIDE

BED BOTTOM

BED HEADBOARD

SHORT DIVIDER

LONG DIVIDER

CHEST SIDE

CHEST BOTTOM

SUPPORT POST

CHEST END

EXPLODED VIEW

1 Cut the parts to size. All of the parts except the chest ends should have the grain running in the direction of the longest dimension. The chest ends should have the grain running in the direction of the 10-inch dimension. The *Layout Detail* shows an economical arrangement of the parts on a piece of plywood.

To minimize the amount of layout and sawing and account for the width of the saw kerfs, lay out the parts as you cut them. Begin with one long crosscut yielding a 21½ × 48-inch piece. Next, lay out the lid top and rip it off. Lay out a chest side and rip it off. Continue with the other chest side and the chest bottom. Trim the chest sides and chest bottom to length. Cut up the remaining piece of plywood in the same way, laying out a part and then ripping it off.

This procedure works well whether you are using a table saw, a portable power saw, or a handsaw. When you've cut all the plywood parts to size, smooth the edges with a file or sandpaper.

The only solid wood in the project is in the four support posts. For the preservation of your fingers, first rip a 16½-inch-long piece of wood to 1 × 1 inch, then crosscut it into four 4-inch-long pieces.

2 **Cut out the headboards and hearts.** Make paper patterns of the heart shapes from the *End View*. Trace the shapes onto the headboards and chest ends. Drill a starting hole inside each heart near the outline. Insert the

CUTTING LIST

Part	Quantity	Dimensions	Comments
Chest sides	2	¼″ × 13″ × 20¾″	Hardwood plywood
Chest ends	2	¼″ × 13″ × 10″	Hardwood plywood
Chest bottom	1	¼″ × 10″ × 20¼″	Hardwood plywood
Support posts	4	1″ × 1″ × 4″	Solid wood
Long divider	1	¼″ × 4″ × 10″	Hardwood plywood
Short divider	1	¼″ × 4″ × 9″	Hardwood plywood
Bed headboard/footboard	2	¼″ × 7″ × 9″	Hardwood plywood
Bed bottom	1	¼″ × 9″ × 19¼″	Hardwood plywood
Bed sides	2	¼″ × 3″ × 19¾″	Hardwood plywood
Lid end	2	¼″ × 2″ × 10¾″	Hardwood plywood
Lid sides	2	¼″ × 2″ × 21½″	Hardwood plywood
Lid top	1	¼″ × 11¼″ × 21½″	Hardwood plywood

Hardware

¾″ brads

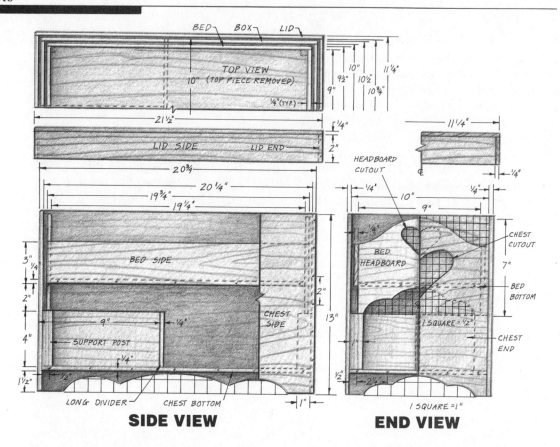

SIDE VIEW

END VIEW

blade through the hole and saw out each heart. Both coping saws and saber saws work well for these cuts. Clean up the sawed edges with files or sandpaper.

3 Cut the curves on the headboards and chest sides. Make paper patterns of the headboard and the bottom edges of the chest sides and ends from the *End View* and *Side View*. Trace the patterns onto their respective parts and saw to the traced lines. When cutting the scallops, cut one scallop and continue the sweep of the cut all the way to the edge. Remove that scrap of wood and then begin the next scallop cut. Clean up the sawed edges as before.

4 Lay out positioning lines. Sand the chest pieces. Draw a line on both the inside and outside of both the chest sides and ends 1½ inches from the bottom edge of the pieces. These lines show where to position the chest bottom and where to drive the brads that hold the bottom. Lay out a similar line on the inside of one of the chest ends to position the divider. This divider layout line should be ⅛ inch from the center, 4 inches long, starting at the bottom line. Put Xs on the center side of the line. The drawings shows the position of the divider. Lay out corresponding lines and Xs on both sides of the long divider, ⅛ inch from the center.

5 **Glue the chest ends to the bottom.** Drive two brads through each chest end ⅛ inch above the line on the outside and about ½ inch in from each edge. Tap them until the points just break the inside surface. Clamp the chest bottom in a vise. Put a small bead of glue along the end of the bottom. Put another small bead of glue just above the inside layout line on one of the end pieces. Position the end piece on the bottom so the bottom lines up with the inside layout line. Tap the brads home. Space three more brads evenly between the first two. This is the basic procedure for assembling the rest of the chest, the lid, and the bed. Repeat the procedure now with the second end.

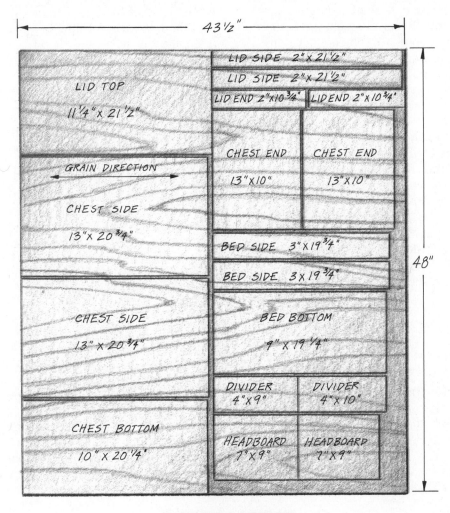

LAYOUT DETAIL

6 **Add the sides of the chest.** Lay the chest bottom and end assembly on its side on the workbench. Glue and nail on a chest side using the same procedure that you used for the ends. This time there will be three edges to glue instead of only one. Nail the sides to the bottom and both ends. The brads should be evenly spaced, about 2 inches apart, starting ½ to ¾ inch from the ends. Keep the parts flush at the corners as you go and be sure to align the bottom with the layout line. When you've finished one side, install the other.

Wipe up all of the squeezed-out glue with a clean damp rag.

7 **Glue the support posts in the chest.** The bed support posts fit in each corner of the chest. Sand the blocks and glue them in place. Clamping them would be difficult, but you can get a reasonably good bond by sliding the blocks up and down about ½ inch while applying moderate pressure. Support the outside of the chest as you do this. After a moment the sliding becomes more difficult and the block will grab. Push the block down in the corner and leave it. Clean up the excess glue after 5 to 10 minutes.

8 **Glue the dividers in the bottom of the chest.** The dividers form a T in the bottom of the chest. Glue and nail the dividers together following the procedure you used to assemble the rest of the chest.

Put a bead of glue along the bottom edge of the two dividers and set them in place in the chest. Be sure to line them up on the sides of the lines marked with Xs. Weight them down until the glue sets.

9 **Glue together the bed.** Glue the bed pieces together the same way that you assembled the chest. Lay out positioning lines across each headboard at the level of the bed bottom. Glue and nail the headboards to the bed bottom, then add the sides.

10 **Make the lid.** The lid should have ⅛-inch clearance all around the chest. To double-check the fit, tape the lid together with masking tape. Put it upside down on the workbench and put the upside down chest inside it. Trim the parts if necessary, or replace parts if anything has gone seriously awry.

Assemble the lid ends and sides with glue and two brads at each corner. Put this assembly on the workbench and glue and nail the lid top to it. Four inches apart is close enough for the brads holding the lid top.

11 **Apply a finish.** Jean painted her bed and chest. Spray paint in a can is a particularly convenient way to paint a project with lots of small parts like this one. If you prefer a natural finish, choose one that hardens, like shellac or polyurethane. Oil finishes sometimes bleed and could stain the doll or its accessories.

LIMBERJACK

This traditional mountain toy came to us from Bobbie Ralphs of Greenlane, Pennsylvania. It may not look like it can do much, but it can dance like nobody's business. Sit on one end of the paddle and insert the handle into the hole in the limberjack's back. Let him dangle with his feet just touching the paddle. Now with your other hand, lightly tap the paddle to make it bounce, and watch the limberjack go. He even seems to make his own music.

With the limberjack's limbs loosely jointed, his movement is free and easy. Oak, as shown in the photo, is a good choice of wood, but other hardwoods also work well. You can be as creative as you like in putting a face and clothes on your dancer. If you want to paint him, do it before the final assembly.

1 **Select the stock and cut the parts.** Choose wood for the limberjack that is dry and free of knots. Resaw the stock to just over the required thickness. Plane it smooth and to thickness before cutting it to the sizes specified by the Cutting List. See "Resawing on the Table Saw" on page 13 for resawing step-by-step instructions. Resaw stock for the paddle first. If you start with 4/4 (four-quarter) stock, the remainder after sawing off the paddle should be more than thick enough for the remaining parts. Prepare one piece for both upper legs and one for both lower legs, as shown in the *Leg Joint Detail*.

2 **Drill the pivot pin hole in the body.** Lay out the ⅛-inch-diameter hole through the lower edge of the limberjack body. Set the body blank on edge on the drill press table and make certain it is 90 degrees to the table surface. Drill halfway through the body. Set the body on the other edge and lay out and drill halfway through again. If the two holes don't meet perfectly, don't worry about it. You'll attach the legs with separate dowels, one from each edge, just as you drilled the holes.

3 **Notch the body for the legs.** Cut the leg notches in the body with a dado blade on the table saw. The dimen-

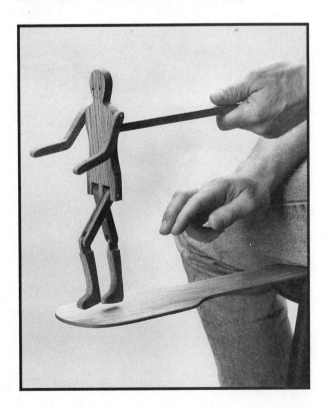

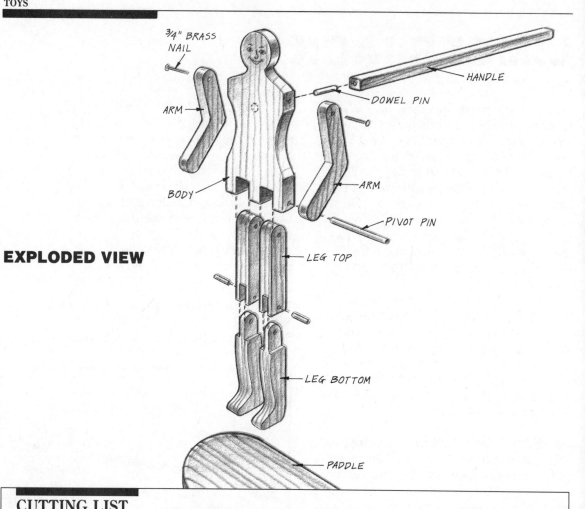

EXPLODED VIEW

Labels: ¾" BRASS NAIL, ARM, BODY, HANDLE, DOWEL PIN, ARM, PIVOT PIN, LEG TOP, LEG BOTTOM, PADDLE

CUTTING LIST

Part	Quantity	Dimensions	Comments
Body	1	$\frac{7}{16}'' \times 2'' \times 5\frac{7}{16}''$	Oak
Arms	2	$\frac{5}{16}'' \times 1'' \times 3\frac{3}{8}''$	Oak
Leg tops	2	$\frac{7}{16}'' \times \frac{7}{16}'' \times 2\frac{3}{4}''$	Oak
Leg bottoms	2	$\frac{7}{16}'' \times 1\frac{1}{8}'' \times 3''$	Oak
Handle	1	$\frac{3}{8}'' \times \frac{7}{16}'' \times 12\frac{5}{8}''$	Oak
Dowel pin	1	$\frac{3}{16}''$ dia. $\times 1''$	Hardwood dowel
Paddle	1	$\frac{3}{16}'' \times 4'' \times 23\frac{1}{2}''$	Oak
Pivot pin stock	1	$\frac{1}{8}''$ dia. $\times 5''$	Hardwood dowel

Hardware

2 brass nails, ¾"

sions are given in the *Front View.* Clamp the body upright against an auxiliary fence screwed to the miter gauge to make the cuts. Cut one notch, then reposition the limberjack body, reclamp it, and cut the second notch.

4 **Cut the body to shape.** Lay out the limberjack body shape on the body blank. Saw the body to shape with a coping saw or scroll saw. Clean up the sawed edges with files and sandpaper. Round-over the outside edges of the body slightly.

5 **Drill the hole for the handle dowel.** Drill a ³⁄₁₆-inch hole in the back of the limberjack's body for the handle dowel. Drill the hole ³⁄₈ inch deep, which leaves only ¹⁄₁₆ inch of wood between the hole and the front of the body. Use a Forstner bit, if you have one, to avoid a hole from the pilot of a bit showing on the front of the body. (The pilot hole would be too high to pass off as a navel.)

6 **Make the arms.** Lay out the arm pattern on the arm blanks. Saw the arms to shape and clean up the sawed edges as you did for the body. Drill a small hole in each arm for the brass nails that hold the arms to the body. The hole should be slightly larger than the diameter of the nail so the arm can swing freely.

7 **Drill the legs for the pivot pins.** Lay out the holes for the pivot pins in the top and bottom leg sections, as shown in the *Leg Joint Detail.* Drill the holes to the diameters shown. Note that two different size holes are required.

8 **Cut the knee joint in the legs.** The knee joint is really a loose-fitting open mortise-and-tenon joint. Because the pieces are short, cut the joints before you cut the leg pieces to length, as shown in the *Leg Joint Detail.* Lay out the bottom leg and foot shapes on the lower leg blank. Then lay out the mortise cuts on the top leg blank and the tenon cuts on the bottom leg blank.

Cut the joint with a tenoning jig on the table saw. First make the ³⁄₁₆-inch mortises on both ends of the top leg blank.

Crosscut the tenon shoulders on the bottom leg blank with the miter gauge. Stand the blank on end in the tenoning jig to cut the cheeks of the tenons. Make sure the tenons fit loosely in the mortises. Saw the lower legs to shape and clean up the edges, then saw the top legs to length. Sand the blanks, rounding all the edges slightly. Use sandpaper around a hardwood block to radius the ends of the legs, as shown in the drawing.

9 **Make the limberjack handle.** The handle is a straight length of wood with a dowel in one end. The dowel fits in a hole in the back of the limberjack so you can hold him above the paddle as he dances. Cut the handle to length. Drill a ³⁄₁₆ × ⁵⁄₈-inch-deep hole centered in one end of the handle. Glue a piece of ³⁄₁₆-inch-diameter dowel in the hole, then cut it off so it won't quite reach the bottom of the hole in the back of the limberjack. Sand the handle, rounding the edges slightly.

10 **Make the paddle.** Draw the paddle pattern on the paddle blank. Saw it to shape, then file and sand the edges clean. Sand the paddle, rounding the edges slightly.

11 **Apply the finish.** If you want to use a finish that builds a film on the surface, like paint or polyurethane, apply it before assembling the limberjack. After applying each coat of finish, before it begins to set, clear all of the pivot holes with a pipe cleaner. If you're using a clear finish, draw or paint the limberjack's face before applying the finish but test to make sure the finish won't cause the drawing to run. Let the finish dry completely before assembly.

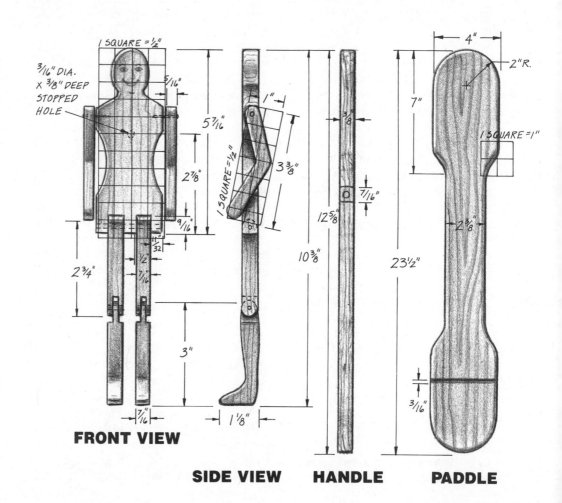

FRONT VIEW **SIDE VIEW** **HANDLE** **PADDLE**

LEG JOINT DETAIL

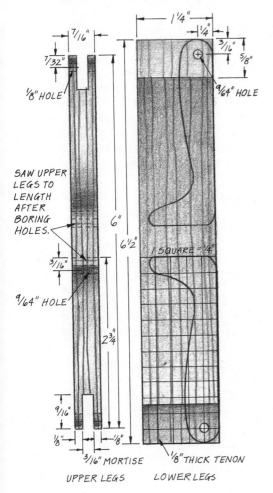

SAW UPPER
LEGS TO
LENGTH
AFTER
BORING
HOLES.

7/16"

7/32"

1/8" HOLE

6"

6½"

3/16"

9/64" HOLE

2¾"

9/16"

1/8"

3/16" MORTISE

UPPER LEGS

1¼"

1/4"

3/16"

5/8"

9/64" HOLE

1 SQUARE = ¼"

1/8" THICK TENON

LOWER LEGS

12 **Attach the arms and legs to the body.** The arms pivot on nails. Predrill a pilot hole in the body for each arm nail to prevent splitting the thin body. This hole must be smaller than the diameter of the nail but not by much. Nail the arms to the body but not tightly; leave plenty of clearance so the arms will swing freely.

To assemble the legs, start short pieces of ⅛-inch dowel through the mortises in the upper legs. Slip the lower leg tenons in place as the dowels start to enter the mortises, then tap the dowels through until they enter the other side of the mortises. Dab some glue in the remaining portion of the dowel hole before tapping the dowel home.

Start a ⅛-inch dowel through one of the dowel pin holes in the bottom edge of the limberjack body. Assemble the leg to the body the same way you assembled the top and bottom legs. Make sure the foot is frontward and drive the dowel only halfway into the center section of the body. Attach the second leg in the same way, right away, before the glue in the center section dries. Test to make certain the leg sections move freely. Sand off the pivot pins where they protrude from the body and legs.

HAND-HELD TABLE TENNIS

All right, sports fans, here it is: table tennis for one. Hold the paddle in one hand and bounce the ball back and forth from one side of the net to the other by turning the paddle. "Easy job!" you say? Try keeping it going during an entire NFL commercial break. You're better than that? A fiver says you can't keep it going for a Super Bowl halftime.

Bobbie Ralphs of Greenland, Pennsylvania, makes the paddle and handle from cherry. The net consists of birch dowels. If you've only got an hour before game time, you could use plywood for the paddle, but a game of this class really deserves solid hardwood.

1 Select the stock and cut the parts. Resaw a 7½-inch-wide piece of cherry to just over ⅜ inch thick for the paddle. See "Resawing on the Table Saw" on page 13 for step-by-step instructions. You'll have to saw the last 1½ inches by hand. Saw the paddle and handle pieces to the dimensions specified by the Cutting List and plane off the saw marks. Saw out a piece ⅜ × ⅜ × several inches long for the net posts, then cut them to length. Saw the dowels for other net parts to length.

2 Drill the net holes. To lay out the holes for the net post pins and netting, draw a centerline across the paddle, dividing it into two courts. Mark the position of the net post pins and netting dowels on the line, as shown in the *Top View*. Drill the ³⁄₁₆-inch holes for the posts and the ¹⁄₁₆-inch holes for the netting on the drill press.

3 Bevel the end of the handle. Draw the bevel on the end of the handle and saw to the line on the band saw. Sand or plane the bevel smooth.

4 Sand and assemble the paddle and handle. Lay out the rounded corners of the paddle and saw to the outside of the lines. Sand the paddle and the handle. Soften the edges of both pieces. The handle should be comfortable to grip.

Glue and clamp the handle to the bottom of the paddle, as shown in the drawings.

5 Pin the handle to the paddle.
Drill two $\frac{3}{16}$-inch holes through the paddle and into the handle, as shown in the *Top View* and *Side View*. Glue the handle pins into the holes to reinforce the glue bond between the handle and

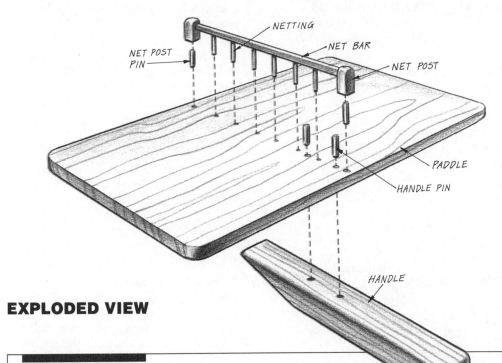

EXPLODED VIEW

CUTTING LIST

Part	Quantity	Dimensions	Comments
Paddle	1	$\frac{3}{8}'' \times 7\frac{3}{16}'' \times 13\frac{1}{2}''$	Cherry
Handle	1	$\frac{3}{4}'' \times 1'' \times 8\frac{1}{2}''$	Cherry
Handle pins	2	$\frac{3}{16}''$ dia. $\times \frac{3}{4}''$	Birch dowel
Net posts	2	$\frac{3}{8}'' \times \frac{3}{8}'' \times \frac{13}{16}''$	Cherry
Net bar	1	$\frac{3}{16}''$ dia. $\times 6\frac{5}{8}''$	Birch dowel
Netting pieces	6	$\frac{1}{16}''$ dia. $\times \frac{3}{4}''$	Birch dowel
Net post pins	2	$\frac{3}{16}''$ dia. $\times \frac{5}{8}''$	Birch dowel

Hardware

1 regulation table tennis ball

the paddle. When the glue dries, sand the top of the pins flush with the top of the paddle.

6 **Make the net posts.** Drill the net posts to receive the net bar, as shown in the *Side View*. Mark the center of the bottom of the net posts and drill holes for the net post pins. Sand the net posts to round the top edges and soften the side edges.

7 **Drill the net bar for the netting.** Make a very shallow V-block to help lay out and drill the net bar dowel. Start with a piece of scrap about 8 inches long, flat and uniform in thickness. Tilt the table saw blade to 45 degrees and adjust the height of cut to ⅛ inch. Rip a ⅛-inch-deep groove in the piece of scrap.

Hold the net bar dowel in the V-block and use the edge of the groove as a straightedge to draw a line the length of the dowel. Lay out the holes for the netting along this line, as shown in the *Top View*. Tape the dowel in the V-block to keep it steady while you drill the holes. Set the depth stop on the drill press so you get holes of uniform depth.

8 **Assemble the net.** First, glue the netting pieces into the holes in the net bar. A tiny dab of glue applied to each hole with a toothpick is enough. Next, glue the net bar into the holes in the net posts. Make sure the netting is in the same plane as the net posts. Then glue the net post pins in the bottoms of the net posts. Now you are ready to glue the net to the paddle.

Put a tiny dab of glue in the netting holes in the paddle and coat the inside of the net post pin holes. Start the net post pins into their holes, then start the netting into the netting holes. When everything is aligned and started, tap or clamp them home.

9 **Apply a finish.** Complete the project by protecting it with a clear finish. Two or three coats of a penetrating oil like Danish oil are quick and easy to apply. If you prefer a film finish, an aerosol can of clear lacquer is convenient. Let the finish dry thoroughly before the opening game of the season.

TOP VIEW

SIDE VIEW

MARBLE TILT GAME

Some games look simple, fun, and relatively easy, and then slowly and inevitably drive you nuts. Welcome to the Marble Tilt.

The object of the game is simple enough. Just roll the marble from slat to slat by manipulating the control knobs on the bottom slat. When you get to the bottom slat, flip the marble up and through the basket on the side. Simple, eh? To make the game a little more interesting, the extended part of each slat, the part that catches the marble when it falls from the slat above, gets a little shorter with each successive slat. All in all, it's a diabolical device.

As you build the game, measure carefully. Make allowances for smoothing saw cuts, then sand the parts to exact finish dimensions. You'll rue the day you made a slat too short.

Bobbie Ralphs of Greenlane, Pennsylvania, makes the game out of cherry, with birch dowels and a birch plywood back. Choose a wood that pleases you; you'll be looking at it a lot.

1 **Select the stock and cut the parts.** Plane the stock flat and to uniform thickness for the sides, top, and bottom. Rip it to width and crosscut it to pieces about 1 inch longer than the final lengths specified by the Cutting List. The extra length will make it easier to cut the miters at the ends. Rip the ladder slat stock and arms from the edge of a ¾-inch-thick board. Plane the pieces smooth and to thickness, then crosscut the slats to the lengths shown on the

Front View. Sand the ends smooth and to the exact lengths specified by the Cutting List. Rip the basket piece to thickness and width but leave it several inches long for the time being. Saw the ¼-inch plywood backing board to size and cut all the pins to length.

2 **Cut the corner miters.** The corners of the frame are joined with doweled miters. To cut the miters, tilt your table saw blade to 45 degrees. Crosscut one end of each frame piece at a 45 degree angle. Use a stop block

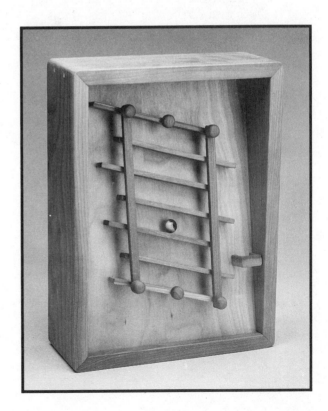

clamped to an auxiliary miter gauge fence when crosscutting the other ends to ensure that both sides are exactly the same length. Do the same for the top and bottom.

3 **Rout the groove for the backing board.** The backing board tilts back so the marble will stay on the slats. The groove for the backing board in the sides is therefore at an angle, as shown in the *Side View.* Lay out the groove on the outside of the frame sides, not the inside where the groove will actually go. Chuck a ¼-inch-straight bit in a table-mounted router and adjust the bit height to ¼ inch. Saw a scrap of ¼-inch plywood or hardboard to 4 inches × 1 foot or so. Adjust the router table fence so this scrap just fits between the bit and the fence. Stick the scrap alongside the groove layout with double-faced tape. Make sure the laid-out groove is outside the scrap, as shown in *Routing Angled Grooves.* Rout the groove with the scrap riding against the fence. Repeat for the other frame side.

Hold the top and bottom boards to the side boards to mark the location of the backing board groove. Rout the grooves on the router table with the fence in the conventional manner.

4 **Bevel the front of the bottom edge.** The small bevel on the front edge of the frame bottom prevents the marble from escaping when it falls from the slats. Hand plane the bevel, as shown in the *Side View.*

CUTTING LIST

Part	Quantity	Dimensions	Comments
Sides	2	$^{11}/_{16}'' \times 3^7/_8'' \times 13''$	Cherry
Top/bottom	2	$^{11}/_{16}'' \times 3^7/_8'' \times 10''$	Cherry
Backing board	1	$^1/_4'' \times 9^1/_8'' \times 12^1/_4''$	Birch plywood
Horizontal corner dowels	8	$^3/_{16}''$ dia. $\times 1''$	Birch dowel
Vertical corner dowels	4	$^1/_8''$ dia. $\times 1''$	Birch dowel
Basket	1	$^1/_2'' \times 1^1/_8'' \times 1^1/_8''$	Cherry
Ladder slat stock	1	$^7/_{32}'' \times 3/_4'' \times 45''$	Cherry
Ladder arms	2	$^1/_4'' \times 3/_8'' \times 8''$	Cherry
Control knobs	4	$^9/_{16}''$ dia. $\times 9/_{16}''$	Cherry
Pivot knobs	2	$^9/_{16}''$ dia. $\times 3/_8''$	Cherry
Control pins	4	$^1/_8''$ dia. $\times 1^3/_{16}''$	Birch dowel
Pivot pins	2	$^1/_8''$ dia. $\times 1^3/_8''$	Birch dowel
Arm pins	10	$^1/_8''$ dia. $\times 7/_8''$	Birch dowel

Hardware

1 marble

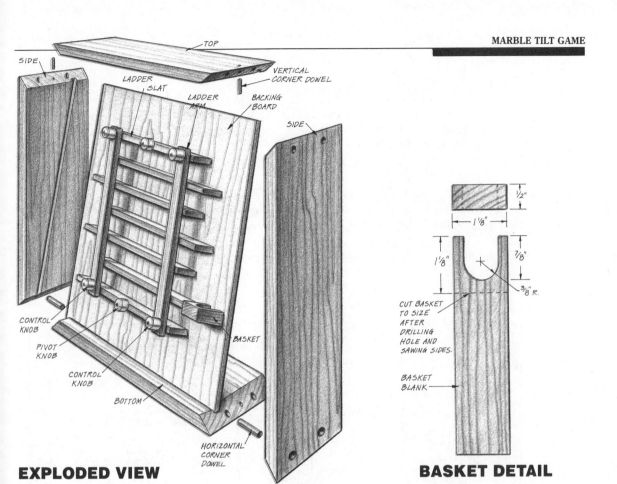

SIDE

TOP

VERTICAL
CORNER DOWEL

LADDER
SLAT

LADDER
ARM

BACKING
BOARD

SIDE

CONTROL
KNOB

PIVOT
KNOB

CONTROL
KNOB

BOTTOM

BASKET

HORIZONTAL
CORNER
DOWEL

EXPLODED VIEW

½"

1⅛"

1⅛"

⅞"

⅜" R.

CUT BASKET
TO SIZE
AFTER
DRILLING
HOLE AND
SAWING SIDES.

BASKET
BLANK

BASKET DETAIL

5 **Assemble the frame.** Sand the frame and backing board. Test assemble the frame with the backing board in place to check the fit. You may have to bevel the bottom front edge and the top back edge of the backing board with a block plane. When the fit is correct, glue and clamp the frame together around the backing board on a flat surface. A band clamp or two is the easiest way to clamp the miters tightly together.

If you don't have band clamps, glue the frame together, as shown in the *Miter Clamping Detail*. Glue the triangular clamping blocks to the frame boards with hot-melt glue. The glue will hold

the blocks during clamping, but the blocks can be pried off with a chisel after the glue in the frame is dry.

6 **Pin the frame miters.** Reinforce the miter joints with dowels in both directions. Lay out ³⁄₁₆-inch dowel holes through the frame sides and ⅛-inch dowel holes through the frame top and bottom. Drill the 1-inch-deep dowel holes on the drill press with brad-point bits.

Brush glue into the holes with a pipe cleaner and tap the dowels into the holes. Sand the ends of the dowels flush with the sides of the frame. Round-over the corners of the frame.

7 Make and install the basket.
Cut the hole in the basket blank before sawing it to length. Drill a ¾-inch-diameter hole in the blank, as shown in the *Basket Detail*. Saw the sides of the blank to open the hole, then clean up the sawed edges with a file and sandpaper. Crosscut the basket blank to length and finish sand it. Glue it in place, as shown in the *Front View*.

8 Apply the finish. Give all of the parts a final sanding, then apply two or three coats of penetrating oil finish. Wipe off any excess oil that is not absorbed into the wood.

9 Drill the holes in the ladder slats. The ladder slats and arms move as a parallelogram. For this to work, the dowels are glued in some of the holes but loose in others. The two

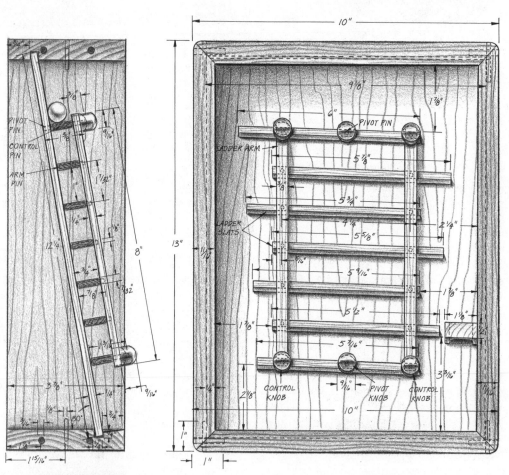

**SIDE VIEW
(NEAR SIDE REMOVED)**

FRONT VIEW

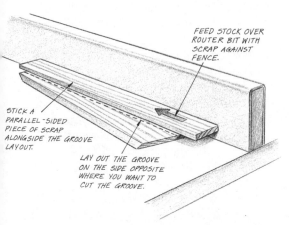

FEED STOCK OVER ROUTER BIT WITH SCRAP AGAINST FENCE.

STICK A PARALLEL-SIDED PIECE OF SCRAP ALONGSIDE THE GROOVE LAYOUT.

LAY OUT THE GROOVE ON THE SIDE OPPOSITE WHERE YOU WANT TO CUT THE GROOVE.

ROUTING ANGLED GROOVES

holes in each of the middle five slats are $9/64$ inch in diameter. The middle holes in the top and bottom slats are also $9/64$ inch in diameter. The remaining two holes in the top and bottom slats where the control knobs attach are $1/8$ inch in diameter. (Dowels are sometimes undersize. If your dowels turn freely in a $1/8$-inch hole, drill all your holes $1/8$ inch in diameter.)

Clamp a fence to the drill press table, as shown in the *Slat Hole Detail,* to position the slats. The fence will make it easier to keep the slats vertical and the holes centered.

Even though all of the slats are a different length, they all have the same hole layout. One hole is centered $5/16$ inch from an end and the other hole is $4^{1}/4$ inches from the first. Lay out the holes on one slat. Saw out a $4^{1}/4$-inch spacer and set up a stop on the fence, as shown in the *Slat Hole Detail.* Drill the end holes in the top and bottom slats with a $1/8$-inch diameter brad-point bit. Change to a $9/64$-inch diameter bit and drill the holes in the remaining slats. Still with the larger bit, drill the middle hole

in the top and bottom slats midway between the two end holes. Drill all of the holes all of the way through.

10 **Drill the holes in the ladder arms.** Lay out the holes in the ladder arms $1^{7}/32$ inches center to center. The easiest way to lay them out is to mark the midpoint of the 8-inch arm, then strike three successive arcs in both directions with a compass or dividers set to $1^{7}/32$ inches. Drill the middle five holes in each arm $1/8$ inch in diameter $\times$ $3/16$ inch deep. Drill the end holes $9/64$-inch diameter and go all the way through.

11 **Make the control knobs and pivot knobs.** You can make these knobs from purchased hardwood dowel or you can turn your own dowel. Either way, round the end of the dowel with sandpaper and then saw off a knob to the correct length. Repeat the rounding and sawing to make four $9/16$-inch-long knobs and two $3/8$-inch-long knobs.

To drill the flat end of the knobs for

MITER CLAMPING DETAIL

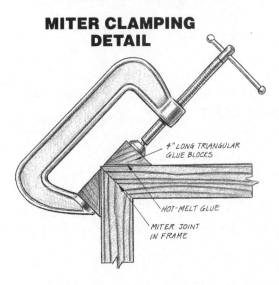

4" LONG TRIANGULAR GLUE BLOCKS

HOT-MELT GLUE

MITER JOINT IN FRAME

the pins, begin by drilling a shallow, $7/16$-inch-diameter hole in a piece of scrap. Cradle the rounded end of each knob in the shallow hole to steady it while drilling the pin hole on the drill press. Drill the control knob holes $1/8$ inch in diameter × $3/8$ inch deep. Drill the pivot knob holes $1/8$ inch in diameter × $5/16$ inch deep. Glue the pins in the knobs.

12 **Attach the control knobs to the ladder arms and slats.** Apply glue to the end holes of the top and bottom slats with a pipe cleaner. Arrange them on your workbench with the long end on the left, as shown in the *Front View.* Put the pins of the control knobs through the end holes of the arms, then tap them into the end holes of the top and bottom slats. Leave a bit of clearance between the knobs and the arms so the parts move freely.

13 **Attach the ladder to the backing board.** Set the arm and slat assembly inside the frame and position it as shown in the *Front View.* Put a small

nail through the middle hole in the top and bottom slats. Tap the nails lightly to mark the location of the pivot pin holes. Drill the $1/8$-inch holes by hand at 90 degrees to the backing board.

Glue the arm pins into the middle five holes in each arm. Put glue in the holes only. Slip the slats over the arm pins and set the completed ladder in place on the backing board inside the frame. Double-check the slat arrangement. The slats decrease in length from top to bottom and the long ends alternate left and right. Put glue in the pivot pin holes, then slip the pivot pins through the center holes in the top and bottom slats and into the holes in the backing board. Push the pivot pins in until the parts have just enough clearance to turn freely.

14 **Apply a finish to the knobs.** Touch up the knobs with sandpaper, if necessary, then oil them the same way you oiled the other parts. The moment of reckoning is at hand. Good luck; you'll need it.

SLAT HOLE DETAIL

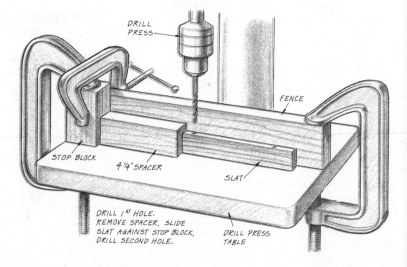

DRILL PRESS

FENCE

STOP BLOCK

4¼" SPACER

SLAT

DRILL 1ST HOLE. REMOVE SPACER, SLIDE SLAT AGAINST STOP BLOCK, DRILL SECOND HOLE.

DRILL PRESS TABLE